Mark Hopkins

Baccalaureate Sermons

And Occasional Discourses. Second Edition

Mark Hopkins

Baccalaureate Sermons
And Occasional Discourses. Second Edition

ISBN/EAN: 9783337160449

Printed in Europe, USA, Canada, Australia, Japan

Cover: Foto ©Lupo / pixelio.de

More available books at **www.hansebooks.com**

SERMONS,

AND

OCCASIONAL DISCOURSES.

BY

MARK HOPKINS, D. D.

PRESIDENT OF WILLIAMS COLLEGE.

BOSTON:
PRESS OF T. R. MARVIN & SON, 42 CONGRESS STREET.
1865.

CONTENTS.

BACCALAUREATE SERMONS:
- 1850. Faith, Philosophy, and Reason.
- 1851. Strength and Beauty.
- 1852. Receiving and Giving.
- 1855. Perfect Love.
- 1856. Self-Denial.
- 1857. Higher and Lower Good.
- 1858. Eagles' Wings.
- 1859. The Manifoldness of Man.
- 1860. Nothing to be Lost.
- 1862. The Living House, or God's Method of Social Unity.
- 1863. Enlargement.
- 1864. Choice and Service.

ADDRESS before the Society for Promoting Collegiate Education at the West.

DISCOURSE commemorative of Amos Lawrence.

DISCOURSE before the Congregational Library Association.—God's Provisions and Man's Perversions.

MISSIONARY SERMON.—The Promise to Abraham.

SERMON at the Dedication of the New Chapel, connected with Williams College.—Religious Teaching and Worship.

DISCOURSE commemorative of Nathan Jackson.

FAITH, PHILOSOPHY, AND REASON.

A

BACCALAUREATE SERMON,

DELIVERED AT

WILLIAMSTOWN, MS.

AUGUST 18, 1850.

BY MARK HOPKINS, D. D.
President of Williams College.

SECOND EDITION.

BOSTON:
PRESS OF T. R. MARVIN & SON, 42 CONGRESS STREET.
1859.

Entered according to Act of Congress, in the year 1850,

BY T. R. MARVIN,

In the Clerk's Office of the District Court of the District of Massachusetts.

SERMON.

HEBREWS xi. 33, 34.

WHO THROUGH FAITH SUBDUED KINGDOMS, WROUGHT RIGHTEOUSNESS, OBTAINED PROMISES, STOPPED THE MOUTHS OF LIONS, QUENCHED THE VIOLENCE OF FIRE, ESCAPED THE EDGE OF THE SWORD, OUT OF WEAKNESS WERE MADE STRONG, WAXED VALIANT IN FIGHT, TURNED TO FLIGHT THE ARMIES OF THE ALIENS.

THE word 'hero,' does not occur in the Bible. Nothing can be more opposite to its spirit than that self-sufficiency, and recklessness of human rights and sufferings, which are commonly associated with this term. Still, there are no higher examples of a true heroism than the Bible presents. In the text, and the chapter from which it is taken, we have an account of great and heroic exploits, performed indeed in ancient times, but such as we should be glad to see emulated, such as ought to be emulated in the midst of the light and advantages of our day. We have a right to expect, as the stream of time rolls on and pours its accumulated wealth at the feet of new generations, that there shall not only be an increase in the knowledge of nature, but that there shall be, at least, no failure in the breadth and compass of a comprehensive wisdom, or in the might of a true manhood that is ready to do and to suffer in the cause of humanity and of God.

But not only may *we* expect this; it is also intimated by the Apostle that it is expected and watched for by those who have gone before us. He represents, in the opening of the succeeding chapter, those worthies and veterans who had finished their own course, as gathered into a vast assembly, forming "a cloud of witnesses," and watching with intense interest the bearing of those who follow them. "Seeing then," says he, "that we are compassed about with so great a cloud of witnesses, let us run with patience the race that is set before us."

This race, my friends of the Graduating Class, I would now invite you to run. *You* are especially called upon to emulate the example of the great and good,—to do deeds that shall not only cause joy on earth, but shall send a new thrill through the vast assembly of those who have gone before you.

But if you are to do the deeds of these ancient heroes, you must be girded with the same armor, be controlled by the same principle, must have the same prize in your eye, and be sustained by the same power. Fruitful as the nineteenth century has been in inventions, it yet furnishes none for making great and good men. The great tree must grow now from the same earth, and under the same sun, and by the same processes and ministrations of dew and rain and storms, as the great tree of old; and so, now, as of old, must the life and might of true greatness be drawn from the same fountains, and work themselves out by essentially the same processes. Were these deeds performed of old only by faith? then only by faith will they be performed now.

What then is Faith? Avowed by Christianity as its peculiar principle of action, ridiculed by the philosophers, is it indeed some new, or peculiar, or blind, or fanatical principle? Or is it one of those grand and universal principles which underlie human action, which are necessary to true heroism, to a right philosophy, to individual and social perfection, and which must, in the progress of light, come more and more into distinct recognition and general acknowledgment?

Whatever faith may be, it must be conceded that the accounts given of it by its advocates have been neither uniform nor consistent. It has been said to be simple belief, founded on evidence, and not differing from any other belief; to be belief in testimony; to be belief for reasons not derived from intrinsic evidence; to be a belief on the ground of probable, as distinguished from demonstrative evidence; to be a belief in things invisible and supernatural; to be a trust; and more recently, and transcendentally, it has been said to be an *organ* of the soul by which it becomes cognizant of the invisible and the supernatural.

To some, this diversity of statement may seem to indicate that there can be nothing in faith very definite or important. To me it indicates the reverse; for while men do certainly differ about things which are indefinite and obscure, yet it is also found that they come latest, if at all, to the investigation of those principles which are the most intimate and essential, and that they are nowhere less likely to come to a uniform and satisfactory result. As in mathematics the truths that are most nearly intuitive are the last and the most difficult to be demonstrated, so here the principles and processes which are so essential that they seem inwoven into our being, are the last to be investigated and the most difficult to be satisfactorily explained. Men are no better agreed what reason is, or what personal identity consists in, than they are what faith is; and yet, as those who think wrongly on these subjects may, and do, exercise their reason, and continue the same persons precisely as they would if they thought rightly, so those who make different statements in regard to faith, all exercise faith, and receive the benefits of faith, in precisely the same way.

That the term faith may not be used loosely and popularly,

to designate the ideas just mentioned, and also others, I would not say; but the inquiry now is, What, generically, and specifically, is that Faith upon which the Bible insists as essential to salvation, and by which the great deeds it records were performed? Can this faith be so defined that our idea of it shall be distinct, that it shall harmonize with philosophy and with reason, and that it shall be adequate to the great offices assigned to it in the Bible?

I propose in the following Discourse, first, to answer these inquiries; and secondly, to speak of the offices of faith—more particularly, as adapted to this occasion, of its office as a principle of action to be adopted by every young man.

The generic definition of faith which I would propose, is, that it is *confidence in a personal being*. Faith lives and moves and has its being only in the region of personality. Whatever we may believe respecting things visible or invisible, on any other ground than our confidence in a personal being, does not seem to me to be faith. It implies the recognition of a moral nature, and a conviction of the trustworthiness of the being possessed of such a nature.

This definition of faith implies a division of this universe into two departments, that of persons, and that of things; and, in connection with this division, will give us a clear distinction between philosophy and faith. The sphere of faith is the region of personality, that of philosophy is the region of things. Each of these spheres addresses our sensibilities and calls for investigation, but in accordance with its own nature and laws.

By things, are called forth in the region of sensibility, the emotions of beauty, of sublimity, and of admiration; by persons, in addition to these, confidence, affection, passion.

In her investigations in the department of things, philosophy is concerned, not with all knowledge, but chiefly with resemblances in those things that exist together, and with uniformities in those that exist in succession. These are the basis of all classification, of all inductive reasoning—and it is through these that we get all our ideas of physical order and law.

Philosophy presupposes a knowledge of things as they exist separately. This being given, she neglects all individual peculiarities, and proceeds to group them according to their resemblances, and to give them collective names. In doing this she acquires for man power, and practical guidance, because a resemblance in external signs denotes a resemblance in essential properties. This gives value to the signs of nature, and shows that in the department of resemblances she is constituted on the basis of truth.

But not only does philosophy notice resemblances in beings and phenomena that exist together, she also notices uniformity of succession; and is thus enabled to foretell the future, and to act wisely with reference to it. She believes in a uniformity of succession according to the order that is established. She investigates the laws in accordance with which this succession moves on. As among things that exist together, she knows nothing of individual peculiarities, so in phenomena that exist in succession, she knows nothing of exceptions, and admits with great reluctance, or not at all, that such exceptions really exist.

Such, except as she may be said to investigate causes, is philosophy. She stands in the centre of things that co-exist, and passes onward and outward to the farthest star, stepping more or less firmly as the resemblances, by which alone she proceeds, are more or less perfect; she stands at the present point in things that succeed each other, and binds the future to the past by what she conceives to be an inexorable law.

But it may be inquired whether philosophy does not extend to the domain of mind. Yes, so far as mind is a thing, and hence under the law of an absolute uniformity, but no farther. The moment a personal being is placed under that law of nature by which that which follows is *necessarily* the product of that which precedes, personality ceases, and you have mere nature—a thing. The very idea of that necessary uniformity upon which philosophy is based, precludes that of personality. It also precludes the idea of faith; for whatever we may believe without the range of personality, and on whatever grounds, there is always wanting that element which enters into faith by which a person may be said not only to have confidence, but to be *confiding*.

The sphere of faith, as opposed to that of philosophy, is, as I have said, the region of personality. Here we find affections, and a moral nature, and a free-will. In the sphere of things we deal with similarities, and uniformities of succession, and laws, and do not necessarily know anything back of these. We *may* indeed refer them all to a personal agent, but for the grounds of our belief we are not necessitated to go beyond the uniformities and laws themselves. We have in these nothing of the great element of character. But in our dealings with personal beings, whatever ground we may have for belief, either of what they say, or of what they will do, must be found, not in any law, not in any unvarying uniformity conceived of as necessary, but in the *character* of the personal being. This is an element entirely different from any found in the sphere of philosophy, and it is upon this that faith fixes. This is the grand peculiarity of faith; it is confidence in a personal being. Like belief, it admits of degrees. As the highest form of belief is certainty, so the highest form of faith is such a confidence in the character of any being as will lead us to believe whatever he may say *because he says it*, and to commit implicitly into his hands every interest of our being.

And as that without us which calls forth faith, is so different from that which is the basis of philosophy, so, it may be remarked, is that within us which is brought into action also different. Doubtless the nature of man is preconformed to the state into which he is to come, and as he naturally conforms himself to the uniformities of nature, so does he, though by a different principle, naturally confide in those to whom his being is intrusted. It is not to be supposed that that feeling of confidence with which the infant looks up into the eye of its mother, with which the new formed angel must look up to his God, is the same as that by which he is adapted to the blind and unvarying movements of nature. It is not to be supposed, as these two great spheres of persons and of things are so distinct, that our nature should not be equally preconformed to each.

If the spheres of faith and of philosophy be thus distinct, it will be obvious that they can come into conflict only at a single point. A personal being may make assertions about facts that lie within the domain of philosophy, and these assertions may seem to conflict, and may conflict, with evidence respecting those same facts derived from philosophy. But in such a case man is not left to the alternative of a blind faith or a presumptuous philosophy. His reason is to decide. By this he is to ascertain, on the one side, that a personal being has spoken, what he has said, what means he had of knowing the truth, and what confidence is to be placed in his character. On the other side, he is to inquire whether he knows all the facts and their relations, and is sure of his inferences. If, after this, there shall seem to be a conflict, or a contradiction, reason must strike the balance, and say whether, under the circumstances, it is more rational to put confidence in a personal being, or to believe in facts and deductions for which we have another species of evidence. Reason recognizes both these grounds of belief; and she, and she only, can decide in cases of apparent conflict between them.

Having thus considered the relations of faith and philosophy, let us now look at those of faith and reason.

It is strange with what pertinacity the opponents of Christianity have insisted that there is, and must be, a conflict between these; and how readily many advocates of Christianity have assented to this view. So far has this been carried, that a recent and much-lauded article in the Edinburgh Review is entitled, "Reason and Faith; their claims and *conflicts.*" But such conflict is by no means to be admitted. There is just as much opposition between reason and faith, as there is between reason and philosophy, and no more.

If we regard reason as giving us only intuitive and necessary truths, then it will act equally in the domain of philosophy and of faith, and there can be no opposition between either of them; unless, indeed, a personal being should assert an absurdity. But if, as is more common, we regard reason as comprising what is rational in man,—those high attributes by which he is distinguished from the brutes, and which must enter into, and preside over, every legitimate act and process of the mind,—then, the sphere of faith and philosophy being different, there can be no conflict between reason as employed in the sphere of philosophy, and as employed in the sphere of faith. Reason presides over both spheres, and can therefore be in conflict with neither. The only possible question is, whether we may, in any case, just as rationally reach conclusions and grounds of action by that process which we call faith, as we can by that which we call philosophy. But on this point there can be no question. We act as necessarily and as legitimately with reference to personal beings by faith, as we do in reference to things by a belief in the uniformity of nature. It is just as *rational* for a man to have confidence in the character and consequently in the word of a personal being, as it is for him to believe in the facts of observation or experience or in those forms and systems of knowledge deduced from these which are called philosophy. It *may*, perhaps, be found to be *quite* as reasonable to believe a fact because it is asserted by God, as to believe one because it is inferred by ourselves, or even as to believe a fact made known to us by those senses which God has given us.

Is there not then such a thing as faith that is not in accordance with reason? Certainly, just as there are inferences and philosophies that are not in accordance with reason, and perhaps it would be difficult to say whether there has been more folly and absurdity under the name of faith or of philosophy. My reason tells me that I may confide in the facts given me by my senses, that I may classify these, and build up a system of knowledge which we call philosophy. Under this impression, men have built up systems of philosophy which we can now see were exceedingly irrational and foolish, but this does not show that there is any conflict between reason and philosophy; but only that reason is not infallible in this department. My reason also, all that is rational within me, tells me that I may, and ought, sometimes to confide in personal beings, and that such confidence is a rational and sufficient ground of knowledge and of action. We may, indeed, here repose confidence where we ought not, and receive irrational dogmas, and submit to useless or ridiculous rites; but this would only show that reason is not infallible in this department.

So far then from separating faith from reason and bringing them into possible and actual conflict, we would say that the sphere of faith is one of the two great spheres over which reason presides, and that faith itself is one of the great and indispensable methods in which reason is manifested. It is a libel upon religion to say that it requires a blind faith, or any other than a rational faith, or that it requires us to believe any thing which it is not more rational to believe than it would be to disbelieve it. There is no tendency in faith to a blind belief. It does not say, and has no tendency to say, 'I believe because it is impossible.' That is mere Quixotism and folly. Faith may, indeed, take hold of the hand of a father, and be willing to step where it does not see ; but then she is willing thus to step, only because she has a rational ground for believing that her father will lead her right. Christianity discards and repudiates altogether, any faith that can come into conflict with reason.

This view of faith gives it a definite sphere, it shows distinctly its relations both to philosophy and to reason, and removes from it all that mysterious or mystical appearance which has sometimes been thrown around religious faith. As an exercise of the mind it is, generically, no way different from that to which we are constantly accustomed. When a child follows implicitly the directions of its father, when a client puts his case into the hands of an advocate, there is an element in the act that is different from simple belief, it is an element that puts honor upon the father and the advocate. This is faith. Faith, then, generically, is confidence in a personal being. Specifically, religious faith is confidence in God, in every aspect and office in which he reveals himself. As that love of which God is the object, is religious love, so that confidence in Him as a Father, a Moral Governor, a Redeemer, a Sanctifier, in all the modes of his manifestation, by which we believe whatever he says because he says it, and commit ourselves and all our interests cheerfully and entirely into his hands, is religious faith. Surely there is in this, nothing irrational, or hard to be understood.

The distinctive element of faith, then, is not belief, but it is confidence from that perception and appreciation of moral character upon which the belief is based. Involved in this there must always be a belief of the trustworthiness of the object of our faith. Hence, if faith were perfect, it would involve, not merely a belief in testimony, but an obedience like that of Abraham. In his case there was simply a command, and strictly no testimony; yet the faith was perfect.

It is this complex nature of faith that has caused the confusion respecting it. It does imply a movement of both the rational and the emotive nature. In this, sometimes the one, and sometimes the other may predominate, but it is never due either to the intellect simply, or to the feelings simply. When outward appearances, as in the case of Abraham, are opposed to the dictates of faith, it will be an affectionate confidence. When there is no such opposition, it will be a confiding affection in which the confidence may seem to be entirely absorbed and transfigured into love. The belief involved in faith, is based on those very qualities which necessarily call forth emotion or affection; and hence, in this act, the two are fused and inseparably blended. Hence too the moral element in faith, which is not necessarily in mere belief, and hence its power as a principle of action. Nor is there any thing strange or anomalous in this. Pity is a complex act, consisting of sympathy for distress and a desire to relieve it. These may exist in different proportions, but if either be wanting there is no pity; and yet no one finds any difficulty in understanding what pity is.

Having thus considered the nature of faith, we now proceed to its offices.

Of faith in general, the great office is to underlie all the social intercourse of personal beings. It is to this higher and distinct sphere of personal intercourse, what a belief in the uniformity of nature is in our intercourse with nature. Without confidence society is impossible. It is the great element and condition of social prosperity and happiness. Universally it will be found that all the ends of society are reached, in proportion as there is mutual confidence between husbands and wives, parents and children, rulers and subjects, buyers and sellers, friends and neighbors. Remove but the single element of distrust, and who does not see that the great cause of human wretchedness would be taken away. Let but the one element of a general and perfect confidence be poured into the now heaving mass of human society, and its agitations would subside, and it would be at once aggregated and crystalized into its most perfect forms. In connection with this, every form of human attachment would strike deep root, every mutual affinity would have free play, and every capacity of man for happiness from intercourse with his fellow-men would be filled.

Of the more specific offices of religious faith we will first consider that, so much insisted on in the Scriptures, by which it accepts a gratuitous salvation. From the nature of faith as now stated, it is easy to see that its relation to such a salvation is a necessary and not an arbitrary one. To be accepted, a gift must first be appreciated, and desired *as a gift*. This, in the case of salvation from sin, involves repentance. And then there must be full confidence in the sincerity of him who offers the gift. This is faith, and, the gift being desired, there can be a completion of the confidence only in its acceptance. In this view of it, faith is not that in consequence of which we receive the salvation, as if the faith existed first and accepted the salvation afterwards, but faith is the very act of confidence by which the salvation is accepted. It is a confidence which can become complete only as it accepts the offer, because it is only as He makes the offer that the Saviour can become the object of our confidence. Faith then, in its relation to salvation, is that confidence by which we accept it as a free gift from the Saviour, and is the only possible way in which this gift of God could be appropriated. How simple! how rational! how strange it should fail to be understood!

A second office of religious faith, as stated in the Scriptures, is to unite man to God, and in so doing, to give him power with God. To this, faith, as now explained, is perfectly adapted. As our relations to God are so numerous and intimate, and as confidence in him can be based only on a perception of those perfect attributes which would call out the highest affection, it must be an affectionate confidence. But it is only by an affectionate confidence that such a being as man can be united to God, or, indeed, that any one moral being can be united to another. Let this exist, and every thing in the relations of the two beings must be pleasant, the relation itself will be the ground of the highest satisfaction which our nature can know, and will lie at the foundation of a higher and nobler idea of being and of order than any other. What is the idea of myriads of orbs circling in harmony together, compared with that of myriads of intelligent and moral beings united to God and to each other in a mutual and affectionate confidence? Here we find the true end of this universe—an order of which all other order is but the symbol.

And while faith thus unites us to God, it is natural and rational to suppose that it should have the great power ascribed to it in the Scriptures. It is one of the strongest impulses and principles of a rightly constituted nature never to disappoint any confidence that is justly reposed in it. This seems to be even the instinct of a generous nature without reference to principle. Who is there that would not protect a dove that should come and nestle in his bosom? An appeal by innocence, by helplessness, by distress, in which the individual abandons himself with entire confidence to *us,* is one of the strongest that can be made to our nature, and will often be met by the greatest sacrifices, not only by individuals, but by whole nations. Let Kossuth escape and come to this country, and confide himself to our protection, and let him be pursued by the combined power of Russia and of Austria, yea by the power of the world, and the nation would rise as one man, would form a living wall around him, and he would be taken only as his pursuers should pass over the dead bodies of those who would stand in his defence. Shall *men* do thus, and shall not God defend those who come to put their trust under the shadow of his wings? Shall any *innocent* creature of God that is in distress come to him and confide in him, and shall not the resources of Omnipotence be held ready for his deliverance? Shall any guilty creature of God, however debased and wretched, yea though he were dyed and steeped in sin, come to him with a confidence authorized by the death of Christ, and cast himself upon him for pardon and adoption, and shall he not be received even as the prodigal son? Shall any servant of God, in this world of conflict, be hardly beset, and, feeling that his own strength is weakness, look up to God with an eye of filial confidence, and shall he not send him succor? Shall his servants say, in the very face of the flames, "Our God whom we serve is able to deliver us from the burning fiery furnace, and he will deliver us, O king," and shall he not deliver them? What are the laws of nature in a case like this? They are but as a technicality compared with a mighty principle. One glance of a confiding eye is mightier than all the laws of nature. Heaven and earth may pass away, but not a hair of him who puts confidence in God shall "fall to the earth." Sooner, far sooner, would God sweep this material framework, with all its laws, into utter annihilation, than he would disappoint the authorized confidence of the most inconsiderable of his creatures. How different is this universe when thus viewed by the light of faith in its relation to a controlling personal being, a Father, and a Friend; and when viewed in the light of philosophy, as mere nature—as an unvarying, undiscriminating, crushing uniformity!

The third office of religious faith is to be a principle of action. And if there be any one thing which a young man about to enter upon life ought to consider thoroughly, it is his principles of action. Upon these his own character, and that of his enterprises, will depend. As you, my friends, adopt, from this time, right principles of action, so, and so only, will you promote your true usefulness, and permanent good.

But certain it is, referring to the distinction already made, that the highest principles of action cannot be found in the sphere of things. The study of these may train the intellect, and make men mere philosophers; they may awaken the desire to possess them as property and make men misers; they may call forth the emotions of beauty and sublimity; and that is all. There is here no confidence, no affection, no sympathy. But bring man, now, into intercourse with free, personal and moral beings, and every high faculty of his nature will come into play. The intellect, and the heart, and the moral nature will act together and strengthen each other. And as the basis of all such intercourse must be faith, so the basis of all intercourse with God must be religious faith.

As a principle of action, religious faith is contrasted with those adopted by the heroes of this world, because it tends to form a complete character. Recognizing an omnipresent and omniscient God, it acts equally at all times, and bears as well upon the minute, as upon the greater actions of life. Minute actions and details must make up the whole life of most men, and the greater part of the life of all men; and what we need above all things, is a principle of action that shall embrace all acts equally, as the law of gravitation embraces the atom and the planet, and that may dignify the smallest act by the principle from which it proceeds. Such a principle is religious faith ; and nothing but this can carry the life-blood of principle into those minuter portions of human conduct on which our happiness here chiefly depends. This would attune the chords of domestic life and make them discourse sweet music ; it would substitute the freshness of sincerity, and the flush of benevolence, for the paint and frigidity of a false and conventional politeness. Carrying out such a principle, an individual may be truly great, however humble his sphere ; and this greatness will bear the test, and grow as it is examined ; while that which takes human opinion as its standard and reward, dwindles and becomes contemptible the more it is known. This latter cultivates the art of concealment ; it is great, and generous, and kind, in public ; and mean, and selfish, and unamiable, at home. Long enough has the world been filled with pretences, and shows, and fair seemings, and whited sepulchres ; but the remedy for these is to be found, not in any ridicule or denunciation of hypocrisy, nor in any splenetic or contemptuous decrial of 'shams,' but only in the cultivation of a true religious faith.

This will be the more obvious if we notice a second, and grand peculiarity of religious faith, which is, that it can work only in harmony with the moral nature. No man can expect to be aided or sustained by God, when he is doing any thing which he is conscious is not well pleasing to him. Confidence in God must imply a constant endeavor to know his will, and must, hence, quicken the conscience, and, as the Scriptures express it, purify the heart. I have already spoken of the essential connection between faith and love, and it is by its intimate alliance with conscience on the one hand, and love on the other, that religious faith is capable of becoming a principle of action so ennobling and so mighty. It is rational and intelligent as recognizing, sometimes the plans of God, and always the grounds of trust in Him; it quickens the conscience as necessarily adopting the law of God for its rule of action; and it gives full play to the affections, by drawing its very life from the holy and infinitely amiable character of God. Thus, he who is actuated by this principle must have the strength that comes from the consciousness of acting rationally; from peace with God; and peace of conscience. Thus has it every element that can be needed to sustain great and heroic action. Let a man feel that he is in sympathy with God in the object of his pursuit, that God approves the means he adopts, and let him have a filial confidence in him, and what deed of a true heroism is there, whether of action or of suffering, which he may not perform? Thus moved and sustained, is it any wonder that they of old " subdued kingdoms, wrought rightousness, obtained promises, stopped the mouths of lions, quenched the violence of fire, escaped the edge of the sword, out of weakness were made strong, waxed valiant in fight, turned to flight the armies of the aliens"? And what this principle was of old, it is now. The same God is above us, and his response to any confidence reposed in Him will not be less full. This only can support the martyr, the moral hero, the hero of meekness, and rightcousness, and love unconquerable. This only can lead men to originate and sustain those great moral enterprises, on the success of which the welfare and progress of the world must ultimately turn. It cannot be that man should set himself fully against the wickedness of his own heart, and the wickedness of the world around him, and resist the allurements of temptation, and defy the powers of nature wielded by persecution, and endure to the end, and overcome, except as " seeing him who is invisible." "This is the victory that overcometh the world, even our faith." Only this can enable the true missionary to forsake country and friends, and devote his life, in a heathen land, to the good of those whom he knows but as redeemed by the blood of Christ; only this can sustain him in attacking forms of sin that seem as ancient and firm as the hills; this alone can enable him to labor on till death, and die in hope, while yet the darkness of midnight lies upon the mountains. Such a faith has nothing to do with nature. She comes down from above into the sphere of nature, she contemplates objects of which nature knows nothing, and when she acts rationally with reference to these objects—to a kingdom and laws that are above nature—nature says she is mad. She is not mad;— the might of the universe is with her; God is with her; eternity shall vindicate her. This, not money, not machinery, or confidence in them, but this it is that the church needs. Let her come directly to God in the strength of a perfect weakness, in the power of a felt helplessness and a child-like confidence, and then, either she has no strength, and has no right to be, or she has a strength that is infinite. Then, and thus, will she stretch out the rod over the seas of difficulty that lie before her, and the waters shall divide, and she shall pass through, and sing the song of deliverance.

From the view of faith now taken, it is easy to see that every system of negations, and distrust, and skepticism, must tend to lower the tone of human action and enjoyment, and must be uncongenial to our nature. Such systems may be useful in pulling down error, but have no constructive power. Their effect must be like that of withdrawing the vital element from the air; and not more certainly will languor and feebleness creep over the physical system in one case, than over the spiritual in the other. There can be no robust and healthy life, either social or spiritual, without a strong faith.

Let me then first counsel you, my friends, to place a generous confidence in your fellow-men. Not that you should be weak, or credulous, but, if you must err at all, let it be on the side of confidence. For your own sakes repress the first risings of a suspicious and distrustful temper. It will unstring the nerves of your energy, and corrode your very heart. Far from you be that form of conceit which attributes to itself shrewdness and wisdom by always suspecting evil. Far sooner would I make it a part of my philosophy and plan, to be imposed upon and cheated, up to a certain point. Let not even intercourse with the world, and the caution of age, congeal the spring of your confidence and sympathy. So doing, you may find much that you would wish otherwise, some you may find that will be as a briar, and sharper than a thorn-hedge, brethren that will supplant, and neighbors that will walk in slanders; but you will also find answering confidence, repose for the soul, green spots, and fountains in the desert.

Let me also warn you especially against all those pantheistic views, virtually atheistic, which are setting in upon us in these days in connection with certain forms of a transcendental philosophy. The great result, if not the object of all such schemes, is to obscure and exclude the idea of personality in God; and hence, of accountability in man. It is around this banner, more than any other, that the migratory hordes of infidelity are gathering, and uniting against the religion of the Bible. These schemes assume the garb of a high philosophy; they put on the sheep's clothing of a religious phraseology. In their outward aspect, they are contemplative, reverent, and especially philanthropic. Their advocates believe in God—but then all things are God, and in the working of all things hitherto, nothing higher than man has been produced. They believe in inspiration—but then all good books are inspired. They believe in Jesus Christ—

and so they do in Confucius, and Socrates, and Mohammed, and Luther, and in all *earnest* and *heroic* men. They believe in progress—but in a progress which neither springs from, nor leads to moral order. They make the ideas of guilt and retribution a bugbear, redemption an absurdity, repentance unnecessary, and faith impossible. Making such pretensions to philosophy, and giving such license to passion, these schemes have great attractions, and form the chief speculative quicksands which the currents of this age have drifted up, and on which the young are in danger of being wrecked. They merge personality into laws, the operations of a wise agent into necessary uniformities. They make the order and stability of God's works testify, not to his wisdom and immutability, but to his non-existence. They change the truth which the creatures thus tell, into a lie, and say, "No God." Thus are the heavens disrobed of their glory, and infinite space becomes a blank, and faith finds no object, and the tendrils of affection find no oak, and human life is without a providence, and conscience is a lie, and death is an eternal sleep. To all such schemes, and their abettors, how appropriate and overwhelming are the reproof and the argument framed expressly for them long ago: "Understand, ye brutish among the people; and ye fools, when will ye be wise? He that planted the ear, shall he not hear? He that formed the eye, shall he not see? He that chastiseth the heathen, shall not he correct? He that teacheth man knowledge, shall not he know?"

And now, my beloved Friends, in bringing to a close my relations to you as an Instructor, what can I wish better for you personally, or for the world in your relations to it, than that you should take for your actuating and sustaining principle, Faith in God. Without this, you will lack the highest element of happiness, and the only adequate ground of support; life will be without dignity, and death without hope. Only by faith can you run that race which is set before *you*, as before those of old. In this world your courses may be different; you will choose different professions, and diverge widely in your lines of life. To some of you, the race here may be brief. One whom I addressed the last year, as I do you to-day, now sleeps in death. But whatever this may be, and whether longer or shorter, before you all there is set the same race under the moral government of God; to you all is held out the same prize. Why should you not run this race? Never was there a time, in the history of the world, when moral heroes were more needed. The world waits for such. The providence of God has commanded science to labor and prepare the way for such. For them she is laying her iron tracks, and stretching her wires, and bridging the oceans. But where are they? Who shall breathe into our civil and political relations the breath of a higher life? Who shall couch the eyes of a paganized science, and of a pantheistic philosophy, that they may see God? Who shall consecrate, to the glory of God, the triumphs of science? Who shall bear the life-boat to the stranded and perishing nations? Who should do these things, if not you—not in your relations to time only, but to eternity, and to the universe of God?

And as seen in the light of faith, what a race! what an arena! what a prize!

Faith places us under the inspection and care of the eternal and omnipresent God, and accepts of him as a Father, a Redeemer, a Sanctifier, and Portion. She enthrones Him above all laws, and to that utterance which she hears coming as the voice of many waters from around the throne, saying, The Lord God omnipotent reigneth, she says, Amen. She introduces us to a spiritual family of our own race, and of superior orders of beings, before whose numbers and capacities the imagination falters. She accepts the suggestions of analogy, that the moral and spiritual universe is commensurate with that physical universe which night reveals, the outskirts of which no telescope can reach ; and for the unfolding and sweep of a government embracing such an extent, she has an eternity. Such is the scene in the midst of which this race is to be run. What is the prize? It is likeness to God—sonship—the inheritance of all things to be enjoyed forever. That such a prize might be offered, Christ died ; that it may be striven for, as the one thing needful, the Holy Spirit pleads. Gird yourselves, then, for this race ; run it with patience, " looking unto Jesus." The world may not notice, or know you ; for it knew Him not. It may persecute you, for it persecuted Him ; but in the Lord Jehovah is everlasting strength. He will be with you ; He will sustain you ;—the great cloud of witnesses will encompass you ; they will wait to hail you with acclamation as you shall reach the goal, and receive the prize. That goal may you all reach,—that prize may you all receive.

STRENGTH AND BEAUTY.

A

BACCALAUREATE SERMON,

DELIVERED AT

WILLIAMSTOWN, MS.

AUGUST 17, 1851.

BY MARK HOPKINS, D. D.
PRESIDENT OF WILLIAMS COLLEGE.

Published by Request of the Class.

BOSTON:
PRESS OF T. R. MARVIN, 42 CONGRESS STREET.
1851.

SERMON.

PSALM xcvi. 6.

STRENGTH AND BEAUTY ARE IN HIS SANCTUARY.

THERE are some things, both in nature and in character, that are incompatible with each other. Such are light and darkness, moral good and moral evil, hope and despair. One can exist only as the other is excluded. There are also some things, as drought and sterility, integrity and firmness, stealing and lying, which are naturally associated, and which we expect to find together. Again; there are qualities which, though not incompatible, have yet a tendency to exclude each other, and which are seldom found combined in any high degree. Such are flexibility and firmness, weight and velocity, energy and good temper, imagination and judgment, judgment and feeling, versatility and concentration, patience and the power of rapid combination and execution.

That the highest excellence, either mental or moral, can be reached only by blending, in their most perfect proportions, qualities which have thus a tendency to exclude each other, may be easily seen. An acute intellect is justly reckoned a perfection, but there is in it a tendency to exclude broad and comprehensive views. The power, on the other hand, of taking the most broad and comprehensive views, not only tends to exclude, but often leads us to despise that acuteness and subtlety of analysis without which no investigation is perfect. But these are not incompatible, and a perfect mind would be able to act equally well in either direction. As a perfect eye would possess both a telescopic and a microscopic power,—now ranging through the universe, and now adjusting itself to the minutest object,—so will mind be perfect only as it can embrace at once the most expanded generalizations and the minutest details. In a perfect mind, great logical power would be united with an affluent imagination; but these tend to exclude each other, and the combination is so rare that he in whom it occurs is always a distinguished man. In moral character, economy is a virtue; but there is in it a tendency to the exclusion of generosity, which is equally a virtue. Boldness is not easily combined with caution, nor sternness with a melting pity, nor zeal with toleration. How seldom is a Boanerges at the same time a Barnabas!

Among the qualities which may thus exclude each other, but which are yet often combined both in nature and in character, are strength and beauty.

In nature, how beautiful is the lily, the tulip, the rose, the honey-suckle! How beautiful is the humming-bird, that poises itself upon its almost viewless wings, and draws from that same honey-suckle its sweet food! How beautiful is the oriole, that weaves its hanging nest in the tree above! These are beautiful, but have not strength. On the other hand, how strong is the ox, and the elephant, and the rhinoceros, and the whale! These have strength, but not beauty. The hugeness of these contributes to their strength, but would seem to exclude beauty; while the lightness and fragility and exquisite structure of the others constitute their beauty, but would seem to exclude strength. This separation of strength and beauty is perhaps more striking when they are contrasted. Of this we find instances in man and woman, in the vine and the oak, in the violet sheltered in the cleft of the rock, in the rainbow overhanging the cataract.

But these qualities, so often separated and contrasted in

nature, are also often combined. They are so in the tree. In the oak strength predominates. Its sturdy and gnarled trunk is the emblem of strength; and yet an oak, with its full coronal of glossy leaves, is not without beauty. In the elm, beauty predominates. With its light form compared with its height, with its symmetrical top and pendent branches, it stands like a veiled bride in her beauty; and yet the elm impresses us with the idea of great strength. The green valley is beautiful, the mountain is strong. The mountain covered with verdure, is strength clothed with beauty. In a horse, to pass to the animal kingdom, these qualities are sometimes strikingly blended. A fine horse is among the most powerful of animals; but when he is left as nature made him, with his flowing mane and tail, and moves with the apparent consciousness of the admiration he excites, he is among the most beautiful. But it is in the human form that these qualities are capable of their highest and most perfect combination. This is the central idea in that conception of the Apollo by the Greeks, which must always remain the model of the physical man. In that, nothing that would contribute to beauty is conceded to strength, and everything that contributes to strength is beautiful. Let the body of man combine these qualities as it may, and it is evidently a fit dwelling for that immortal spirit which is made in the image of God. Such a body, filled with life, the features radiant with intelligence and love, would realize the highest conception that man can form of the power of the material, both to veil and to reveal the spiritual.

But while we thus find this combination in each separate department of the works of God, it is perhaps most striking in the general impression which those works make upon man. To the whole structure and movement of nature the Greeks gave the name '*kosmos*,' signifying beauty; but looking as they did upon the earth as fixed, what could give a stronger impression of strength in the form of stability? But if we look upon the earth and planetary system as now understood, this impression is greatly heightened. While we have the same round of the seasons, the same 'pomp of day' and glories of the night, the same green hills and sparkling waters, and the same bow in the heavens, with them, nothing can be more beautiful than the conception which our astronomy gives us of the uniform, circular, harmonious movements of the shining orbs above us, and nothing can give us a higher conception of force, or strength exerted, than their amazing velocity.

With such a combination of these elements in the works of God, we might expect that they would be combined in any physical structure which he should direct men to build. Accordingly we find that strength and beauty were in his sanctuary. Probably these were more perfectly combined in the temple of Solomon than in any other building ever erected. This, however, was not for its own sake; but, under a typical dispensation, it was doubtless intended to symbolize that spiritual strength and beauty which were to belong to the spiritual and only true temple of God.

Let us then look at strength and beauty as they may exist and be combined in the character of man.

The idea of strength is simple, admitting of no analysis; but strength itself may be manifested in either of two ways. It may either make an impression, as when the "sun shineth in his strength;" it may overcome obstacles, break down barriers, and march forward to the attainment of a proposed end; or it may stand firm as the hills, when it is said that "the strength of the hills is His also;" it may bear burdens, it may resist impressions that are attempted to be made upon it.

The whole strength which any man will be able to exert in either of these modes will depend in part on the faculties he may possess, and in part on the energy of the will.

The faculties will vary in their power according to their original constitution, and their training. Nothing that I see would lead me to suppose that the powers of all men are originally alike. In this respect, as well as in others, God gives to one five talents, and to another one. But certain original powers being given, their subsequent strength will depend on their training. Here the great and only law is, that the legitimate use of any power given by God strengthens that power. This is true of the body and of the mind; and here we see the difference between the works of God and those of man. The works of man are impaired by use; those of God are improved. For his original faculties man is not responsible, but only for their improvement.

But while there is nothing praiseworthy in the possession of great original powers, we yet contemplate them with admiration and delight, as we do a great tree, a great mountain, a great river, as we do the ocean. We watch with delight the march of the mind of Butler, we wonder at the apparent intuitions of Newton, and at the spontaneous creations of the genius of Milton. It is vain to complain of the admiration of men for talent and genius as such. That admiration is legitimate. It may be overwhelmed and merged in sorrow, or in horror from their perversion; but interest will concentrate where great power is manifested, whether it be physical or mental, whether for good or for evil. A tornado, prostrating trees and unroofing houses, a volcano pouring forth its destructive lava, a burning city even, regarded simply as a display of energy, are witnessed with pleasure. But this strength of the faculties, this energy with which they are capable of working, however impelled, is entirely different from strength of character. This it is for which we are responsible, and with which we are chiefly concerned.

But man can have strength of character only as he is capable of controlling his faculties; of choosing a rational end; and, in its pursuit, of holding fast to his integrity against all the might of external nature.

Without self-control there can be no strength of character. Its first condition is the subjection of the impulses and appetites and passions of all the faculties, to the control of the personal power—of the man himself. " He that hath no rule over his own spirit is like a city that is broken down and without walls." He has no strength to do, or to resist.

This power of self-control being supposed, strength of character may be manifested by a continued and concentrated energy put forth for the attainment of a given end. This strength, however, can be manifested fully only as obstacles are met, and external influences are resisted, and the power, not only of active effort, but of patient endurance, is tested to the utmost.

Of such strength of character, both in active effort and in patient endurance, Washington is a good example. During the long years of the revolution his activity was incessant, and that too in the midst of every form of discouragement; yet he never faltered. Still, strength of character was not as severely tested in him as it might have been. There were many who understood his object, and sympathized with him. The eyes of a nation were upon him. It never came to be a question whether he should relinquish his purpose or his life. But if we suppose one of exquisite sensibility, the most keenly alive to suffering and to every form of reproach, whose object is great and worthy, but not understood, who has no sympathy from any human being, who is either opposed or deserted by all mankind, and that the question with him is whether he shall abandon his purpose or go to a death of torture and of ignominy, we shall then have the highest conceivable test of strength of character. Of this there has been but one perfect example in our nature; but of this, man is capable. He was once in harmony with nature and with all external agencies. In a perfect state he would be. But through moral, and consequent physical derangement, all expressed sympathy, and all external agencies may be against him, and they may press him to the last extremity; but still he may have such a sense of duty, and such faith in God, as to enable him to stand firm, and to meet a certain death. The spiritual may triumph over the sensual and the material—the immortal over the mortal. If man is not the master of nature, as here he is not, he is yet not her slave. Against his own will, no power on earth or in hell can make him so. As spiritual and free, he is not properly of nature, but stands over against her. He is no part of a linked and necessary series of cause and effect, but may find in himself grounds of activity that will enable him to resist every impulse and motive that can be brought from without. When pushed fully up to 'that line where degradation and slavery commence, he has only to stand firm, and God himself, by the hand of death, will open a gate by which he may pass out unstained and unhumbled into perfect freedom. Here is his true dignity, here is strength. So have the martyrs stood. What is the strength of the hills compared with this?

Strength thus shown in resistance to impressions, and in standing firm, is in some respects less striking, and at the time is less admired, than that which shows itself in active effort, producing directly great results; but it may be doubted whether, in a world like this, it is not more heroic, and ultimately more fruitful of good and more honored. To illustrate this, and express for it the admiration of mankind, the simile of all ages is that of a rock standing immovable in the midst of the tumultuous waters. And certainly when we think of the sea of human passion, and of the fury into which it may be lashed, and of the strong desire for approbation, and of the fear of death, and of the natural distrust of men in their own opinions when they stand alone, it is one of the sublimest of all spectacles to see a man stand firm against all possible allurements and threatenings, and, reckless of consequences, hold fast to truth and to duty.

Perhaps it should be mentioned here, that energy in active effort, and the power of patient wating and endurance, may be blended in different proportions, and that they have some tendency to exclude each other.

Such are the nature and sphere of strength of character. What are those of beauty?

As the idea of strength is simple, so is that of beauty. The emotion can be known only by being felt, and only experience can teach us what it is that causes the emotion to arise. Doubtless there is something of inherent beauty in all the forms of moral goodness, but in some more than in others. If it is said, as it may be, that there is beauty in justice, yet other elements preponderate, and it has far less of beauty than benevolence. On such a subject, the imperceptible shading of one thing into another will not permit us to draw sharp lines; but it may be said, in general, that while strength of character depends on the will, beauty depends on the affections. The affections are beautiful, because they are spontaneous, and the general truth here is that strength is to be found in the voluntary action of the mind, and beauty in its spontaneous action.

We are all conscious of these two modes in which our faculties work. A student may pursue a science from fear, or from the love of praise or of gain. In this case the faculties will be impelled as by a force from behind, and the moment that is withdrawn they will cease to act—perhaps will react with strong aversion towards the science itself. Here the will must labor—it must row against the current. Much of the activity in this world is of this kind, and this it is that makes it *labor* and drudgery.

But again, a student may pursue a science from a love of the science itself. In this case there is an affinity—an attraction. There is a current of the soul setting in that direction, which the will may indeed resist, may perhaps wholly arrest; but it will require an effort to do so. The will must indeed now give its assent, but it need not row the boat. The movement of the mind is spontaneous, and without apparent effort. It is as when

"The river windeth at its own sweet will."

Such activity and effort are not esteemed a labor. There will be in it a deep joy. With the movement of the faculties as they perform it, there will be a music like that of the spheres. It is from the attempt of the will to resist these currents, that some of the profoundest struggles of which our nature is capable arise.

Now all such spontaneous movements, if legitimate, are beautiful. They are beautiful as spontaneous. Such are all the emotions of taste which respond to the beauties and sublimities of nature and of art. Such are all the natural affections, and such pre-eminently are all those high moral affections which find a complacency in their object from its own intrinsic character. Thus it is that benevolence is beautiful, and pity, and tenderness, and a regard for the feelings of others in the minutest particulars; thus sympathy is beautiful, and love, and a clinging trust. Let these be genuine, spontaneous, like the free gushing up of a fountain, and there is a beauty in them such as there is in no verdure or sparkling waters. They are to those sterner qualities which give strength, what the leaves and blossoms are to the tree, making it beautiful in the eyes of men, and sending up a fragrance to heaven.

But spontaneousness is not the only element of beauty. If the beauty be a moral one, as it must, to be strictly a beauty of character, then the affections must be confirmed to the law of conscience, and will have an intrinsic beauty as moral. The beauty of holiness is the highest of which the mind is capable, and this implies the conformity of the affections to a perfect law.

What has now been said applies to particular affections; but beauty of character, as a whole, must include not only spontaneousness and moral rectitude, but also symmetry. There is a tendency in spontaneous movements to extravagance and wildness. This must be repressed. The river, to be beautiful, must indeed wind "at its own sweet will," but it must wind within its banks. A just proportion must be preserved between the affections themselves and between the affections and the other powers. Symmetry, involving completeness, is a most important element of beauty of character.

With these elements, individual mind possesses a beauty far transcending that of nature. And if this be so in a single individual, how much more in a spiritual system where every relation is responded to, and every duty met! What is the harmony of music to the concord of souls in a true affection? What is the breaking up of light into its seven colors as it meets with the surfaces of matter, compared with the modifications of benevolence as it meets with the varying forms of sensitive and intelligent life? What is the beauty of natural scenery, with its clustering objects, and contrasted flowers and trees, compared with the meeting of a family, upon no member of which a stain rests, and where you see the gray hairs of the patriarch, and the infant of the third generation? What is the beauty of satellites circling around primaries, and primaries around the sun, compared with the order of families and the state—compared with the order of that moral government of which God is the centre and sun, and of which a holy love is at once the uniting force and the glory and beauty.

Thus the strength and the beauty which impress us most, are the strength of the will, and the beauty of the affections.

That the tendency already noticed of strength and beauty in matter to exclude each other extends also to mind, is too obvious to need illustration; and it is equally obvious that the most desirable character can be reached only as these are combined in the most perfect manner. And what is there that this combination would not include? As perfect strength and beauty of the body would imply and include all that is desirable in the body, so would perfect strength and beauty of the mind and of character include all that would be desirable in them. What is there higher or better that we can wish for our friends? What higher or better at which a young man can aim?

The question then arises, how this combination can be reached. And this brings us directly to the assertion of the text that strength and beauty are in his sanctuary. Adopting its spiritual import, the doctrine here indicated, and which I wish to enforce, is, that it is only within the fold and under the banner of the religion of Christ, that strength and beauty of character can be perfectly combined. Aside from Christianity there may be strength combined with the beauty of the natural affections, but strength combined with the highest beauty there cannot be.

That true religion would produce this combination appears because God desires it. This desire he has indicated, as we cannot doubt, in the structure of his works already referred to. Does he then value strength and beauty in these? Has he made them the foundation of all that we admire, and of most that we value in material forms? And shall he not value that in mind which is so analogous as to be called by the same name? Yea, is not nature typical? Was it not so constituted for the very purpose of leading us on gradually to ideas of this higher strength and beauty? Is it not but as the Mosaic dispensation to lead us to something higher and better than itself? As certainly as nature was intended to lead us at all to a knowledge of the perfections of God, so certainly were physical strength and beauty intended to reveal to us that in Him which is the substance, and of which these are but the reflection. Hence, only as there is spiritual strength and beauty, can his own image be produced in his creatures.

But on this point, if nature could leave us in doubt, revelation does not. We are commanded to "be *strong* in the Lord;" and the Psalmist prays that the *beauty* of the Lord our God may be upon us. It is the object of the Saviour to present to himself a glorious church, without spot or wrinkle, or any such thing. Does God then desire this? Then must it be the duty and aspiration of every religious man to strive for it. So only is man religious, so only ennobled, as he strives in coincidence with the purposes and plans of God—as he works 'according to the pattern showed him in the mount.' Does God desire this? Then will He who is the foundation of all strength and beauty ultimately impart them to those, and to those only, who shall come to Him for them. Thus coming, that process of assimilation will take place, by which, as they behold the glory of the Lord, they shall be changed into the same image. Approaching the sun, they will shine brighter, and the strength of their movement will be increased. God will clothe them with strength and beauty, and thus these shall be the completion and glory of his spiritual, as they are of his material creation.

Again. That the religion of Christ must produce this combination of strength and beauty, is obvious from the character of Christ. To be a Christian, a man must not only receive the doctrines and admire the precepts of Christ, but must be like him. He can be a Christian only as he actually follows Christ and is like Christ. In this is found a grand peculiarity of Christianity as distinguished from other systems. But there has never appeared on the earth any character which approximated to that of Christ, in the union of strength and beauty. In him we see the strength of achievement, and the strength of endurance. He moved with a calm majesty, like the sun. The bloody sweat, and the crown of thorns, and the cross, were full in his eye; but he was obedient unto death. In his perfect self-sacrifice we see the perfection of strength; in the love which prompted it we see the perfection of beauty. This combination of self-sacrifice and love, thus perfect in Christ, must be commenced in every Christian; and when it shall be, in its spirit, complete in him, then will he also be perfect in strength and beauty.

But once more. That this doctrine is true, appears from the very nature of true religion. This is no mere impulse; and strength of character is not a blind obstinacy, which, if it does show strength of will, shows also, in equal proportion, weakness of intellect. No: an intelligent *faith* is at the foundation of Christian character. Such a faith will "work," that is, it will produce obedience, and it will "work by love." But it is in obedience to a perfect law, from love, that we find the highest expression of strength and beauty. Law demands the approbation of the moral nature, and the intelligent action of the will in obedience; but it comes as an external force, and when it conflicts with inclination, obedience will have in it something of constraint; it will not be perfect freedom; it will be shorn of its beauty. But let a perfect law no longer stand without as a law of constraint; let it enter in and become the internal law of the mind, so that every inclination and current of the soul—all its love—shall set in the same direction, and then will there be a confluence of all in man that is rational and moral, with all that is emotive—of all the elements which produce strength with those which produce beauty. This is the consummation which the world waits for, the deliverance and the rest. So only can man be at peace with the law, and at peace with himself. So only can the most intense activity become a harmony and a joy, become rest and peace. So only can the nuptials be celebrated of inclination with conscience, of liberty with law. It is of the essence of Christianity to produce this identification of activity and repose, this union of inclination and conscience, of liberty and law, and thus of strength and beauty. So doing, it must be true; for it so accords with the nature of man as to embosom his highest good here, and to contain the elements of heaven. If it be not true, falsehood is as good as truth, for no truth could more demonstrably save man. Starting with these combinations, the immortal spirit will need nothing but the expansion of its powers to enable it to move on in its unending way with the strength of a giant and the beauty of an angel.

This is a point on which we may well dwell. You know, my hearers, what a terror to us law is, especially the law of God; how severe and onerous, even while it commends itself to the conscience, its requisitions seem. You know what that fear of its penalty is that hath torment. Now, could we come to see the stern features of this law so radiant with loveliness that we would not have one of them changed; could we see within its domain such a perfection of holiness and of happiness that no wish would stray beyond that domain; could we adopt this external law as the law of the mind, so that it should become the life of our life, how plain is it that all the harmonies of the soul would be restored, and that in its every movement there would be strength and beauty. But this enthronement of the law of God, or as I would choose to say, of the God of the law, in the centre of the affections, must come from a perfect Christianity—it can come from that alone; no other system even proposes to itself such a result; and hence we may regard the doctrine as established, that strength and beauty are in his sanctuary, and only there.

But if this be so, it may be asked why more of moral beauty has not been manifested in the lives of Christians. It is well known that evangelical religion especially has been regarded by some as distasteful, and the lives of its professors as severe, and harsh, and the reverse of beautiful.

To this two answers may be given. The first is that the real beauty of Christian character that exists is not known, nor appreciated. It is not known,—for this is no conservatory plant fostered by human culture and admiration. It springs up under the eye of God on the mountain-side, and in the retired valley. For Him it blooms, and He who notices the violet that no human eye ever sees will notice this. It is not appreciated,—for the standards of this world are wrong. The beauty which the world admires and idolizes, is that beauty of fashion and of art which may minister to vanity, to sensuality, to superstition—that beauty of manners which may cover a corrupt heart—and that beauty of nature which may become a part of a pervading pantheism. To these the Christian would give their due place, but he thinks little of them compared with the beauty of the affections and the life. To him the character of Christ is supremely beautiful. He is the "chief among ten thousand," but how is he to the world? It was foretold of Him, perfect in beauty as his character was, that he should be a root out of dry ground, and that when we should see him there would be no *beauty* in him that we should desire him. This was fulfilled. The beauty of the character of Christ was not appreciated in his own day; it is not now; and it is to be expected that the disciple shall be as his Lord. It cannot be expected that the selfish, the sensual, the ambitious, the proud, the vain, or the frivolous should admire that which is so opposed to their own temper and character. Especially cannot this be expected when holiness lays aside its abstract form, and is seen in actual life opposing and casting down cherished corruptions and interests. Then, instead of admiration and praise, all history shows that moral goodness and beauty are vilified; they are cast out as evil; are persecuted and crucified. What do bigoted persecutors and infuriated mobs know or care about moral beauty?

A second answer is, that Christianity is here but incipient, militant, imperfect. It begins in repentance, in tears, in struggles against sin, in self-denial and renunciation of what the heart had clung to. In this state of struggle there is a beauty to the eye of God, but not to that of the world. But beyond this there are many Christians who do not get—nay, they seem to cease to struggle, and stereotype a form and aspect of religion fit for neither a sinner nor a saint, that is neither of the law nor the gospel. There is in it slavery and penance. The face of duty is austere. They abstain from gayety, from fashion and folly, too much through fear, or conventionalism. They have no consistency. They attend church on the Sabbath, but show little of the spirit of religion during the week. They have more of the form of religion, than of the spirit of benevolence. The love of the world in them is not slain by the cross of Christ. There is no free and full and joyful consecration of themselves to God. They know nothing of the "joy of the Lord" as their strength. But religion,—if anything with a preponderance of these elements can be called such,—can be beautiful only as the conditions of beauty are met. It must be from the heart, and it must be symmetrical. The miserable notion of duty as imposing tasks, which is so prevalent, must pass away. Every thing harsh and austere must vanish from her countenance. The Christian must look upon her with the eye of a lover. At her voice his heart must throb, and his chest heave; her call must be to him as the sound of the trumpet to the war-horse. Then would each individual Christian have not only strength, but beauty; and that conception in Holy Writ of the embodied church, so beautiful, and so accordant with the spirit of our text, would be realized. In her *beauty* she would be "fair as the moon and clear as the sun," and in her *strength* she would be " terrible as an army with banners."

In the preceding discussion, a distinction has been indicated between that strength and beauty of the faculties which belong to genius and talent and taste, and that strength and beauty of character which involve moral excellence. This distinction is, perhaps, sufficiently obvious; but genius and talent have been, and still are, so much deified, and have cast such an illusive attraction around moral deformity, that I wish to draw to it particular attention.

The distinction is that between the agent and the instrument, between a person giving direction and that which is directed. This relative place of these is to be carefully noticed, because of the peculiar difficulty there is, in the present moral state of the world, in combining talent and genius with a high and reverent regard for duty. This is not that there is any natural opposition between them, but because that admiration and influence which are so dear to men possessing talent and genius, are expected to follow them without much reference to moral integrity. Now what we say, is, that we are not to over-estimate the mere instrument, however brilliant. We say that our chief regard is due to that sacred personality, that moral presence, which has both the power and the right to direct talent and genius, and before which it is their place to wait and to bow. We say that in any other relation talent is a curse, and that the light of genius can only "lead to bewilder, and dazzle to blind." We would honor genius and talent as gifts of God; we would make large allowance, if they must have them, or think they must, for their peculiarities, their idiosyncrasies, their weaknesses even; but when those who possess them would regard themselves, and be regarded by others, as privileged persons, whose moral delinquencies are to be allowed or winked at, and that, too, on the very ground that should be their highest condemnation, we would utter our solemn protest. We say that the influence of no other men can be so hostile to the best interests of the community—if they be public men, to the liberties of a free people. We say that no rebuke can be too prompt or severe when any man would practically dignify or even palliate meanness, or trickery, or falsehood, or profaneness, or licentiousness, or corruption, by associating them with high intellectual gifts. In the judgment of God, nothing can compensate for the want of moral strength and beauty of character; in comparison with these, every thing else is as nothing. This should be so in the judgment of man, and to this position we would fain hope that public opinion is slowly finding its way.

This discussion, which I now close, is my last labor for you, my dear Friends of the Graduating Class, in my relation to you, which has been so pleasant to me, as your instructor. If, in the course of your education, with us hitherto, more direct labor has been bestowed on your literary acquisitions, yet our chief anxiety has been for your character. That is the great thing. On that your happiness and influence here will mainly depend; by that your whole interest, under the government of God, will be ultimately decided. My object in this discourse has been to bring to your definite apprehension a standard of character at which you might safely aim, and to show you how that standard might be reached. I have wished to give you a motto to be inscribed upon your banner, which might give you strength in the hour of conflict. And what can I give you better than *strength and beauty?* What can you do better than to seek the highest combinations of these in the characters you are to form and to manifest?

And in doing this, you are not to suppose, from any thing that has been said, that you will be laboring to blend things that are naturally opposed to each other. No; in the deepest view of them they are but the varying forms of the manifestation of one force. They are not one as opposite polar forces are one; but strength, though not necessarily manifesting itself in the form of beauty, though it has a centrifugal force that tends to carry it off from its true curve, does yet underlie it, and is essential to the formation of that curve. Rightly directed, strength seems to attenuate and expand itself into beauty as the trunk of the tree, which is strong, attenuates and expands itself into the branches and the leaves, which are beautiful. It is strength alone that can elaborate itself into beauty; and only as it does this can we have evidence of the perfection of strength. The exquisite finish of the leaf of the tulip, is from the circulation within it of the divine omnipotence, and is as essential to the perfect evidence for that, as the spheres that roll above. So can you give the highest evidence of strength of character only as that strength can so restrain and control its own workings as to elaborate itself into beauty. The strength that we want is not a brute, unregulated strength; the beauty that we want is no mere surface beauty, but we want a beauty on the surface of life that is from the central force of principle within, as the beauty on the cheek of health is from the central force at the heart. This is the combination and the character that the world needs, that you need. Going forth with this, the wildernesses and solitary places of the earth will be glad for you. With this you will fill, up to the measure of expectation, and beyond it, every position of domestic and social and public life. You will be more appreciated as you are more known. The natural influence of uncommon powers or acquisitions will not be hindered or marred by those sad blemishes that every body must speak of in a whisper, but that every body will know. If you should have greatness of character, it will not shoot up into those isolated and startling peaks that attract notice indeed, but are barren; but it will rise up into those broad table lands that are covered with verdure, and where the springs arise that gladden the valleys. You will work in harmony with God, and He will give you success.

But you are to remember that the strength and beauty that can do this are not those of nature. The strength is the strength of faith, and the beauty is the beauty of holiness. As I have said, it is only through the religion of Christ that this combination can be reached. Here is our only hope. But through this it may be reached. We bless God for the hope that to reach this, is, in the hearts of some of you, the controlling aspiration. We bless him for the hope, that to some of you it has become so recently. We would remember and signalize, in this parting hour, the grace that has effected this. But if this be so with some, why should it not be with all? This combination of strength and beauty you may all reach, every one of you: and eye hath not seen, nor ear heard, nor hath it entered into the heart of man to conceive the blessings that will flow from it in the track of ages. Other strength will decay, other beauty will fade, but this strength will only grow stronger and this beauty more beautiful as eternity shall roll on. " They that wait on the Lord shall renew their *strength;* they shall mount up with wings as eagles, they shall run and not be weary, they shall walk and not faint;" and " the *beauty* of the Lord " their "God shall be upon them." This, my Beloved Friends, this is the strength, and this the beauty that I desire for you. In your characters may they be blended, and in all the pilgrimage of life that is now before you, may you be girded with strength from on high, and may the beauty of the Lord your God be upon you.

RECEIVING AND GIVING.

A

BACCALAUREATE SERMON,

DELIVERED AT

WILLIAMSTOWN, MASS.

AUGUST 15, 1852.

BY MARK HOPKINS, D. D.
PRESIDENT OF WILLIAMS COLLEGE.

SECOND EDITION.

BOSTON:
PRESS OF T. R. MARVIN, 42 CONGRESS STREET.
1855.

Entered according to act of Congress, in the year 1852,

By T. R. MARVIN,

In the Clerk's Office of the District Court of the District of Massachusetts.

SERMON.

ACTS xx. 35.

IT IS MORE BLESSED TO GIVE THAN TO RECEIVE.

As a dependent being, man is, and must be, a receiver. From God he must receive life and breath, and all things; and no one can so elevate or isolate himself, that he shall not need to receive from his fellow men those things which only their sympathy and kindness can bestow.

Man being thus necessarily a receiver, we should anticipate, from the goodness of God, that it would be blessed for him to receive. And so it is. It is blessed for the creature to receive from the Creator. It is blessed not only from the enjoyment which the gift itself may confer, but as awakening admiration, and gratitude, and love. It is blessed for the child to receive from the parent, for the friend to receive from his friend. It is always blessed to receive when the gift is born of affection.

This blessedness our Saviour knew. We are told that Mary Magdalene, and Joanna the wife of Chuza, Herod's steward, and Susanna, and many others, ministered to him of their substance. He received of them what he needed, and, so far as appears, he consented thus to receive at the hands of gratitude and affection, and was doubtless blessed in so receiving, his whole support.

But if it is thus blessed to receive, it is more blessed to give. This is one of those great truths, uttered by our Saviour, opposed to the whole spirit and practice of the age in which he appeared, which, like his inculcation of the forgiveness of enemies, and universal philanthropy, and seeking first the kingdom of God, showed a divine insight. It is a great practical truth, which, as it is received or rejected, must affect the whole spirit and all the results of life.

This blessedness was that pre-eminently known by our Saviour. "The Son of man came, not to be ministered unto, but to minister, and to *give* his *life* a ransom for many." He gave, not property, but himself. He gave instruction, and gifts of healing, and a divine sympathy. He gave the energies of his being in activity and in suffering for the welfare of man.

But here the inquiry arises, what it is to give. As now used this term carries the mind chiefly, if not wholly, to property; but this cannot be its main reference in the text, for then neither Christ nor his Apostles, would have illustrated their own precepts, or have known, to any great extent, the blessedness of giving. It is worthy of notice, that no direct record is made, that either Christ or his Apostles ever gave any thing in the form of property; and that would be a sad interpretation which would restrict the pleasures and benefits of giving, to the rich. To give, is not merely to transfer property without an equivalent from him who receives it.

This may be done from a regard to public opinion, to quiet conscience, to purchase heaven, to get free from annoyance. Property is not affection, it is not self-sacrificing energy, it is not the heart or the life. No; *to give, is to impart benefits freely, out of good will.* This Christ and his Apostles did. Said Peter to the impotent man, " Silver and gold have I none, but such as I have give I thee. In the name of Jesus Christ of Nazareth, rise up and walk." Here was a gift which money could not purchase, and such were all those great gifts which Christ came to bring. Thus understood, the pleasures and benefits of giving are open to all, even to her who is poorer than the poor widow who cast in her two mites. All can impart benefits of some kind, freely and from good will; and the proposition which we now wish to illustrate is, that thus to give is more blessed than it is to receive.

That this is so may appear, first, because God is a giver only, and not a receiver. Of the modes and conditions of the divine blessedness we know, indeed, very little. To our conception, God must have been perfectly blessed in himself, when, as yet, no creative act had rendered the blessedness of giving possible. We must conceive of God as self-sufficing in all respects, as having within himself the spring of his own activity, and finding in that activity the source of his blessedness. Without activity in some form, blessedness is inconceivable, for absolute quiescence is death. But if we know little of the modes of activity possible to God, and hence of the modes of his blessedness, we may yet be sure that in all the forms of that activity there is blessedness, and pre-eminent blessedness in those which are pre-eminently his. But, as has been said, he manifests himself only as a giver. He is so in creation. To the universe of matter, overwhelming us as it does by its vastness and variety and glory, he gave its being. From the resources of his own omnipotence he caused that which was not, to be, and no doubt there was a sublime blessedness not only in the result, when he beheld and pronounced it good, but also in the energy by which it was accomplished. And having created this universe with all its properties and adjustments, he gave it to his sensitive and rational creatures to be the theatre of their being and a source of enjoyment. To the sensitive and spiritual universe also, through all its ranks, from the insect up to the seraph, God has given being, with its infinite diversity of forms, and modes of perception, and capacities, and responsibilities. Throughout the universe there is nothing that any being is, or that he possesses, that is not the gift of God. And not only has God given in creating, but he gives continually. Whatever we may say of second causes, he is the constant upholder and governor of all things, the ever present, conscious giver of every good and perfect gift. This is the highest conception we can form of any being, that he should not only have the spring of activity within himself and be self-sufficing, but that he should suffice for a universe, and find a conscious blessedness in giving without limit and without exhaustion forevermore. Here we find a conception that bears us far above the glories of night, and of all telescopic heavens. Here we find the source of the river of the water of life, clear as crystal, that overflows and sparkles and spreads itself to the outmost limits of the creation. What are the starry heavens to Him who is enthroned as the infinite and only original giver in this limitless universe!

To give thus without exhaustion, would seem to be the natural prerogative of God; but there is also a form of giving that implies self-denial and self-sacrifice; it implies that we forego a good for the sake of the good of others. How this may be compatible with what we conceive of the infinite and perfect blessedness of God, it may not be easy to see; but that he is capable of this form of giving, the Scriptures plainly assert when they say, that He "so loved the world that he gave his only begotten Son." Possibly the highest blessedness of a benevolent being can be known only through self-sacrifice. Blessedness is more than pleasure; it is the consciousness and exercise of the highest goodness. This is the highest form of giving, and constitutes Christ the great gift of God. It makes him not merely the outflow of his natural attributes, but the manifestation of his heart.

And while God thus gives, he does not receive. "Who hath first given unto Him and it shall be recompensed to him again?" By the right of an original creation, and of a constant preservation, all things are already his. "He is not worshiped with men's hands as though he needed any thing, seeing he giveth to all life, and breath, and all things." He may be said to accept of our services; that is, he may be pleased with our dutiful affection, but we can bestow upon him no gift; he can receive nothing from us so as to become the owner of that which was not his before. We can never requite him by paying back an equivalent; we can lay him under no obligation.

If then God finds his own blessedness in giving, and not at all in receiving, we should naturally expect, that those who are made in his image would find it more blessed to give than to receive.

But, secondly, it may not be amiss to mention that this is one of those great truths which seem to find their prefiguration and twilight in the material creation. The sun, the grandest and noblest of all material objects, is only a giver. Age after age, from his high place, he imparts, without exhaustion, light and heat, and receives nothing in return. In the coldness of our philosophy we say, indeed, that this involves no blessedness. This is true, just as it is true that there is no color spread over the surface of bodies; and yet is the sun a silent preacher of a truth that is not in him, because we are so made that we must diffuse over matter our own conceptions and vitalize it with our feelings. Let the natural emotions speak, and they say at once, that the sun is "as a bridegroom coming out of his chamber, and *rejoiceth* as a strong man to run a race." We attribute to this sublime body power and dignity, and feel that, if it were conscious, it must rejoice in its greatness and in its dispensing power. This teaching becomes more impressive by contrast. The sun gives only; the sandy desert only receives, and hence we regard it with aversion, and as fit only to symbolize the drearier desert of a heart thoroughly selfish and absorbing.

But I observe, thirdly, that this truth is enstamped upon our very constitution; it grows out of the frame-work of our being.

To see this, we have only to examine a little the kinds and sources of the blessedness of which we are capable. As has been said, all blessedness must come from activity; and of this there may be three kinds. One of these we need not consider, because there is in it nothing of giving or receiving. It is the activity of the mind within itself, in contemplation and thought, when it receives no impression from without, and puts forth no outward activity. Laying this aside then, we find that man is a centre of activities, from which influences, originating in his will, flow outward, and affect the world without; and also that he is a centre of susceptibilities, to which influences flow in from the world without, and by which he is affected. In the first case he is truly active, putting forth powers, and may be said, in a large sense, to give; in the second, he is as passive as a perceiving and sentient being can be, and he receives.

It is in conformity with this general idea that the physical frame, even, is constructed. The nervous system is a railway with a double track. It is now well known that there are two sets of nerves, those of motion, and those of sensation, running side by side, apparently intimately blended, yet entirely distinct in their origin and office, by one of which influences pass from within outward, and by the other from without inward; by one of which we receive, and by the other, give. By the one, we receive materials of instruction, and impressions pleasing or painful; by the other, we exert our wills as agents, and give forth our own proper activity.

When we open our eyes to the light, when we behold the trees and the mountains, the waters and the flowers, the stars and works of art, we receive; when there comes to us the perfume of flowers, or the fragrance of the new-made hay, we receive; when we taste the strawberry, the peach, the melon, we receive; when we hear the song of birds, the rustling of leaves, the rippling of waters, or the music of the flute or of the voice, we receive; when we open our minds, through the senses, to thoughts and impressions from others, we receive. Here the movement is from without, inward; and if no folly or wickedness intervene, it is always blessed, and only blessed, thus to receive.

To this process God has attached pleasure, as he has to that of receiving food, but both the process and the pleasure are as clearly subordinate in one case as in the other. We receive food that the body may be built up and strengthened, and the pleasure is incidental. So here, the object of the importing railway, or rather railways, is to bring to the mind those materials upon which it may work and be strengthened, which may be elaborated into speech and action and enable man to become a giver, freighting the outward railway with the products of knowledge and of love.

This last is the true sphere of man. He was not made to be merely a passive receiver of pleasure, a bundle of sensibilities, to be madly wasted or artistically and prudently exhausted, beginning with a fountain full and sparkling, and ending, as all mere pleasure must, with the vapid and bitter dregs of decay and exhaustion. He was made to be an agent, with powers having the spring of their activity within themselves, and having it for their law that they shall increase in strength by their own legitimate activity. This it is that allies man to the angels, and makes him of inappreciable worth, and fits him to become increasingly a giver, and to walk with waxing strength in an upward path, even the path of the just, that shineth more and more unto the perfect day. This it is in man that lays the foundation for that most magnificent of all figures, used by our Saviour concerning the righteous, that they shall shine forth as the sun in the kingdom of their Father.

But if this be so, if the sphere of activity and of giving be higher than that of passivity and of receiving, then must it be more blessed to give than to receive; *for where should any being find his highest blessedness but in the legitimate exercise of his highest powers?* This is the law of all beings; so, and so only, can their highest blessedness be reached.

Intimately as the pleasures of receptivity and of activity are blended, we yet find in the distinction just drawn, a line of cleavage dividing the race into two classes. To the one belong the lovers and seekers of pleasure as distinguished from blessedness or happiness; for pleasure arises from some congruity between us and that which is without. In it the movement is from without, inward, and we are receivers. The lovers of pleasure are those who make it their business to find that without them, which shall act on their susceptibilities and minister to their passive enjoyment. To seek this predominatingly is the fatal mistake and besetting sin of most. To do so is compatible with the highest forms of civilization and of worldly respectability. It rather implies the cultivation and patronage of the elegancies and refinements of life, and skill in the most agreeable forms which self-love and selfishness can assume. The elite of the class may worship beauty and art, but the mass will worship sensual pleasure. What they seek for on earth is the highest combination of these, and they would desire no heaven but a Mohammedan paradise. Give them the means of gratification, and they are courteous, liberal and tolerant; interfere with these, and they are intolerant, deceitful, malignant, cruel; and thus vices and cruelties more shocking than those of barbarism may mingle and alternate with the highest forms of luxury and refinement. With such an object of life, immortality and accountability disappear from its back-ground, and its value is estimated in sensations; the individual loses his self-respect and his confidence in others; and though society may seem to be crowned with verdure and flowers to its summit, yet that summit will be the crater of a volcano.

Those, on the other hand, who make their activities the basis of their character, seeking blessedness rather than pleasure, need, indeed, to have those activities rightly directed; but they are on a basis which is capable of sustaining the highest and most solid structure of individual and social greatness and blessedness.

We have now considered man as having sensibilities on the one hand, and a will on the other,— a receptivity and an activity in correspondence with which his physical frame is formed. But we find a similar correspondence of faculties in the mind itself, with no corresponding physical organization. Man has not only sensibilities and a will, but also desires and affections; and as he receives by his sensibilities and gives by his will, so does he receive by his desires and give by his affections.

Having shown that to give forth activity and influence is higher and more blessed than to receive impressions, we may now leave behind us, in our search for the highest blessedness, all mere passive enjoyment, and, while we estimate that at its proper value, consider only the different forms of activity. All activity from within, outward, can be regarded as a form of giving only in the wide sense already mentioned; but all giving is a form of activity that springs from the affections, and we say that this is more blessed than any form of receiving through the desires.

It is of the very nature of the affections that they give, and of the desires that they receive. The affections have persons for their object; they arise in view of worth or worthiness in them, real or supposed, and we seem in their exercise to give our very being. They are disinterested, they flow out from us, they give, and appropriate nothing. That is not affection which is not disinterested, and it is only because this is not a world of open vision that any outward token, flowing from a secret regard to self, can ever be supposed to give evidence of affection. In the sphere of affection every outward token is valued as the evidence of a gift more precious than itself. When we give affection we truly give; and what is commonly called giving, is really so only as it is an evidence of this.

The desires, on the other hand, have, as their distinguishing characteristics, that they appropriate to themselves the things desired, and that their object is things and not persons. They appropriate wholly; they receive, and give nothing. Here self is the centre, and nothing is valued except as it can be made to revolve towards the vortex of this whirlpool.

And here again it is blessed to receive, and only blessed, if the desires be kept within their own sphere. Not alone is there the music of enjoyment from the correlation and adjustment of external things with a sensitive organization, of the harp with the breeze, but in the attainment of its object by each of the desires. There is a legitimate enjoyment in receiving wealth, and admiration, and fame, and power.

But here, no less than previously, do we find an obvious subordination. Not more obvious is it that food should be received to be given back in strength and activity, or that sensation should minister to knowledge, than it is that the desires were intended to receive that they might minister to the affections. Let a man pursue wealth and power, not for their own sakes, but solely that he may do good to his fellow creatures, and there is no danger that the desires, thus subordinated, will be in excess. But the moment he pursues them, I will not say with some reference to self, for God intended we should provide for ourselves, but the moment he pursues them selfishly, the servant becomes the master, and slavery begins.

And here, too, there is made a great and general mistake. The ends proposed by the desires, instead of being held subordinate, become ultimate, and thus the desires become the main spring of activity and the basis of character. We all know how each of the desires creates for itself a world of activity, in which it becomes not only the pervading, but too often the dominant principle; and when this is so, man seeks to balance himself and society upon a false centre, and can never be at rest.

In the world of business the desire of wealth rules, and in the eager pursuit of this the vision of its votaries becomes narrowed, so that they see and care for nothing else. The fraudulent man, the rum-seller, the slave-trader, the panderer to appetite, the inexorable landlord, have, it may be, no malignity, but in the intenseness of this desire, they bow so eagerly to the god of their idolatry that they see not the scattered wrecks of property and of character strewed around them, and hear not the wail of distress that comes up from fathers and mothers agonized, and from wives and children made desolate. They hear but the cry of this desire, saying, Give, give, and all the better forms of intellectual and moral life are contemned and wither away, and their hearts become as the nether millstone.

In the world of fashion it is the desire of admiration that reigns. The value of dress as a necessary and a comfort, becomes subordinate to that which it receives from the eyes of others, and from the position it is supposed to give. Health and comfort are disregarded. Each desires to become a receiving centre, and the party, the ball, the assembly, where they have been admired, and especially more admired than others, has been a pleasant party or ball or assembly to them. It is in this sphere that vanity, self-complacent, yet meanly dependent and apprehensive, finds its food. Here every thing is on the basis of receiving, and this gives it its heartless and unsatisfying character. Even all copartnerships for mutual admiration, whether between individuals or in regular societies, give, only that they may receive as much again.

In the world of ambition the desire of power is supreme. No ties of kindred, no obligations of faith and sacred honor, no pleadings of humanity, no fear of a righteous retribution, can stay the course of him who has once entered the lists for this glittering prize. Reckless and remorseless as a cannon-shot, he moves towards his object, shattering and prostrating every thing in his way. "The land is as the garden of Eden before him, and behind him a desolate wilderness." A miser of power, if he is less despicable than the miser of wealth, it is only because he is more formidable; for though he may be admired by the unthinking, he is yet equally false to his nature, and to the true ends of life. He may be a battle-axe in the hand of the Almighty to punish the nations, but a true *man*, knowing his Maker, and voluntarily co-operating with him, he cannot be.

And what is true of the desires thus specified, is true of them all. The slightest knowledge of them will show that they cannot be the basis of either individual or social happiness. The isolated summits which they would reach are glittering and attractive at a distance, but there is there no spring of water for the thirsty soul, and no green thing. Their constitution is such that they grow by what they feed on, never reaching, like the bodily appetites, a limit of satiety. "He that coveteth silver, shall not be satisfied with silver." He that conquers one world, will weep that there is not another for him to conquer. Hence a character which has the desires for its basis, must be hard, and dry, and unamiable, and selfish; and the individual must be restless and unhappy. As, too, the desires are appropriating and necessarily exclusive, if they are the basis of character in the community generally, it must become the theatre of a general conflict, in which every malignant passion and dissocial element will mingle, and society will be dissolved into its original elements.

But with the affections, the reverse of all this is true. In their exercise, we find ultimate ends that are legitimate; nor is there in them any tendency to excess and disproportion from their own activity. They arise from an apprehension of some worth or worthiness in the person towards whom they go forth; and the only danger is, that the imagination will clothe their object in false colors. Let the person be seen as he is, and the measure of his worth, or of his worthiness, is the natural measure and limit of the affection; and in this there can be nothing exaggerated or excessive. If the object be greatly worthy, the affection ought to be great; and the greater the affection, the greater the blessedness. Among the highest forms of blessedness conceivable by us, is that of a perfect affection resting with full complacency upon a worthy object.

But if the individual will thus be made happy through the affections, much more will society. This scarcely needs to be shown. The affections are not only the true bond of society, the only element and sure guarantee of peace, but as burning coals burn more brightly when brought together, so must there be intenser blessedness where the affections are drawn out by intimate and complex social relations.

From what has been said under this head, it would appear that to give, is to put forth power under the guidance of love. In doing this, there will be a union of the activities with the affections. Hence giving is the culminating point, the blending and fusion of those activities and affections which we have shown to be the two highest sources of human blessedness. If, therefore, we will but notice it, we shall find, as was already said, that it is enstamped upon our constitution—that it grows out of the very frame-work of our being, that it is more blessed to give than to receive.

I cannot leave the discussion under this head without observing, that we may gather from it the limit and law of all our receiving faculties in their relation to those that give,—of all receptivity in its relation to activity. It is that that only should be received, which will enable us to give; that the limit of receptivity should be the point where it ceases to minister to activity.

This gives us the law of temperance in all things—its universal law. Nature is not arbitrary, or capricious, or cynical. We are at liberty to receive into the body anything, and in any quantity, that will, on the whole, best minister to the strength and activity of the body. The mistake of intemperate men, of every degree, is to receive for the sake of passive impression those things which depress and injure the powers of activity. The student is at liberty to receive into his mind as much promiscuous reading, and to hear as many lectures, as will give him the most active and vigorous mental powers. Let him read as much as he will, provided it be assimilated, and there be nothing of the crudities or tumidity of mental indigestion. Let the desires stretch forth their arms as they may, and gather wealth and admiration and power, provided there be nothing gathered to be hoarded and gloated upon and worshiped; and that the disposition to communicate go hand in hand with the ability, and thus the great law of stewardship come in, and every man, as he has received, be a good steward of the manifold grace of God.

It is, indeed, in this relation and law of receiving and giving, that we find the true ground of the subordination of different enjoyments, and the true theory of human well-being. This last consists, essentially, in the right activity of the powers. The right activity of her powers, is that which makes the King's daughter all glorious within; and if this be so, the King will see that her clothing shall be of wrought gold. For the completeness and fullness of well-being, there is needed not only the inward harmony and joy, but the investment and regalia of a world without, that shall testify through every sense and susceptibility to the sympathy and approbation of Him by whom that world was organized and is sustained. We reject not, nor undervalue the investment; but we find in this law a necessity, that he who would attain true blessedness at all, should make the basis of his character the activities and the affections, and not, as the many do, the sensibilities and the desires. In the prevalent type of character, reason and conscience and the affections are subordinated to some one of the desires, pleasure being pursued so far as may be compatible with that. But if true blessedness is to be attained, this order must be reversed; and the love that gives, sustained by reason and conscience, must take the place of the desires that would receive; and all mere pleasure, all desire for passive impression, must give way when love, so sustained, shall call for active exertion.

I have thus illustrated, as I was able, the weighty and comprehensive saying of our Saviour, that "it is more blessed to give than to receive;" and we find it confirmed by the example of God himself; by the mute teachings of his works; and by the best examination we can make of the constitution of man in its relation to the modes and kinds of possible enjoyment. The essential elements of giving are power and love—activity and affection—and the consciousness of the race testifies that in the high and appropriate exercise of these there is a blessedness greater than any other.

And what is thus taught by precept and confirmed by philosophy and by consciousness, it is most pleasing to find perfectly illustrated by example. With the interpretation now given, it could not be more perfectly illustrated than it was by our Saviour and his Apostles. He "loved us and gave himself for us." He saw that the world was in such a state, that by giving himself he could save men; and with the full knowledge of what was before him, the poverty, the reproaches, the buffetings, the mockings, the scourging, the crucifixion, he gave himself freely. This he did in the conscious exercise of power. He had power to lay down his life, and he had power to take it again. He gave, not as he gives whom giving does not impoverish, but he gave of his heart's blood till that heart ceased to beat. He planted his cross in the midst of the mad and roaring current of selfishness aggravated to malignity, and uttered from it the mighty cry of expiring love. And the waters heard him, and from that moment they began to be refluent about his cross. From that moment, a current deeper and broader and mightier, began to set heavenward, and it will continue to be deeper and broader and mightier till its glad waters shall encompass the earth, and toss themselves as the ocean. And not alone did earth hear that cry. It pierced the regions of immensity. Heaven heard it, and hell heard it, and the remotest star shall hear it, testifying to the love of God in his unspeakable gift, and to the supremacy of that blessedness of giving which could be reached only through death—the death of the cross. This joy of giving it was that was set before him, for which he endured the cross, despising the shame.

And not only did our Saviour exemplify this precept, but also his Apostles. They were first receivers, and then givers. They filled their urns at the fountain of light and power, and then rayed these forth with an energy that made them the great benefactors of the race. Standing simply as men, without wealth, or power, or learning, or genius, they gave their being in its entireness to the diffusion among men of God's method of salvation, and thus took their stand at the head of the mightiest moral movement the world has ever seen. Nor have they failed to have successors in men of a like spirit, faithful, self-denying, ready at any moment to seal their testimony with their blood. All down the ages there have been those who have given, not property only, but themselves, to this cause of God and of man.

My dear Friends of the Graduating Class, I now turn to you. Our intercourse of the past year has been one of mutual giving and receiving. You have not, I am thankful to say, merely received, but in kindness, in courteousness, in faithfulness, in progress, have also given ; and in this there has been a blessedness which I am sure will be cherished in mutual remembrance. And now, in closing my labors for you, it has been with the hope of commending to your more careful attention, and to your full adoption the reach and spirit of the text, that I have entered upon the preceding discussion. I would that you should be givers. To you the exhortation comes with peculiar appropriateness, "Freely ye have received, freely give." You have received from God high endowments—not merely the susceptibilities of the animal, by which you are capable of pleasure, but the powers of the angel, by which you are capable of an eternal blessedness—not merely the desires which would grasp and appropriate their objects, but also affections by which you may give love and its fruits, voluntarily joining hands in that line of receiving and giving which begins at the throne of God and terminates only with animate being. You have received a country, vast, prosperous, progressive, whose future towers up into an undefined magnificence. Freely you have received the heritage of free institutions bought with blood, for which the nations of the old world sigh in vain. Under these fostering institutions you have received your early education, and now, through the wise beneficence of others, are completing your collegiate course in the free air of these mountains. You have received the hoarded wisdom of the past, a key of knowledge that fits the wards of nature's locks as never before, that is daily unlocking, and will unlock, treasures and resources undreamed of in former days, and surpassing fable. Above all, you have received "freedom to worship God," and a knowledge of the way of life and salvation through Jesus Christ our Lord. O ye plants in the very garden of the Lord, have ye thus received his rain and his sunshine, and shall ye not yield fruit? Shall there be among you one empty vine, bringing forth fruit unto himself; one frivolous, pleasure-loving, self-seeking, world-worshiping idolater? Are you not satisfied that the law of giving is the true law of our being? And do you not see how hopeless it must be to go against those deep tendencies which God has wrought into our frame—that to strike against the adamant of his laws is to be "dashed in pieces?" "Freely ye have received, freely give." Poor you may be, and many of you are, in the riches of this world. But there is a giving higher than that decorous giving that meets public expectation, but not the requirements of good stewardship; there is a giving higher than that of wealth to any extent. The time has come when a man is "more precious than fine gold; even a *man*, than the golden wedge of Ophir." Give *yourselves*, give as Christ gave, as the Apostles gave. Pierce to the kernel those Christian paradoxes, that we save by losing, and live by dying, and receive by giving. Go where duty calls, where there is ignorance to be enlightened, suffering to be relieved, vice to be reclaimed, character to be improved. These are works which must be done by living men. Wealth alone cannot do them; the labors of the dead past cannot do them. It is not the touch of the bones of a dead Prophet that can give moral life. In every age it is a sympathizing love that must stretch itself upon the body of this death, and then it will live. So give, and in the day of the Lord Jesus "you shall receive a crown of glory that fadeth not away."

PERFECT LOVE.

A

BACCALAUREATE SERMON,

DELIVERED AT

WILLIAMSTOWN, MS.

AUGUST 15, 1855.

BY MARK HOPKINS, D. D.
President of Williams College.

SECOND EDITION.

BOSTON:
PRESS OF T. R. MARVIN & SON, 42 CONGRESS STREET.
1859.

Entered according to Act of Congress, in the year 1855,

BY T. R. MARVIN,

In the Clerk's Office of the District Court of the District of Massachusetts.

SERMON.

1 JOHN iv. 18.

PERFECT LOVE CASTETH OUT FEAR.

The happiness which men seek, is not like gold, which, when once found, can be kept; it is the result of some activity; it must cease when that activity ceases; and the happiness that is highest and best, can spring only from the activity of those faculties that are highest and best. Here is the true theory of human happiness. With all normal activity, God has connected enjoyment; and the more exalted the faculties, and the more intense the activity, the higher the enjoyment. If then the highest happiness can come only from those faculties, or forms of activity, that are highest and best, it becomes a paramount question what those faculties are.

The general modes of activity are three. We think, we feel, we will. The will, however, need not be considered here, because it is a means of good only through thought and emotion. Aside from mere sensitive good, it is from thought and emotion that all willing springs, and it is to thought and emotion that it ministers. We have, then, in seeking for the immediate sources of enjoyment not sensitive, to compare only our intellectual and emotive nature; and our first inquiry is, What is the relative rank of the intellect and the emotions?

It has been the tendency of the world, and especially of students, to exalt the intellect. Under this, all agree in including our perceiving and reasoning powers; and I would also include our powers of intuition, and of comprehension. These, especially those of intuitive reason and comprehension, are high powers. By them we are made in the image of God, we become partakers of his thoughts and purposes, and are enabled intelligently to serve him. They place us in the same rank as the angels, and involve the capacity, and thus the implied promise, of an indefinite progression. In their exercise, there is a consciousness of inherent and native dignity that sets us apart from the brutes that perish.

Connected with the activity of the intellect there is naturally an appropriate and a high enjoyment, that still has no name as a specific emotion. Its wheels do not creak and complain, as they revolve; they sing. Doubtless there might have been a cold and unimpassioned perception, a merely dry insight and comprehension; but we are not so made. "It is a pleasant thing to behold the sun;" it is pleasant to perceive and trace relations, to discover or follow an argument; all insight and comprehension are pleasant. Shall we then say that the pleasure thus received is itself an emotion? In its widest sense, we may; but not thus can we practically discuss this subject. The pleasure connected with the mere activity of the faculties, is one thing; the specific emotions, as of admiration, beauty, sublimity, which depend on the activity of the faculties under certain circumstances, are another; and there is plainly no fixed ratio between perception or comprehension on the one hand, and any specific emotion on the other. There are those with great powers of insight who feel little admiration; who can stand before beautiful and sublime objects with but slight emotion. An astronomer may weigh a planet, or measure its orbit, or cast an eclipse, with as little admiration as a shop-keeper would weigh a pound of sugar, or measure a yard of cloth, or cast up his day-book; while a person with but little insight, knowing nothing but facts and results, may contemplate the heavens with constant admiration and delight. We even hear of the cold philosopher; as if there were some incompatibility between intellect and emotion; and we constantly observe the greatest variety in the intensity of emotion, when persons are in the presence of the same beautiful or sublime objects. It is true that all elevated and worthy emotion must depend on the intellect; yet so distinct are they, that we may cultivate the intellect exclusively, and repress the emotions; or we may riot in emotion, while the intellect is comparatively neglected.

But since both intellect and feeling are essential parts of our being; since thought is the condition of feeling, and feeling stimulates thought; it may be asked, how we are to decide their relative rank.

This we can do, as in all other systems of related parts that have reference to an end. In these, that which precedes as a condition and a means, is subordinate to that which is accomplished as an end. Hence, that the intellect is subordinate, appears from the very fact that it is the condition and basis of the emotions, and that they are later in the order of nature and of time. In the order of creation, and of all individual development,

"Time's noblest offspring is the last."

Man, in whom all other things are epitomized and culminate, came last; and that in him which is highest and noblest, the powers of reflection and of reason, with their consequent emotions, also come last to perfection. In the vegetable, the fruit and the flower come last, and all that precedes is conditional for these. Emotion is, indeed, as the flower to the stalk, as the fruit to the flower. It is the verdure, that clothes the skeleton trees; it is the expression, that lives and glows upon features otherwise rigid and motionless; it is the sweet smelling savor of every acceptable offering, that is laid upon the altar of God's service or of the service of man; it is the incense that should go up as a cloud from this world of marvels and of beauty. To say that there is no happiness without emotion in some form, seems hardly adequate. It might be nearer the truth to say, that it *is* happiness—for what do we know of happiness, except as an emotion? And yet there is no distinct emotion of happiness that is known by that name, and that can be distinguished from those several emotions by which it is enwrapped, and which it perfumes.

The emotive nature of man, thus pre-eminent, has a wide range; and we next inquire what it is in *that* that is highest and best.

In perceiving external nature, every degree and kind of perception has its emotion, from the faintest whisper of beauty, sublimity, admiration, delight, to their highest notes. It is, however, only when we pass to sentient and rational beings, that the emotions take the name of affections, and swell and surge in the passions. Here it is that we find love; but in assigning its rank, we must make some discriminations.

From the poverty of language, things but remotely related to each other are often indicated by the same word. So it is with love. In its broadest sense, it indicates the tendency of beings capable of enjoyment towards that in which their enjoyment is found, whatever it may be. It includes all animal appetencies and instinctive affections, as well as that attachment which has its primal seat in the will, and involves rational and moral elements. The ox is said to love the grass, the mother bird its young, the ambitious man loves fame, the miser loves money, and the seraph loves God. It is used to express the purest affections of spiritual beings, and to sanctify the grossest and most criminal passions. Like 'fitness,' it is used to express a general relation, and not the nature of the things related; and the attraction of gravitation is not more unlike that of two loving hearts, than are some of the different forms of what is called love, from each other. But the love spoken of in the text, has no connection with appetite, or passion, or instinct, or any thing sensitive; but springs wholly from our rational and moral nature, and is drawn forth wholly by that which is rational and moral. It is the love of man for the spiritual and unseen Creator. It is love, not as an instinctive tendency, or a mere affection, but as a principle. As in conscience there is a rational element, by which we recognize the right, and an emotion, by which we approve it; so in the higher forms of love there is a rational apprehension of worthiness, of moral beauty and excellence, and that peculiar and strong and undefinable emotion which is the soul of love. These may be distinguished from each other, but they cannot be separated and the love remain. It is their union that constitutes the one substantial and working principle that we call love, as it is the union of oxygen and hydrogen that constitutes water; and it is this fusion of the intellect and the affections, that is called 'love' in the text. This is the highest form of human, and we may say, of rational activity. The light of the intellect is cold and cheerless; it is the warmth of love that brings out the verdure, and awakens the voice of the swelling song. This is the high and pure principle by which we are drawn towards all that is capable of happiness in its proper sense, by which we are not only attracted towards all that is amiable and generous and pure and holy in character, but by which we abide steadfast in our attachments. It is the highest form of activity drawn out by the highest objects. Taken with the happiness which it enfolds, which pervades and forms a part of it, it is the highest result, the brightness, the crown and consummation of the works of God—nay, it is the great mode of activity and ground of happiness in God himself. "God is love, and he that dwelleth in love, dwelleth in God, and God in him." "He that loveth not, knoweth not God."

But perhaps we may best gain a conception of the true rank and functions of love, from the agencies of nature which are required as its symbols. No one of these is adequate. To symbolize it fully, requires the three great elements or agents, on which all enjoyment, and life, and order depend.

Of these, the first is light, which represents the intellectual element in love. How grand a symbol is this all-encompassing, all-revealing element! It gives to the earth and heavens all their beauty and glory. Without it, the distant universe would be to us as though it were not. This is the only symbol of that conscious certainty and satisfying knowledge, without which all affection is degraded to an instinct. But as there may be and is, knowledge without love, as light without warmth, we will not dwell upon this.

The second great element needed to symbolize love, is heat. Not chiefly as concentrated in fire, or as radiating immediately from it, is heat known as a beneficent agent. It pervades all matter, giving fluidity to water, to the sap of vegetables, to the blood of animals, quickening every seed that germinates, and is an indispensable condition of all life.

Without it the universe would be solidified in eternal frost, and motionless in death. But suppose, now, there were in this universe no warmth of affection, no throb of kindness in any heart; that God himself were, as some would make him, but an iceberg of intellect, chilling the universe, and that men were made in his image; and there would be a frost and a death, which the withdrawal of its vital heat from the frame of nature could but faintly shadow forth. Not one pulsation of love in the universe! How awful the desolation! But where love is, all icy chains are dissolved, all dormant life is quickened, every rivulet sings, every flower opens its petals, and to breathe is to be happy. An intelligent love is the blended light and warmth that gives to all things in the spiritual world their life and beauty.

But not less essential in nature than light and warmth, nor less perfect as a symbol, is another power that pervades the universe, and binds all nature together. This is the power of attraction. It shows itself in various forms, now uniting the particles of smaller masses in the embrace of a cohesion which no force can sever, and now binding together families of worlds as they pay homage to their centre, and move on with reciprocal attraction and seeming affection in the fields of space. Without this, particle would be loosed from particle, and world from world. The earth, the planets, the sun, the fixed stars would be sifted into space, and would disappear. Not a spot where the foot might tread would remain in the universe. And this does but represent the uniting and harmonizing power of love, in an intelligent and moral system. Within a limited range, and under higher control, a system of balanced selfishnesses may move on for a time; but as a great uniting principle, that will hold every individual in his place and sphere, and work out any rational good, nothing but love can be imagined. This only can unite the family, the church, the state. Only this can insure harmony among nations, only this can bind the creature to the throne of the Creator. With a God thus enthroned and reigning by love, and every rank and order of being walking his circuit by the attraction of love, not merely around the throne of God, but around all those social and governmental centres which God has ordained, we have moral order, the only order that can be permanent, or that has intrinsic worth.

The union thus of three, and perhaps even of two great elements in nature, as the symbol of a principle or mode of activity in the spiritual world, is entirely without example. Of these three elements and forces, the sun is, in our system, the centre. From him goes forth the light, from him the warmth, from him chiefly, though it be reciprocal, the attraction. What a fountain of radiance! How does that radiance stream forth as in genial marriage with the vitalizing heat! What a centre, we might almost say, of loving attraction! And when we look at the splendor and pervasiveness of these elemental forces, at their gentle, yet ceaseless and resistless agency, and at their results in the sphere of matter, we may form a conception of the place which that love must hold in a moral and spiritual system, which can be symbolized only by all of these; and we may realize more fully the grandeur and force of those most simple, yet most sublime expressions of the Bible, "God is a Sun," and, " God is Love."

It is to this great principle of love, thus shown to be the highest form of human, and indeed of rational activity, that I would now, my dear Friends of the Graduating Class, call your especial attention. It is of this, that I desire you should become radiating centres; it is under the control of this, as flowing out from the great centre of all, that I desire you should fully come. In order to this, then, let us, as would be required by the text, consider first, what it is that love must exclude.

And here I observe, in the first place, that love would exclude fear. " Perfect love casteth out fear." It is chiefly in fear, and not without reason, that the son of Sirach makes that " great travail " to consist, which he says " is created for every man, and that heavy yoke which is upon the sons of Adam, from the day that they go out of their mother's womb, till the day that they return to the mother of all things." " Their imagination of things to come," says he, " and the day of death, trouble their thoughts, and cause *fear* of heart; from him that sitteth on a throne of glory, unto him that is humbled in earth and ashes; from him that weareth purple and a crown, unto him that is clothed with a linen frock." How then may fear be removed? Its opposite is commonly said to be hope, and it is by this that most would attempt to exorcise this spectre. But the philosophy of the Bible is profounder than this. Hope is so far from being the opposite of fear, that it implies it. So long as there is that want of certainty which hope implies, there must be some lingerings of fear. Nor is it all love that can cast out fear. On the contrary, much of our love tends to increase and multiply our fears. The more objects of affection we have in a world like this, and the more tenderly we love them, the more open are we to suffering, and the more ground we have for fear. It is only the love of God, as a Father, involving perfect confidence in his wisdom, and goodness, and almightiness, that can stay the risings of distrust and apprehension. This, a perfect filial love not only can, but must so do, that all fear shall flee away, as the mists of the morning before the sun. To him who loves *thus*, God will be a " refuge and strength." He need not, and he will not fear, " though the earth be removed, and though the mountains be carried into the midst of the sea."

And not only would perfect love exclude fear, but also hate. This it does towards the being loved, by the very force of the terms. But he who has a perfect love of God, can have no more hatred of any of his creatures, than God himself has. He may—from the very fact of his loving a moral quality he must—have a strong hatred of its opposite; but in that there will be no corroding passion, no malignity, which alone is properly hate, and in which alone, and in remorse, is there involved essential misery. As love is pervaded by an inseparable happiness which, as an original part of it, emanates from it, as the fragrance from the flower, or the light from the sun; so is malignity pervaded by an inseparable and an inevitable misery. This element love would exclude; and thus, under its sway, both fear and hate, those two great foes of human good, would disappear.

Once more. The perfect love of God would exclude that undue regard for self, into which all malignity properly human strikes its roots. Both fear and hate are passions, and imply intense feeling; but selfishness is a principle, and may be the basis and substratum of life. Practically, this is, indeed, the great antagonist force to love. Consciously or unconsciously, impliedly or avowedly, we must make either self or God the centre; and in the conflict of self with the claims and will and interests of God, consists the great moral battle of this world. Originally self has the ground; but the entrance of divine love is as the opening of spring, where the winter has reigned. The beginning of the spring is often unperceived; its progress is slow; there are long and fierce struggles of contending forces; sometimes it may seem to go back. But the sun does not go back. His advance towards the northern tropic is steady; the snows disappear, the conflict of the wind ceases, the earth is quickened, and in due time the long, quiet, fruitful days of summer are sure to come. Such is the progress, the triumph, the summer of a divine love reigning in the soul. Now it will bring forth fruit unto God, and all undue regard to self will be excluded.

Having thus spoken of what a perfect love would exclude, we now come to that which is positive, and will first consider it as a motive to action. As such, it is higher and purer than any other. To work from fear, is slavery; to work under the compulsion of animal want, is a hardship, and if not a positive, yet a relative curse; to work for personal ends, as for pride, or ambition, or the accumulation of property, either for *its* own sake, or *our* own sake, is compatible with freedom, but has in it nothing either purifying or ennobling; it finds and leaves the soul dry and hard. But activity from love, is the perfection of freedom and of joy. Love has the power to make the greatest labors seem light, and the greatest obstacles trifling. When Jacob served seven years for Rachel, " they seemed unto him but a few days, for the love he had to her." How free and cheerful is the labor of a mother for her child! And even among animals, where instinct simulates and foreshadows moral love, we are attracted towards it, we sympathize with it, we think it beautiful, we regard it as wanton and cruel to disturb its natural flow. Its very semblance is the highest form of animal life; and when the rapt seraph adores and burns, it is this that gives to the flame its brightness and its power.

But in a world and a universe where obedience is so required by the cardinal relations in which we are placed to parents, to civil society, and to God, the place of love, as a motive to obedience, requires special attention. In a moral system it would seem that the point where obedience is required, must be that and that only, where there can be pressure, friction, derangement. Obedience requires the sacrifice of will, of pride, often of apparent self-interest. And of these there is no solvent but love. Fear may hold them in abeyance for a time; policy may disguise and temper their workings; but only love can come up and undermine them, and float them away, and dissolve them in its own depths. Obedience from love, is that alone which is honorable to him who is obeyed; and there is no other principle, there can be no other, that will bind a free and rational being to obey, and make that obedience a source of happiness. Hence the Bible, always true to the constitution and wants of our nature, anticipates and recognizes no other obedience. "This is the love of God, that we keep his commandments." "If ye love me, keep my commandments," making the love first, and the keeping of the commandments a natural fruit and out-growth of that. Thus it is that love, where action is not possible, and where it is, love expressed in action—"love, is the fulfilling of the law."

Nor, in addressing students, may I omit to mention the relation of love to the intellect as a moving power. All high emotion is indeed preceded by the action of the intellect; yet that emotion reacts upon the intellect, and from it alone must come the impulse that will lead to steady and intense application. Here, as in the body, the powers act in a circle. Digestion forms the blood, the blood gives power to digestion. It is a prejudice, as disastrous as it is unfounded, that there can be a schism between the heart and the intellect, to the advantage of either. The world is not ready to receive it, but it lies in our structure, and must ultimately appear, that the love of God is the highest ground of enthusiasm, not only in the study of his word, but of his works. They may indeed be studied from curiosity, from ambition, from a desire even to disprove the being or the moral government of God; and thus we may have sharp, disputatious, dogmatical partisans of theories; but the genial, patient, comprehensive, all-reconciling thinker, will be most often found where the pale and dry light of the intellect is tempered by the warm glow of love. How can he who has no love, interpret a universe that originated in love? The works of God are all expressions of his attributes, and thoughts, and feelings. Through them we may commune with him. So far as there is thought in the works of God, it is his thought. He it is that, through uniformities and resemblances and tendencies, whispers into the ear of a philosophy, *not* falsely so called, its sublime truths; and as we begin to feel, and trace more and more those lines of relation that bind all things into one system, the touch of any one of which may vibrate to the fixed stars, this communion becomes high and thrilling. Science is no longer cold. It lives, and breathes, and glows, and in the ear of love its voice is always a hymn to the Creator.

And not only is love a motive of action, it is also a guide. The modes in which conscious beings are guided to their good, are two. They either comprehend the good, and the means of attaining it, and so are guided by reason; or, without comprehension, are guided to the good by a blind and unreasoning instinct. Of these, reason is the higher, but instinct is the more sure; and proud as we are of our reason, it not seldom happens that that very reason would call upon us to give up the guidance of ourselves, not merely to faith in God, which some object to, but even to the instinct of a brute. The traveler on horse-back, returning home and losing his way in the darkness, will most wisely give his horse the reins. He who winds his way over the fearful passes of the Andes, on the back of a mule, where a single mis-step would precipitate him a thousand feet, must interpose no suggestions of reason between the sagacity of instinct and his own safety. Now what man needs, is a guiding principle, that shall combine the security of an instinct, with the ardor of passion, and the freedom and dignity of a rational wisdom. And such a principle he has in the love of God. It is rational and free, because, in the fullest light of his reason, man chooses God as the object of his confidence and love; it has in it the element and impulsion of passion, because we are drawn towards him by his own inherent loveliness, as the river to the ocean; and it is sure, because God must deny himself, before he could suffer an action, prompted by genuine love to him, to result in ultimate disaster. It is through this irresistible conviction of security, that a perfect love must cast out all fear and its torment.

In a world like this, where we know so little of the connections and dependencies of things, a case can never occur in which the highest reason would not require us to follow the promptings of love to God, rather than any calculations of what we may call prudence, or understanding, or reason. It may lead to the martyr's stake; but the end will justify it. It is from the predominance of love in the character of woman, that what seem to be her instincts, but which are something higher, are often so much wiser than the reason of man. Woman loves, and trusts, and so prays; man reasons, or thinks he does, and scoffs. The perfection of character and of action will be found, as it was in Christ, in the highest combination of reason and of love.

But not only is love a motive and guide of action, it is the basis and essential element of character. The *characteristics* of a man, are those things by which he is known; his *character*, is his moral state, and this depends on the paramount love that is in him. If the paramount love be of sensual pleasure, the man is a voluptuary; if of fame, ambitious; if of money, a miser; and if of God, he is a religious man. According to his paramount love, will be the image and superscription that shall be set upon every spiritual being; according to this the quality of his inner life, his affinities, his companionships, and his ultimate destiny. The perfect love of God, is the Christian religion perfected in us; it gives us affinity for him, complacency in him, and gives us naturally, the inheritance not only of all things which he has made, but also of the direct brightness and glories of his character.

And this leads me to speak, in the last place, of love as a source of enjoyment.

Happiness, as has been said, does not consist chiefly, in the possession of any thing, but in the activity of the faculties upon their appropriate objects. The intellect is not for itself; it apprehends objects adapted to produce emotion, and the emotion comes to us loaded with happiness, as the air with fragrance. We seem at times, indeed, to know it only as happiness.

But of the emotions, the moral love of a Being that is infinite and perfect, is the highest possible. Has man the capacity to apprehend such a Being directly, and can such a Being thus become, by his own presence, the immediate cause of emotion? That he can, the Bible clearly asserts; and this is the Christian solution, unique and grand as the telescopic heavens, of the great problem of the highest good of man. No philosophy and no religion had conceived of any thing so lofty as this. It is his chief distinction, his highest dignity, that he is capable of such direct communion.

In this life we see all things by reflected light, often in utter unconsciousness of the source of that light. The tendency is to see the creature, and forget the Creator. Men behold all things in their unity and beauty, the 'cosmos,' without reference to God. The world is in their heart. But infinite love has provided for his creatures something better than this. We shall not only, as here, see God by reflected light, we shall behold his face. The light that is now below the horizon will arise full-orbed, and shine with direct rays. It shall flood the universe, and shall never go down. There shall be no night there. Not that we suppose that the whole joy of heaven will consist in the direct contemplation of God. Christianity excludes no source of happiness of which our higher nature could render us capable. It includes the pleasures of knowledge, of the social state, and the swelling anthem. But all must see, that if we are admitted, not only to an apprehension of the universe, but also to an immediate and direct apprehension of that goodness in which the universe originated; if we may know the Infinite as a friend knows his friend, the emotion must be far higher. This is the goal, the limit of imagination and of possibility. Than this nothing higher, nothing more ultimate or more satisfying can be conceived.

And now, my Friends, in bringing my labors for you to a close, what better can I do than to commend to you the cultivation of the affections, and especially of that highest of all affections, the love of God. I do not give you advice, but seek to bring you under the guidance of a great principle, that will bear you on to your true good, as the river to the ocean. Adopt this, and I would simply say to each of you, by way of advice, as Samuel said to Saul: 'Do as occasion shall serve thee, for God is with thee.' So far as instructors can give direct aid in education, it is in that of the intellect. In this you have, to a great extent, walked with each other, and with us; and if the way has been toilsome, it has also been pleasant, and the toil strengthening. We rejoice to have walked with you; we hope it has been profitable for you, and that it may hereafter be pleasant in the remembrance, that you have walked with us. But when the intellectual part is finished, and the point of transition from thought to emotion and affection is reached, there is no longer unity. We have then the expression of the individuality of each, and the same appearances and facts and knowledge may be transmuted into motions and affections, as different from each other as an anthem is from a sneer. I exhort *you* to sing the anthem, and if there must be those who scoff and sneer, not to be of their number. There is no source of happiness like a loving heart. He that has found a worthy object of a true affection has found a treasure, and he that has found one of infinite worth has found an infinite good. Therefore it is that I address you in no language of stoicism, of caution, of repression, such as age and experience often adopt. It is peculiar to the love of God, that there is in it no danger or possibility of excess. It is with loving, as with glorifying him. "When you glorify the Lord," says the son of Sirach, "exalt him as much as you can; for even yet will he far exceed: and when you exalt him, put forth all your strength and be not weary, for you can never go far enough." Here there is no need of repression, no conflict of reason with the affections. The highest office of reason is to minister to a divine love, and if this, in which there can be no excess, be enthroned, there can be no danger of excess in any other affection or passion. It is not reason, that is the natural governor of the passions. The office of reason is to enthrone an affection rightfully supreme. When this is done, all other affections take their proper places. Then light, and warmth, and attraction, coalesce; then, not from coercion or repression, but from co-operation and harmonious action, will there be peace, and an infinite joy. I exhort you, then, to no cold caution, but to the intensest energy, both of thought and of feeling. Let reason tread her outermost circuits; she shall gather nothing that will not kindle and go up as incense at the touch of divine love. Have zeal, have enthusiasm. There is a sphere for you; there is a true treasure. There are gold and pearls and diamonds and rubies that perish not. There *is* something worth living for. Mount up as on eagles' wings, up—up—to the expanse above you there is no limit.

But while I thus exhort you to this love, as the permanent good of man, I would also urge it as especially needed now in our relations here—in the present tendency to sectionalism in politics, and to sectarianism in religion. If discordant elements are to be fused, it can be only by love. Entire unity of view, in regard to modes and rites and forms, may be hopeless; but may not these be put and kept where they ought to be? May not minor points be so merged in essential truth, that harmony shall not be disturbed? May not God be so loved, that all who love him shall be loved also—that all shall be loved as he loves them? And who should do this if not you? This is demanded of you by the spirit of your training here; the age demands it of you; God demands it. Who can better bring the diversity that springs from free thought into the unity of an intelligent love? Diversity is before unity, as chaos is before order, as solution is before the crystal. But has not diversity touched its limit? Is it not time that thoughtful and good men should find a common centre in Him who foretold the diversity, but prayed for the unity. To Him we must look. He is the true head, the leader, the champion, the restorer of the race. Not human systems or organizations, but Christ only, can be a living centre of unity. His kingdom is one of obedience and love—of obedience from love. Of these he set the great example. He became obedient unto death; he loved us unto the end. My friends, I feel deeply, at this solemn moment, that the complacency of God in us—that our co-operation with him—that the results of our living that will stand the fire, will be as our love. This will purify us. This will strengthen us for self-denying labors. This will make us missionaries wherever we may be. This will enable us to unite substantially with all good men. This will make it light when we go down into the dark valley. And when your work is done; when, one by one, you shall go down into that valley, may that light be around you; may you each have that "perfect love" that "casteth out fear."

SELF-DENIAL.

A BACCALAUREATE SERMON,

DELIVERED AT

WILLIAMSTOWN, MASS.

AUGUST 3, 1856.

BY MARK HOPKINS, D. D.
President of Williams College.

Published by request of the Class.

BOSTON:
T. R. MARVIN & SON, 42 CONGRESS STREET.
1856.

Entered according to Act of Congress, in the year 1856,

By T. R. MARVIN,

In the Clerk's Office of the District Court of Massachusetts.

SERMON.

HEBREWS II. 10.—MATTHEW XVI. 21.

For it became Him, for whom are all things, and by whom are all things, in bringing many sons unto glory, to make the Captain of their salvation perfect through sufferings.

If any man will come after me, let him deny himself, and take up his cross, and follow me.

WHAT is it that makes a hero? Not simply labors performed and sufferings endured. The slave labors and suffers. The labors and sufferings must be voluntarily assumed. Nor is this enough. The fanatic, the superstitious devotee, voluntarily assume labors and sufferings; but they are not heroes. The labors and sufferings must be voluntarily assumed, from benevolence, a pure affection, or a sense of duty. Labors and sufferings thus assumed and perseveringly sustained, make a hero; and it is the turning point in the destiny of men, when they freely decide whether they will, or will not, assume that self-denial and suffering, without which nothing great or good can be accomplished. Not more surely does the tree come to its flowering and its fruitage, than man comes to freedom of choice, intelligent action, moral responsibility, and through these, to that moment of decisive and governing choice which shall control his professional career here, to that which shall give direction to the current of his moral life forever. At this point, the *set* of the current may be undecided. It may be as water on the summit of the Andes. A pebble, the finger of a child, may turn it; but that moment decides whether it shall mingle with the stormy Atlantic, or rest and glitter on the bosom of the broad Pacific.

You, my beloved Friends of the Graduating Class, stand, to-day, upon the summit of a moral Andes. It overlooks, on either hand, the plains you are to traverse, and the ocean you are to sail. Not as drops of water, are you impelled by a necessitating force; but with the comprehension of reason, with the responsibilities of freedom, with the advantages of education, in the freshness of opening manhood, you are to decide whether you will tend towards that dark and troubled sea which can not rest, whose waters cast up mire and dirt; or towards that bright and peaceful ocean, where sleep the isles of the blest.

This connection of heroism with labor and suffering preferred for a high end to ease and pleasure, and this turning point in life, heathen mythology has presented in the choice of Hercules, between Virtue and Pleasure. I wish to present them to you under the clearer light and higher sanctions of the religion of Christ. This would make every man a hero. The text asserts that the work of Christ was accomplished through suffering, which we know he chose to endure, and that those who would follow him, must deny *themselves*, must *take up* the cross! Is then the end worthy of these sacrifices? Are they inherent in the system? How does this principle of self-denial compare with those which regulate the world? That we may answer these questions, let us look

I. At the object of Christianity, as presented in the text—to bring "many sons unto glory."

II. At the process by which this is to be accomplished—a process of *salvation* implying a previous liability and tendency to ruin.

III. At the consequent fact that self-denial and suffering, voluntarily assumed, must enter as essential elements into Christianity.

And IV. Compare the principle of self-denial with those which regulate the enterprise and pleasures of the world.

First, then, the object of Christianity is to bring "many sons unto glory."

This is its more immediate and direct object, though, as has been said of the atmosphere, it "consolidates uses." The atmosphere evaporates water, distributes it, reflects light, bears up birds, wafts ships, supports combustion, conveys sound, is the breath of our life, and the azure of our heavens. So Christianity, while it magnifies the law, and enthrones mercy, and reconciles us to God, and makes known to principalities and powers in the heavenly places his manifold wisdom, is also the regulating and renovating spirit in the relations of time. It alone inspires and guides progress; for the progress of man is movement towards God, and movement towards God will ensure a gradual unfolding of all that exalts and adorns man. It excludes malignity, subdues selfishness, regulates the passions, subordinates the appetites, quickens the intellect, exalts the affections. It promotes industry, honesty, truth, purity, kindness. It humbles the proud, exalts the lowly, upholds law, favors liberty, is essential to it, and would unite men in one great brotherhood. It is the breath of life to our social and civil well-being here, and spreads the azure of that heaven into whose unfathomed depths the eye of faith loves to look. All this it does, while yet its great object is in the future. The river passes on, but the trees upon its banks are green and bear fruit.

The glory spoken of in the text, and which is the direct object of Christianity, consists in an immortality in the moral likeness of God, and in the consequent enjoyment of him and of all that he has to give. It implies conscious rectitude, and the approbation and love of all the good in the universe of God. This is true glory; and the love of this, Christianity does not repress. That love *is* Christianity, and it calls out in its pursuit the whole strength of the human powers. It opens to the flight of the eagle a boundless firmament. Here is one difference between the Christian and the worldly hero. "Now they do it," says the Apostle, "for a corruptible crown, but we for an incorruptible." It is a " crown of glory that fadeth not away." It transcends, as it should to be most effective, as it must to be adequate, our highest conceptions. Even inspiration can only say, as only inspiration would say, "We know not what we shall be." " Eye hath not seen, nor ear heard, neither have entered into the heart of man, the things which God hath prepared for them that love him." This is the highest possible object for man, and hence there is in it his true end; for the true end of any thing which God has made, is the highest of which it is capable.

Christianity does not, indeed, claim that it shall bring *all* unto glory. Here is a mystery that hangs over this revelation, and a ground of its rejection by many. It speaks of sin with a sternness, and of its unaverted results with a terror, with which those who have but slight conceptions of the holiness of God have no sympathy. Still, it is entirely a system of salvation, and will bring unto glory every one who will receive it. Men may reject it, and then charge upon it the very ruin from which it came to deliver them; but it is wholly beneficent. Through it must come all the ultimate good that shall come to the race; and if there must be those who perish, yet the sons that shall be brought unto glory shall be many. They shall be "a great multitude which no man can number, of all nations and kindreds and people and tongues."

Such is the object of Christianity; and I now observe, in the SECOND place, that this object is to be reached by a process of *salvation*, implying a previous liability and tendency to ruin.

This proposition all do not accept; and, among those who believe in the being and agency of a personal God, the question respecting its truth involves a division more radical than any other. It involves a difference in the foundation on which men build, in all the aspects of the present system, in the supposed tendencies of our nature and of human affairs, and in all plans for reform. This is the parting point between the Evangelical system of religion and all others; for Evangelism, being the proclamation of good tidings, can properly involve only what is announced from without as coming into the system, and not any thing already in the system and that could be evolved from it. Is the ship moving towards the port, or drifting upon the rocks? Left to itself, will that aggregate of capacities and tendencies which we call human nature reach its true good as instinct reaches its end? Do we become sons of God, and shall we be brought unto glory by our first birth, or must we be born again?

I know well how strange the state is in which this doctrine supposes our world to be, and into what mysteries of the past, and perplexities of the present, and fears of the future, it must run; and how strong in us all, is that naturalism by which we hold, as with the grasp of death, to what is called the world. I know with what intense hatred and scorn this doctrine and its adjuncts are regarded, often by learning and philosophy, and especially by genius, that well knows how to weave its bitter derision of them into the tissue of its fiction and its poetry. I know how strong the argument against it is, both from feeling and from a seeming analogy.

How bright and beautiful is that nature by which we are surrounded, and with which we feel ourselves in sympathy? We stand abroad when the day is gone, and the stars are coming out in the clear heavens, and the crescent moon hangs in the west, and the dark foliage sleeps in the still air, and the faint light lies upon mountain and valley and river like a white veil upon the face of beauty, and Feeling asks, Can it be *this* upon which revelation has written, " Reserved unto fire" ?

We see the orbs of heaven moving, unerringly, as if of themselves ; we see the tree pushed upward by an internal force, and the animal following its instincts, and thus reaching their ends. They have no need to be born again ; and Analogy asks, Is not our nature also good ? If we give ourselves up to the guidance of its instincts and impulses and passions, shall it not be well with us ? To enjoy, is it not to obey ? May we not give nature her bent, and eat and drink and enjoy ourselves and die, and feel that death is but a sleep before a pleasant waking ? O what joy it were to mingle ourselves with the elements and forces around us, in their on-going, without responsibility, or care, or fear ! Can it be that we must deny ourselves ? Have we that in us which needs to be repressed, crucified, and must we make strenuous effort or be lost ? O how gladly would we believe that the broad road of nature does *not* lead to destruction — that her current would float us down to no rapids, and to no cataract.

But not so speaks the revealed word. That says that the broad road does lead to destruction. Not so says conscience. When the still night of reflection comes, she does hear the roar of the cataract towards which sin is floating. Not so say history and fact. When we contrast the idols of heathen nations, and their objects of worship, with the true

God; and their frivolous and debasing superstitions with his holy and spiritual worship; and their aims and hopes with the Christian heaven; and their wretched forms of intellectual and social life, their wars and licentiousness and revenge and deceit, with the intelligence and purity and love which Christianity would produce; when we see how Christianity itself is thwarted, baffled, perverted, rejected; we must feel that here is moral perversion and moral ruin. Not so speaks the voice of nature, in her sterner and more terrific aspects; not so in the uncertainty and hazard upon which she puts us in regard to our interests here; not so in her unswerving laws and unpitying inflictions when the fatal point in transgression is reached. Not so speaks death, in its present aspect and form, with its sin-envemoned sting. Not so speak the law of God, and those dreadful words, guilt, and remorse, which are in human speech because what they indicate was first in human consciousness. Not so, especially, speak Gethsemane and Calvary. There can be no healing without sickness, no redemption without captivity, no pardon without guilt, no finding of those that are not lost, no salvation without exposure to ruin. If nature and Christianity did so speak, the first altar built by the gate of Paradise, and every bleeding victim under the Jewish economy were a lie, and Christianity would deny the necessity of its own existence. There would not be, as there is now, a salvation, and a Captain of our salvation made perfect through sufferings.

With such ground for the proposition that the process of Christianity is one of *salvation*, let us look,

III. At the *consequent* fact that self-denial and suffering, voluntarily assumed, must enter as essential elements into Christianity.

The self-denial and sufferings essential to Christianity as redemptive and restorative, are those of Christ, and of his people. Both were necessary, but on different grounds. When the Apostle says of Christ that he was made perfect through sufferings, he must mean, not that he was made perfect as a man — for as a man he was always perfect — but that by these he became officially perfect, that is, qualified for his work. Why it became God thus to qualify him, we are not here told; but this expression implies that in his qualification the sufferings were an indispensable element. That they did meet an exigency in the divine government, and are of peculiar efficacy, appears from the fact that he did *so* suffer; from the whole sacrificial economy, patriarchal and Jewish; from most direct assertions of the Bible; from the peculiar basis of Christian obligation; and from the songs of the redeemed.

But all the sufferings of Christ were not redemptive. He met with opposition and reproach, and felt under them as man may feel. He "was in all points tempted like as we are," and there are self-denials and sufferings which his people must share with him. The soldier must follow his Captain.

That self-denial enters into the preceptive part of Christianity, no one can doubt. It is remarkable how unflinchingly she proclaims her gate of entrance to be strait, and her path to be trodden, narrow. She calls upon men to count the cost before they begin to build. Unqualifiedly and universally does Christ announce the condition of discipleship: 'If *any man* will come after me, let him deny himself, and take up his cross and follow me.' 'It is enough that the disciple be as his Master.' 'If they have persecuted me, they will also persecute you.'

But is not this a harsh and an unexpected feature in a religion which originated in love? Is there not in it something of arbitrary appointment? Might not Christ have endured all? We say, No. We say that self-denial not only may, but must enter into Christian life—that so far as Christianity is redemptive and restorative, every act originating under it is, and must be, an act of self-denial. Christianity is not the absolute religion. That is freedom, health, strength, joy. That is the religion of heaven, where every power sings in the joy of a spontaneous activity. But as redemptive and restorative, Christianity exists only as antagonistic to sin; and hence there must be conflict and consequent self-denial till sin shall be eradicated.

Self-denial is not, as some seem to suppose, a conflict between different forms of selfishness. It is not self-denial when the miser concentrates his selfishness into one absorbing passion, and through that denies and subjugates his appetites; but self-denial is the triumph in man of that which is higher over that which is lower. It is, first, the exclusion of selfishness, and then the renunciation of any form of enjoyment, or of natural good, from duty or from love. Christian self-denial is the denial of self for Christ's sake. It is love going forth to reclaim the sinful, and relieve the wretched.

Now Christianity finds man in the intense activity of a spiritual death, and her work is to make him spiritually alive and healthful; but all moral death and moral disease so involve a love of sin and its pleasures, a wrong bias of the will, that conflict must attend every step of the process in eradicating sin and restoring the image of God. The disease is in the will—in the very self. Hence that self must be denied; and it is the beauty of Christianity that the great transition-acts by which man passes over to it are not arbitrary, but imply just this denial. Repentance, especially in that element of it by which we forsake sin, is always the denial of self; and this must continue as long as sin shall remain. The very act of faith by which we receive Christ is an act of the utter renunciation of self, and all its works, as a ground of salvation. It is really a denial of self, and a grounding of its arms in the last citadel into which it can be driven, and is, in its principle, inclusive of every subsequent act of self-denial by which sin is forsaken or overcome.

But if it must require self-denial to resist and overcome sin in ourselves, so must it when the sin is in others. To a sinner, the very life of his life seems involved in the selfish bent of his will, and hence the war between sin and holiness is one of extermination. The true expression of the opposition of sin to reproof, of its blind determination and unfaltering malignity, is to be found in the crucifixion of Christ. It slew the Son of God. When man saw perfect goodness, he crucified it. That act showed the character of man; the life and sufferings of Christ showed the kind of effort needed to reclaim him. His mission was wholly for the good of others, including their radical reformation, and was *therefore* one stupendous act and manifestation of self-denial. Of the same general character were the labors of the Apostles and their successors, and such must be all true missionary labor. In doing this, men renounce the love of property, of ease and enjoyment, and give, and labor, and suffer, for the good of others.

This essential inherence of self-denial in the Christian system is a doctrine that has faded, perhaps is fading, from the consciousness of the church, and greatly needs to be freshened and revived. Having its root in the moral ruin of man and his possible restoration, it must enter into the elimination of sin and its consequences from any system. It is the distinctive characteristic of Christian activity as opposed to a life of mere nature, or of absolute wickedness. It excludes, on the one hand, all penances and self-righteousness; and, on the other, the love of ease and self-indulgence. Thus viewed, there is about it nothing arbitrary, or harsh, or austere. It is no mere negation of good for the sake of the negation, but rather the regimen necessary for the restoration of health. Not with the eye of a cynic or of a stoic is any enjoyment scorned or rejected, but only as duty and love fix their eye upon something higher and better. God is not a hard master. The infinite love of the gospel is dashed with no spirit averse to enjoyment, or that would mar the unspeakable gift.

But if self-denial must thus enter into the Christian life, let us, as was proposed in the FOURTH place, compare it with the principles which govern the world, especially with that which governs it in its enterprise and business.

The principle which regulates the enterprise and business of the world, is that of *demand and supply;* and the spirit of the times requires, when this would come in conflict with self-denial, that they should be brought fully into contrast, that you may choose intelligently between them.

That this principle of demand and supply has a legitimate sphere, I do not question. Among beings capable of supplying each other's wants and demanding nothing injurious, it would be wholly legitimate. It does now, and must always, regulate trade, as gravity does the level of the ocean; and to apply it skillfully, is the great means of success in honorable traffic and in all forms of business. The young man inquires what it is that the world demands and is willing to pay for — whether to supply its wants, or to gratify its tastes — and as he can furnish this, and the world is willing to pay for it more than it costs, his gains will increase. In doing this, he can meet with no opposition from the very fact that there is a demand; and though he may thus accumulate a fortune, he is often regarded, if not as a benefactor, yet with complacency and approbation. Especially is this so if he have met a want unsupplied before, thus opening new sources of enjoyment, and new channels of industry. How long did the ice of our rivers and lakes form and dissolve, and contribute nothing to industry or comfort? And he who first had the enterprise to take it to the tropics, deserved a fortune. Thus we trust it will be, more and more; that as the great ocean currents circulate the waters of all zones and equalize temperature, heat creating the demand and cold supplying it, so, in the legitimate application of this principle, the productions of all zones shall more and more contribute to bring unity into the seeming diversity of nature, to supply the wants and augment the comforts of man.

But wholly legitimate as this principle would be in a race unperverted, it has its root in the doctrine that the world needs no moral change—that we are to take it as it is, and make the most of it. This it is that supplies, and insists on its right to supply whatever demand may exist, regardless of the wickedness or the woe it may cause. This it is that will sell the assassin his knife, and the drunkard his drink, and the slave-dealer his slave. It says, there is a demand; I only supply it; if I do not, another will. Thus the business of great companies and firms, nay the very institutions of society become impregnated and cemented by iniquity, till interest conspires with appetite and passion to blind the conscience and silence rebuke. Confining yourselves prudently within the range of this principle, you may pass on easily, and gain wealth, and be respected. Men will praise him that doeth well for himself. You will not be of those who turn the world upside down. You will not trouble the world, and the world will not trouble you.

But, my friends, when the Captain of our salvation came into this world, he came not to supply a demand. There was none. He came to meet a deep, though unacknowledged want. He came to those who did not receive him, who rejected him and his teachings, and crucified him. Universally it is the characteristic of wickedness and of the ignorance it engenders, that they desire to be let alone. Unhallowed traffic says, let me alone, and slavery says, let me alone, and drunkenness, and licentiousness, and Sabbath-breaking say, let us alone, and superstition and heathenism say, let us alone. If we wait till there come up from these a call for reclaiming influences, we shall wait forever. And not only do they not demand these, but they will resist them, and persecute those who bring them, and the unconsciousness of need and the strength of resistance will be in proportion to the depth of the ignorance and of the wickedness. In the face of a state of things like this, what is your sagacious, prudent, prosperous, demand and supply-man good for? His principle is that the supply should be as the demand, and when the demand is great his labors are great, and so is his harvest. But just the opposite of this is the principle of self-denial. Not in proportion to the demand but to the want of it; to the depth of the insensibility, or the fierceness of the opposition, will its sensibilities be quickened and its energies stirred. It will run at the articulated cry for help; but when there is no cry, it will abide long, even as the missionaries in the South Sea islands sixteen years, and chafe the temples of seeming death. Said one who proposed to be a missionary, " Send me to the darkest and hardest and most degraded place in your field." There spoke the spirit of the Captain of our salvation; there the spirit of every true missionary and minister and pastor. Where is the pastor even, who so preaches the truth as to search the conscience, and enforce every duty, and exalt God, and lead to a life of humility and self-denial because there is a demand for such preaching? Where is there one who is not constantly tempted to substitute the principle of demand and supply that calls for smooth, or learned, or entertaining, or exciting preaching, instead of that which would fix his eye steadily on the true end of preaching? The object of this principle is, not to take the world as it is and make the most of it, but to transform the world; and it can never rest till that world shall reflect the image of heaven. The leaven, if it *be* leaven, must *work* and cause *fermentation* till the whole be leavened.

After the contrast now drawn, it will hardly be necessary to compare this principle of active and voluntary self-denial with those which govern the seekers of pleasure and of personal distinction. For the principle of demand and supply, there is a legitimate sphere; but a love of pleasure or of personal distinction as a paramount end, has no such sphere. They have self for their centre. Their object is to *use* all things, not to improve them.

Incidentally and casually useful, they are necessarily disturbing forces in any great system of order. They link not themselves with God, or with any rightly constituted community, and so, when the springs of nature fail, they wither. There is about them nothing redolent of immortality. No man, whatever his wealth, or position, has a right thus to live to himself. No man has a right to excuse himself from active self-denial for Christ's sake. " If *any man* will come after me, let him deny himself, and take up his cross, and follow me."

From what has been said, it appears that if there is in Christianity an element of self-denial and suffering, it is because there is also in it the heroic, and the redemptive element.

The heroic element is a firm purpose to do and to endure all that love may prompt and duty require; and implies obstacles great and long continued. It is born of conflict, is manifested through labors and sufferings, and hence, but for sin and its consequent evils, could have had no place. It is not rash, or quixotic, or vain; it is not superstitious or ascetic. Needless conflict or suffering it avoids; but when its hour is come, it dares to the utmost, it endures unto death. Its full perfume is known only when it is crushed. What wonder, then, that there has been hero-worship? What has the pantheist that is nobler? Yea, what is the very highest manifestation of being, the sublimest object of contemplation? Not oceans, not mountains, or precipices, or cataracts, or storms. Not the blue vault above us, with planets and satellites and countless suns; not the awful depths of infinite space. It is not power in its creative or upholding agency; it is not skill in its minutest or in its broadest exhibitions; it is not even God himself ruling by love over an intelligent, free, harmonious, happy universe. No; it is *self-sacrificing Love*. Clothe this and the issues connected with it, as does Christianity, with the attributes of infinity and eternity, and you have a manifestation of God such as nothing else can give. It is Love unto death; Love conquering through death; Love conquering death itself, and bringing up from the struggle, and bearing aloft the gift of eternal life for a race that was lost. Here is the power of a divine Redeemer—in this the voice of the Captain of our salvation to a redeemed race, calling upon them to follow him. For something of this—for self-sacrificing love according to his measure, there is a capacity in every man, and to this, in the great conflict between moral good and evil of which this world is the theatre, every man is called. It requires no favoring exigency, no special endowment, no applauding throng, no results even which may not seem to sleep with the body of the humblest Christian till the resurrection. Its theatre is time, its issues are in eternity. This is the true battle of life. That is, not with the elements, to gain food and shelter; it is, not with the selfishness around us, to gain wealth and position; it is the conflict of every man with that within and around him which would drag him and others down, and would debar him and them from their rightful inheritance and position as children of God. And what element of heroism can there be which does not here find theatre and scope? There is an enemy to be conquered, great struggles are required, great results are pending. Here are needed both endurance and achievement; and if hitherto, in Christian heroism, endurance has seemed to preponderate over achievement, it is to be remembered that they spring from the same root, that endurance is often the nobler and more difficult, and that in this cause endurance *is* achievement. " He that endureth unto the end, the same shall be saved." Wonderful is it that Christianity, which so humbles man, should also so stimulate and exalt him — that it should be the only thing that brings within the reach of all, the struggles and rewards of a true heroism.

We see also, from the preceding discussion, the peculiar source and character of *Christian* joy.

Man is naturally capable of joy in its lighter forms. There is a joy in wit, and pleasantry, and mirth; and with these Christianity is not incompatible, except as the sight of the great mountains, or the piloting of a boat down the rapids, or earnest engagement in any business is incompatible with them. They are a part of our humanity; they have their place, and let them have it, varying with temperaments and with times. There are also the more serious and deeper joys of success, of gratified desire and affection in any form. But Christian joy is joy under the Christian system, which exists only in opposition to sin and in conflict with it. It is not, therefore, the joy of the absolute religion, when the kingdom shall be delivered up to God, even the Father, but of a cause yet militant, moving on in discouragement and perplexity, and often meeting with apparent defeat. It is the joy of repentance, of humility, of hope, of conflict; for in the conflict itself there is often a stern joy not to be exchanged for those that are lighter. There is in it the joy of earnestness, which is man's natural element. Negation, skepticism, distrust, have no joy. There is joy as the truth grows brighter, as temptation is overcome, as appetite and passion and evil habits succumb, as there is news of success and of the power of God's Spirit over the vast and varied field. An Apostle could say, "I have no greater joy than to hear that my children walk in truth." The Christian is in sympathy with Christ; and as the captive Jews remembered Jerusalem, so he remembers his cause, and weeps and rejoices with the alternations of its success. He is as the patriot soldier watching the turns of parties and the fate of battles. This may give him a sober and an apprehensive eye, but there is in it a deep and solemn joy. This is high in itself, but is chiefly to be regarded as prophetic of that which shall be, when these straits and shoals and currents of time shall be past, and we shall look out upon the calm ocean. That will be the time for joy. And O, what joy, when, in view of the full range of this mighty conflict, of the parties engaged, and of the issues involved, we shall see the last enemy destroyed, and many sons shall be brought unto glory. That will be the time for joy; now is the time for labor, for self-denial, if need be, for suffering.

Once more, we may see what must be the characteristic of effective labor in the Christian ministry.

Something is said at the present day, perhaps not too much as it is intended, of making the ministry an inviting field of labor to young men, and thus in these days, when the world draws so strongly, of inducing more to enter it. But nothing is gained by fighting the world with its own weapons. The ministry has its own joys and rewards, higher than any other; but let me say to you, my friends, who propose to enter it, that in its true spirit it can never be made an inviting field to flesh and blood; and unless you expect to take upon you this burden of self-denial, and to look for your reward chiefly to the Captain of your salvation when the conflict shall be over, let me entreat you not to enter it.

But not only in the ministry is self-denial required; there is one rule and standard for all. And now, my dear friends, let me ask each of you, standing where you now do, Will you deny yourselves in this world for Christ's sake? I call you to no superstition, to no austerity, to no fostering of pride and self-righteousness, but to the acceptance of this essential element of the Christian system as Christ left it. As you answer this question, you will settle the cast and general direction of your influence for life. So far as you are Christian men, and have insight into your own state and moral wants, you must adopt this as an element of your own secret, spiritual life. Only thus can you be transformed into the image of Christ. Only thus, too, can you do any thing to hasten the triumphs of a redemptive and restorative system on the earth. In proportion to this, must be your interest and ownership in the future kingdom of Christ. This is the spirit in which Paul prayed and labored, the spirit in which Mills and his companions prayed under the 'hay-stack' fifty years ago, and devoted themselves personally to the work of missions; and only in this spirit can you be associated with them.

Your course of study here is now ended; and these scenes, which I shall remember, which I trust you will remember with gratitude and pleasure, are now closing. The voice of your great Captain is calling you to other posts in the ranks of his army. Go to your posts. You are needed there. Long has that army marched in feebleness and in gloom. Through the long night of the past I hear its muffled tread, and the low notes of its complaining music. I hear the groanings of its prisoners, and see the light of its martyr fires. But now the morning is spread upon the mountains. Catching the strains of prophecy, the music strikes up inspiring notes, and the tramp of the host as it emerges from the gloom, begins to shake the earth. Every where the standard of the Captain of our salvation is thrown to the breeze, and the ranks are defiling as on the plain of the final battle. Go to your posts; take unto you the whole armor of God; watch the signals and follow the footsteps of your Leader. That Leader is not now in the form of the man of sorrows; not now does the sweat of agony rain from him. Him the armies of heaven follow, and he "hath on his vesture and on his thigh a name written, King of kings, and Lord of lords." The conflict may be long, but its issue is not doubtful. You may fall upon the field before the final peal of victory, but be ye faithful unto death, and ye shall receive a crown of life.

HIGHER AND LOWER GOOD.

A

BACCALAUREATE SERMON,

DELIVERED AT

WILLIAMSTOWN, MASS.

AUGUST 4, 1857,

BY MARK HOPKINS, D. D., LL. D.

President of Williams College.

PUBLISHED BY REQUEST OF THE CLASS.

BOSTON:
PRESS OF T. R. MARVIN & SON, 42 CONGRESS STREET.
1857.

Entered according to Act of Congress, in the year 1857,

BY T. R. MARVIN,

In the Clerk's Office of the District Court of the District of Massachusetts.

SERMON.

MATTHEW vi. 33.

BUT SEEK YE FIRST THE KINGDOM OF GOD, AND HIS RIGHTEOUSNESS; AND ALL THESE THINGS SHALL BE ADDED UNTO YOU.

The blessings which man can enjoy may be divided into two classes. Of these, one class comes to him without his seeking them. If he is to live at all, he *must* see the light and feel the warmth of the sun; he must breathe the air, and smell the fragrance of flowers, and hear the voices of men and of birds. These things he may, indeed, seek; but for the most part they come to him without any seeking or agency of his.

But there is another class of blessings in respect to which the voice of nature and of revelation is, "Seek, and ye shall find." They are to be had *only* by seeking—often only by the most assiduous and energetic application of those powers which God has given for their attainment. To most men this is true of wealth and its advantages; and it is universally true of all high knowledge and of all those personal acquisitions and qualities of mind by which a man becomes truly great.

But these blessings that must thus be sought, may also be divided into two classes, according to the *direction* in which they are sought. We may either seek to produce outward changes and to acquire possessions, or we may seek to produce inward changes—to become wiser and better. We may seek to derive our happiness chiefly from what we *possess*, or from what we *are*. The greater part of men evidently direct their activity chiefly to the production of outward changes and the acquisition of possessions. This, as it is the sin, is also the great error of the race. A few only seek first to make the tree good, and leave the result with God.

That "the kingdom of God and his righteousness" are among those blessings that must be sought, is very plain. In this respect they differ even from knowledge. Some knowledge is gathered unconsciously and involuntarily, but the kingdom of God and righteousness *can* come only through the activity and consent of the affections and the will. It is also equally plain, that the direction of the activity to be put forth in attaining these must be within. "The kingdom of God," says our Saviour, "is within you." It does not consist, in any degree, in the possession of any thing. It has nothing to do with wealth, or station, or learning, or place, or time. It consists wholly in our state; in what we really *are* in our relations to God as he is revealed in his law, and in his gospel.

And such a state—a right state in our relations to God—is not only to be sought, but is the highest end which man can seek. That this is so regarded by God, is evident from the very fact and plan of redemption. All the motives and efforts and energies of his moral government have been, and are, adapted to produce in man a change of *state*. For this Christ came; for this the Spirit is given; for this the gospel is preached; for this angels minister; this causes joy in heaven; in this God is more glorified than in all the works of his hands. What God desires of us, is a right state of the affections and the will—that we should take the place of his children, and *be* his children. Such a state, moreover, is the perfection of man himself in that which is most intimate and essential to him. It constitutes him a centre of light and of power. It is the brilliancy of the diamond, and all else is but the setting.

Having thus seen what the kingdom of God is, in what direction we are to seek it, and that it is the highest end at which we can aim, we now proceed to consider the assertion of the text, that if we seek this, " all these things " shall be added unto us. What is included in " these things," we learn from the context. " Therefore take no thought, saying, what shall we eat; or, what shall we drink; or, wherewithal shall we be clothed ? (for after all these things do the Gentiles seek ;) for your Heavenly Father knoweth that ye have need of all these things. But seek ye first the kingdom of God, and his righteousness ; and all these things shall be added unto you."

We have here a promise, in this specific case, that in seeking a higher good, adequate subordinate good shall be incidentally secured. But do these words of our Saviour express an isolated fact ? Is it not a general truth, that he who in any department aims at and attains the highest good, will also, and in so doing, attain, not merely an adequate amount, but the highest amount of subordinate good? This we suppose to be a general principle, and we propose to show that it is confirmed, first, by the Scriptures; secondly, by all that we observe in life; and thirdly, by the very constitution and processes of nature itself.

And first, if we test this principle by the Scriptures, we shall find it fully confirmed in the Old Testament. Of this no more striking instance could be given than that of Solomon. When he was permitted to ask what he would, and asked an understanding heart, "the speech pleased the Lord that Solomon had asked this thing. And God said unto him, Because thou hast asked this thing, and hast not asked for thyself long life; neither hast asked riches for thyself, nor hast asked the life of thine enemies; but hast asked for thyself understanding to discern judgment; behold, I have done according to thy words: lo, I have given thee a wise and an understanding heart; so that there was none like thee before thee, neither after thee shall any arise like unto thee. And I have also given thee that which thou hast *not* asked, both riches, and honor." He sought that which was higher, and God added the lower.

But of this principle the whole history of the Israelites is an exemplification. During the period of the Judges, whenever they sought the Lord and served him, they prospered. The earth yielded her increase, and their enemies were subdued; but when, ceasing to seek the higher blessings, they turned to idolatry, the lower were also removed. So in the history of the Kings, whenever one of them "did that which was right in the sight of the Lord," the Lord was with him and made his way prosperous; and when one of them "did evil in the sight of the Lord," disaster was sure to follow. This is the one great lesson taught by their whole history, and intended for the warning of individuals and of nations.

In the New Testament, spiritual blessings are more regarded; but even there, this principle does not fail of being announced in its general form. We are told that "godliness is profitable unto all things, having the promise of the life that *now is*," as well as "of that which is to come."

Being thus confirmed by Scripture, let us test this principle by a reference to the common objects of desire and pursuit in life.

Health is a subordinate good. To some extent, certainly, it is a good in itself, but it is chiefly so as enabling us to perform fully the duties and labors of life. How then is health best promoted? Not by making it a direct object, and exercising for the sake of exercise, but by seeking, through all the exercise of body and mind which they involve, to accomplish those higher ends for the attainment of which health was given. It was not by attention to health, but by labor, that our fathers secured the constitutions they had. It is when people have little to do, or do little, that they become nervous, and make out a daily bulletin of their feelings; and if they are not sick think they are, and in the end become so. It is recognized by every physician as a general principle, that the best condition and means of health is such activity in the pursuit of other ends as shall cause health to be unthought of.

Again, sensitive pleasure is a subordinate good, and how may this be best obtained? The body may be used either for the higher purpose of promoting the moral ends of life, or as a machine with the direct object of manufacturing the various forms of pleasurable sensation; and what we say is, that it will yield more of this form of good in its higher, than in its lower use. Pleasure results, not from the body alone, nor from that which acts upon it alone, but from the relation of the two. It is as the music from the Æolian harp. Let the harp be well strung, and it matters little what wind may blow. So of the body. It is only when this is well strung by temperance, and has that general vigor and perfection of all the senses by which it is best fitted to serve the mind, that it is most perfectly in harmony with all those natural objects which are adapted to give it pleasure. The sensitive organization of man was made to respond to the whole of nature. It is all his counterpart, and natural inheritance. But when he begins to make upon his system drafts of artificial excitement for the express purpose of pleasure, his relations to those sources of temperate and lasting pleasure which God has provided are changed. Quiet and simple pleasures become insipid; passive impressions become weaker; stronger and still stronger excitement is required; and the dividends of pleasure are increased only by drawing on the capital stock. The natural birthright of the senses is then rejected—sold for a mess of pottage. Thenceforward the man knows nothing of sun-risings and sun-settings, and the glories of night, and the march of the seasons, and the singing of birds. Sensation is more and more divorced from that union with intellect and sentiment by which it may be transfigured. Instead of being mingled in the feast of life as a condiment, it is concentrated with an unwholesome drug that stimulates and bewilders its victim for a time, and then palls upon the sense. Even Epicurus could say, that the greatest amount of pleasure could be reached only by temperance.

Thus it is that the use of the sensitive organization for a purpose lower than that for which it was intended, is not only wickedness but folly. This point should be fully settled by every young man, for it is just here that many make shipwreck.

We next inquire how this principle applies to the acquisition of wealth. Would a lawyer, or a physician, or an artist gain wealth, how will he do it most successfully? Certainly by attaining something higher,—great excellence in his profession or skill in his art,—and then wealth will flow in as a matter of course. But if any should say that the skill is subordinate to the wealth, let me speak of a character for prudence, for energy, for high integrity and honor, for righteousness generally. To such a character wealth is certainly subordinate, and yet the cultivation of that will be found one of the surest ways of acquiring wealth. This includes all that is meant by the proverb, that "honesty is the best policy," and something more.

Not only is *honesty* the best policy, but there is a tendency in all righteousness, or, as the Scriptures term it, wisdom, to produce wealth and the outward means of enjoyment. "Length of days is in her right hand, and in her left hand riches and honor." Righteousness must exclude all habits of vice and of vain and injurious expense; it would insure industry and a sense of responsibility, and would secure that confidence which is so important an element of success with business men.

In the present disordered state of things, there may be, and are exceptions to this in individual cases; but, on a large scale, where alone the principle can be fairly tested, there can be no exception. Let a nation, let this nation become righteous, and it is as certain as any law in physics, that it would be the most effectual means of increasing its wealth and worldly prosperity. The heavy weights of crime and pauperism, that now drag society down, would fall off; its productive power would be greatly increased; property would be more valuable as more secure; and the imagination can hardly conceive the extent to which such a nation might enjoy all that can make this life happy.

Again, how may a man best take care of and extend his reputation? Not by aiming at it directly, by anxiously nursing it, eager to show every unfavorable rumor to be false, and to fan every spark of good opinion into a flame; but by going on in an independent course of duty, leaving unfounded reports to die out of themselves, and the sparks to kindle into a flame, or not, as they may.

And if this be true of mere reputation, it is much more so of any great and lasting fame. The highest form of greatness, and, of course, the highest legitimate fame, can never belong to a man who has fame for his chief object. He is no true artist, who pursues his art for the sake of fame. The patriot, whose highest object is fame, is no patriot.

Health, pleasure, wealth, reputation, fame, these are all subordinate objects, and to them all the principle now laid down applies. As a general rule, they are best attained when some higher end is the immediate object of pursuit.

Here, then, we have a great law for human action. Is it also a law which God has prescribed for himself, which runs through nature, and is incorporated into all the processes and methods of his natural and moral government? Does he always, in securing higher ends, incidentally secure the lower?

In securing specific ends, and giving unity to his works, God has two methods. One of these we may call the method of additions, the other that of development. In the first, he passes onward and upward, from step to step; at each step adding something new, but also bringing forward, either in itself or its results, all that had preceded.

To illustrate this, we must go back to the beginning of time, when we may suppose matter to have existed chaotically in space, having properties but not laws. And it may be well for our present purpose, to represent the world to be constructed as a pyramid with a broad base, and ascending by successive steps or platforms, each above less extensive than that below.

What then, in such a state, must have been the first and lowest step by which matter could have been rendered available? Evidently it was to bring it together into masses; and so the first law in the order of nature, if not of time, must have been that of gravitation. This lies at the foundation. It is simple, universal, and seems to pervade all space; but, acting alone, it would simply hold the particles in proximity.

The object next higher would be, to form from these loose particles solid bodies. This is done by what is called the attraction of cohesion; and bodies united by this will form the second platform. But here it will be observed, that the higher includes the lower. Not all particles that gravitate cohere, but all that cohere gravitate.

The object next higher would be, to cause particles not merely to cohere, but to combine and to form compounds. Bodies thus united would form the third platform. But here, again, this higher is not attained without the two lower. All bodies united by chemical affinity also cohere and gravitate.

The next higher and more specific object would be, the production of regular forms, as in crystals; but every body that has a regular form also gravitates and coheres, and has its particles united by chemical affinity.

These are the first four platforms in the upward progress of the creation, and they include only inorganic matter.

The platform next higher is composed of regular forms endowed with organic life. This includes all plants—the whole vegetable creation. But in every plant we find not only organic life, and regular form, but also chemical affinity, and cohesion, and gravitation.

The next step upward is to sensitive life—that which is capable of enjoyment and of suffering, with the instincts necessary for its preservation. This greatly narrows our platform; but here again the attainment of the higher both includes and presupposes that of the lower. In every being possessed of sensitive life, we find also organic life, and regular form, and chemical affinity, and cohesion and gravitation.

There is but one step more. It is that which carries us from the sensitive life with its instincts, up to the higher rational and moral life of man. Here we find every end attained that we had below, and something added. Man is subject to every law to which the minutest portion of matter is subject, and has, generically, every characteristic of every order of being from the animalcule up to himself. In him we find operating gravitation, and cohesion, and chemical affinity; in him we find regular form, and sensitive life, and instinct, and, added to these, the higher gifts of reason and of conscience, by which he is made in the image of God.

Thus do we pass from that which is subject to law, to that which also comprehends law. Thus is man placed on the summit of the pyramid of these lower works, and fitted to link himself with that which is above. Thus is he the natural ruler, the epitome and crown of this lower world. Thus is he fitted, as partaking of the nature of all, to be the representative and priest of every thing below him, and to gather up and give a voice to that inarticulate praise which goes up from every part of it to the Creator. Thus it is that the seven steps of the creation up which I have endeavored to lead you, may be compared to seven notes in music sounded successively, and then in harmony. In the first step, there was a single note; in the second, the same note was taken up and another that accorded with it was added; in the third, another still was added to these, till man came, and every thing was prepared for the full chorus that rang through the arches of heaven when the morning stars sang together and all the sons of God shouted for joy.

We see then how perfectly, in this method of additions, God adheres to the principle which we are now considering. He never does secure, according to the constitution which he has adopted it would seem impossible he ever should secure, a higher end or good, without securing at the same time, incidentally, every subordinate end and good.

But, besides the method of additions, I have spoken of that of development. This applies only to organized beings, each of which is a system having parts and functions, some of which are subordinate and others ultimate. To such a system nothing is added from without, except as there is development from within. It supposes something to be enveloped; and that to which all the other parts are subservient, will be that which is originally enclosed in all the rest, and which is the last to come to perfection. So it is with the brain in man, so with the flower and the fruit in the plant.

But that the principle in question must hold under this method is evident because, here, that which is highest becomes perfect only through the ministration of the parts that are lower; and the more perfect the parts are that minister, the more efficient must their ministration be. This is the general rule. Limitations there may be, but not exceptions. Would God secure to any man the highest, the best balanced, and the longest continued action of the intellectual and moral powers, he does it only by giving him a sound physical constitution. When Moses, the servant of the Lord, was a hundred and twenty years old, " his eye was not dim, nor his natural force abated." So has God constituted every organic being, that " if one member suffer, all the members suffer with it, and if one member rejoice, all the members rejoice with it;" and if he would secure the perfection of the higher parts that are ministered unto, he must do it by securing the perfection of the lower parts that minister.

So far, then, as we can observe the works and methods of God, there is no exception to the principle now stated. Within the sphere of this world, it is evidently a great, guiding idea, in all that he does. It was so in its construction, giving it unity; it is so in its government, and how much farther it may extend, we cannot say. It may be, taking the universe together, and going back to the very birth of time—not of our time, but of all time—that the first world, or sun, or system that came into being, gave the key-note to the whole. It may be that that note has been repeated with additions from that time onward, till at length it may require the ken of the highest archangel to read the extended scale, and the voices, as of many waters, that surround the throne, to utter the swelling anthem.

But, it may be asked, is not the great doctrine of voluntary self-denial, a doctrine taught equally by nature and by Christianity, an exception to this principle? Is it not of the very essence of self-denial, that instead of attaining a subordinate good by pursuing one that is higher, we attain the higher only by renouncing the subordinate?

This is a difficulty; but it will be observed that it arises wholly from the disorders and unnatural state introduced by sin. This disorder and perversion are sometimes so great, as in martyrdom, that it is necessary to sacrifice every subordinate good, even life itself, for the attainment of that which is higher. Paul found it necessary to suffer, and did suffer, the loss of all things for Christ's sake.

Still, a fair statement of what is required by the law of Christian self-denial, will show that such cases are but exceptions. This law is not arbitrary. It is no law of fanaticism, or enthusiasm, or self-torture. It simply requires, first, that we deny ourselves every thing that is sinful in itself; and, second, that we deny ourselves subordinate good not sinful in itself only so far as it would exclude a higher good. The first of these is no exception to the principle of the text, because pleasures, sinful in themselves, are not a subordinate but an incompatible good — incompatible with any true good. Under the second requisition there may be exceptions, but they commend themselves to our reason and give us our true law at a point where there has been serious error. The Christian may attain any subordinate end, as wealth, may enjoy any subordinate pleasure, as that of the senses, to the highest point of non-interference with that which is higher and better. You are at liberty, my friends, to pursue wealth, and pleasure, and fame, as far as you please, provided that pursuit be not incompatible with the attainment of a higher good. You are at perfect liberty to follow amusements to any extent, if there be nothing higher or better, which, as men, and as Christians, you can do.

While, then, we admit that exceptions may arise in this way, still, the general rule will hold that subordinate good is best attained by the pursuit of that which is higher.

Having thus illustrated and confirmed the general doctrine implied in the text, from the Scriptures, from what we observe in life, and from the constitution of nature, I turn, my Beloved Friends of the Graduating Class, to you. Together, and I trust not without some success, we have pursued the investigations of science, and have sought the foundations of truth and of duty. But now the relation, very pleasant certainly to me, in which we have stood to each other, is to cease. To you there has come a period of transition—one of those doublings of a great head-land, when it becomes the voyager to make up his reckoning, and to take his bearings anew. In doing this, do not fail to remember how treacherous is that sea upon which you are to sail. One, of high promise and hope, who heard me the last year as you hear me now, sleeps in death. The name of Lamberton should admonish you that the voyage may be but brief. But whether it be brief or protracted, whether with gales prosperous or adverse, I wish to put into your hands an infallible chart. Here it is: "Seek ye first the kingdom of God, and his righteousness." Since the world began, there was never a sentence penned or uttered which I should prefer to give you as your guide. In it is the essence of all wisdom for man, for the individual and for society, the wisdom of all reform and of all growth.

In following this chart you will, first, see the necessity of seeking something. " Seek ye," says our Saviour, " seek." Have an aim, definite, specific. Without this there can be no comprehensive plans, no unity, no true decision, no earnestness, no moral power. The whole history of the race, the arrangements of nature, the constitution of man, all proclaim that man can reach his true good only by the voluntary activity of his highest powers in seeking a chosen end. Some things you may have without seeking; some you may seek, and not find; but there are things, and those which you most need, that you will never find without seeking.

Seek *ye*—ye, who are placed on the summit of the pyramid of these lower works; ye, who may, if you will, link yourselves with that which is still higher; ye, who have but one life in which to make the great choice; ye, who have been redeemed by the precious blood of the Son of God, seek *ye*.

But *what* will ye seek? This is the great question, here and now. What *will* ye seek? What will ye seek *first?* Not for its own sake, but for its bearing upon this question, have I asked your attention to the preceding discussion. I wished that my appeal to you to seek first the kingdom of God, might come, not only from his word, but that it might be seconded by a voice from all his works. I wished you to see that the principle involved in the text is so inwrought into all those works, that it cannot fail to avenge itself upon those who shall disregard it. I wished you to see that the works of God are but as a great whispering-gallery, along which, if you will but put your ear to it, the words of Christ are constantly echoing. Seek, then, not that which is below you—you were not made for *that*— but that "which is above, where Christ sitteth, at the right hand of God." Seek *first* the kingdom of God, and his righteousness. Seek it first in the order of time. Let no business preclude it. Seek it first in the strength of that purpose by which you devote yourselves to its pursuit. The kingdom of God! His glorious and eternal kingdom! His righteousness! The moral likeness of God! Seek these, and all other things, truly good, shall be added unto you. That this shall be so, there comes a voice, not from the word of God only, but from the very beginning of time, and it is uttered with increased force at every step in the process of the creation. No, my Beloved Friends, it is not *I* that speak to you; it is the whole process and method and structure of the creation of God. For him all his works testify. When the Saviour says, " Seek ye first the kingom of God, and his righteousness; and all these things shall be added unto you," there is not one of them that does not utter its Amen.

And why should not he who attains the kingdom of God and his righteousness, have all other things added? It must be so. If there may be exceptions and limitations in the present temporary scene of sin and disorder, I beseech you think not so of God as to suppose there can be any ultimate exception. " Though it tarry, wait for it; it will surely come; it will not tarry." Think not of God as unwilling that his creatures should enjoy all from his works that they can enjoy, without sin. Vast as this universe is, he has made it, the whole of it, for his creatures. He owns, not the earth only and the planets, but the sun, and the milky-way, and the far-off nebulæ. And what use has he for all these but to make his creatures happy? And whom should he make happy but those who, in his appointed way, seek first his kingdom and righteousness? So doing, you shall become his children; and if children, then *heirs;* and then it is the voice of reason as well as of Scripture, that utters that promise—the most magnificent that language can embody—ye " shall inherit all things." Ye shall be children and citizens in the kingdom of God, and shall have the free range and use of all his works. The clouds and darkness which now seem to rest over his moral government, you shall see roll away; and from the first faint whisper at the birth of time, to the full and triumphant chorus of a finished creation and redemption, you shall catch and repeat the song that shall come up to God from all his works of creation and providence and grace. With wonder and joy you shall witness every new step in the process of creative power, and of the manifestation of the divine character. You shall be present at that next and higher manifestation to which all things are now tending and hastening, and of which he speaks when he says, " Behold, I make all things new." You shall sit down at the marriage supper of the Lamb.

A

BACCALAUREATE SERMON,

DELIVERED AT

WILLIAMSTOWN, MS.

AUGUST 1, 1858.

BY MARK HOPKINS, D. D.
President of Williams College.

PUBLISHED BY REQUEST OF THE CLASS.

BOSTON:
PRESS OF T. R. MARVIN & SON, 42 CONGRESS STREET.
1858.

Entered according to Act of Congress, in the year 1858,

BY T. R. MARVIN,

In the Clerk's Office of the District Court of the District of Massachusetts.

SERMON.

ISAIAH XL. 30, 31.

EVEN THE YOUTHS SHALL FAINT AND BE WEARY, AND THE YOUNG MEN SHALL UTTERLY FALL: BUT THEY THAT WAIT UPON THE LORD SHALL RENEW THEIR STRENGTH; THEY SHALL MOUNT UP WITH WINGS AS EAGLES; THEY SHALL RUN, AND NOT BE WEARY; AND THEY SHALL WALK, AND NOT FAINT.

Have we then, here, an exception to the great law of decay? Is there any thing that begins to be, and grows, that does not reach an appointed limit, and then go back? Is not the daily movement of the sun in the heavens the fit emblem of every living thing that he looks upon in his circuit? He comes out of his chamber in the morning; he climbs the eastern sky; he reaches his meridian height, and then declines to his setting. So it is with every blade of grass, with every shrub, with every tree; so with every insect and animal, from the animalcule to the elephant; so it is with the physical system of man, and so with his mental faculties. And not only do change and decay affect every organized being, but also the empires of men and their monuments, and even the face of nature itself. "And surely the mountain falling cometh to nought, and the rock is removed out of his place; the waters wear the stones; thou washest away the things that grow out of the dust of the earth; and thou destroyest the hope of man."

Throughout this universe nothing is at rest. There is permanence only from change. The stability of the heavens is from their motion; the permanence of our bodies is by constant waste and supply. Whether the movements in the heavens will be perpetual we know not, but in the march of life every step is towards death. The movement there tends to a cessation, and that cessation is death.

It is this certainty of decay that gives a tinge of sadness to the scenes that are the most full of life. In the deepest green of the mountain side, the prophetic eye sees the " sere and yellow leaf;" in the gayest assembly of the young, it sees the gray hair and tottering age.

But to this law we find in the text, and in the Bible generally, an exception. We are told that " the path of the just is as the shining light, that shineth more and more unto the perfect day "— that " the righteous shall hold on his way, and he that hath clean hands shall be stronger and stronger "— that " they shall go from strength to strength "— that " they shall mount up with wings as eagles; they shall run, and not be weary; and they shall walk, and not faint."

So, likewise, the kingdom of Christ is not to be subject to the decays of other kingdoms. " Of the increase of his government and peace there shall be no end." " And the kingdom shall not be left to other people, but it shall break in pieces and consume all other kingdoms, and it shall stand forever." " His throne shall be established forever as the moon, and as a faithful witness in heaven." " His dominion is an everlasting dominion, which shall not pass away; and his kingdom that which shall not be destroyed."

Here, in those who wait on God, we have an alleged exception to the law of decay.

What then is it to wait on God? It is not to wait *for* him in an indolent passivity. It supposes that "all our springs are in him," and that there is an open channel of communication between him and us; so that the resources of his omnipotence may flow in to us, and supplement our weaknesses and infirmities. Its elements are expectation and trust. It implies ends sought in sympathy with God, and a sense of dependence on him actively expressed. It is as when a captive, who cannot redeem himself, waits on and earnestly implores the help of one who can redeem him. We do not suffice to ourselves. On every side we are surrounded by agents and elements that we cannot control. Beset where we stand, opposed when we would go forward, we find ourselves powerless in the presence of obstacles and foes. Then we wait upon God; our strength is renewed, and we go forward. Plainly, those "who wait on the Lord" are the same as "the just," "the righteous;" and the doctrine is, that the moral and spiritual nature of man is an exception to every thing else on this earth; and that moral goodness not only need not wane, but that it may have an uninterrupted progress.

To establish the doctrine just stated will be our first object; and to do this, we must find the ground on which the exception is made. This is found in the very nature of moral goodness. Moral goodness has its seat in the affections and the will, and these do not so decay with the strength of the body and the power of the intellect, that that goodness is impaired.

It is a brave and a beautiful thing, if indeed it be not rather sublime, when a man, in the fullness of health and of strength, is required to abjure his faith in Christ, and in the face of the tyrant he says boldly, and even defiantly, No. But when the inquisition puts its victim on the rack, and the power of endurance is tested to the utmost, and there remains only strength of mind to apprehend the question, and only strength of body to whisper the feeblest No, there is in *that No*, a power that is mighty in proportion to the very feebleness of its utterance. Yea, if we suppose any power of apprehension, and of expression even by the feeblest sign, to remain, the indication of firm principle and enduring affection and moral goodness can become strongest and most affecting only at the point where the powers of the body and of the mind flicker on the very verge of death, and at the moment when they go out in its darkness. The love of the Saviour for this world reached the crowning point of its expression only at the moment when he " bowed his head and gave up the ghost."

In these cases the exhaustion and feebleness are indeed from torture, but the principle is the same in natural decay. Had the affections of that aged and dying Christian grown weaker as his powers decayed, who, when he was asked if he knew his friend who spoke to him, said, " No,"—if he knew his children, " No,"—if he knew his wife, " No,"—if he knew the Lord Jesus Christ, " Yes," and a smile from heaven lighted up his countenance; "Yes, he is all my hope." In such cases, the embers of a wasting animal life gather over the "vital spark of heavenly flame," and obscure it. It seems to be lost; but when it can be thus reached, as sometimes it may, it is seen to be all a-glow, and the light which it shoots up is but the brighter from the darkness out of which it comes.

It is conceded that the strength of virtue and of trust are most tried in adversity, and when the natural desires are thwarted. "Though he slay me, yet will I trust in him," is the strongest possible expression of confidence. Let, then, the decay of the powers from age commence and go on, and let there be perfect acquiescence in this till their apparent cessation; and how does the power of goodness, as thus seen, differ from that which is seen in submission to a voluntary death, and in holding on, through exhaustion from torture, till the very end?

The truth seems to be, that an accountable being, remaining such, can be placed in no circumstances in which moral goodness, the principle of duty, of submission, of faith, may not be brought into exercise; and if exercised, then, by a natural law, must they be strengthened; and the more difficult and trying the circumstances are, the more strength may be gained. It is through and in the very weakness of the natural powers, that the moral powers may show their strength. Only at the moment of the seeming triumph of the tyrant, of disease, of decay, can humanity pay its highest homage to goodness and to God.

In the struggles of men against evil and for the

right, there is doubtless given the special and supernatural aid of God ; but, in addition to this, it would seem, from what has been said, that the exception made by the Scriptures to the great natural law of decay, is itself sustained by a natural law.

Having thus shown that there may be constant progress in moral goodness, we next inquire whether such progress is not a condition of the highest possible strength and perfection of the intellectual faculties. If we regard man simply as intellectual, will he not, both as an individual, and as a race, mount higher, in proportion as he cultivates his moral powers, and waits upon God ?
This is a question that deeply concerns every scholar ; and that it should be answered rightly, is of much consequence, both because it lies at the basis of all right education, and of all true self-culture ; and because there is, to some extent, an impression that skepticism and wickedness are naturally associated with intellectual power.
In what has been said it has been taken for granted, that the powers of the intellect really decay. This may be doubted. Of mind in its essence we know nothing, and of the laws of its connection with the body, very little. What seems decay may be from the body, and be only as a temporary drowsiness. Certain it is that the intellectual, are indispensable to the moral powers ; that in the nature and sphere of each, there is equally a provision for an indefinite progress ; and that the aged must be supposed to carry into another state, not the imbecility of a second childhood, but the

results of their mental, as well as of their moral action. Still, these powers do *seem* to decay; between them and the moral powers, as has been shown, there is a broad distinction; and what we say, in either case, is, that the condition of their highest attainment is the cultivation of the moral powers.

That this is true we believe, first, because of the obstacles to intellectual growth and progress that would be removed by the ascendency of the moral powers.

These obstacles are prejudice and vice, both of which are inseparable from the sway of passion and appetite, and both of which would disappear in the full ascendency of the moral powers. If prejudice may not be said to weaken the mental powers, it misdirects, perverts, and limits their action. The power of the eye is one thing; a clear atmosphere is another. Prejudice is, to the mental eye, an indistinct, a colored, a distorting medium. But while prejudice misdirects, vice enfeebles, or wholly prevents the action of the intellect. From the drunkard, the glutton, the licentious man, the gambler, we do not look for continuous thought, or for any rich fruit of intellectual culture. They have the instincts and sagacity of the animal, heightened by their connection with rational powers; but they are engrossed by their vices, and their intellects have no range beyond the activity necessary for self-gratification. Through these vices much of the finest intellect of the race has been lost. And so it must be. If the swallow would fly, its wing must not be draggled in the mud; if the eagle would continue to mount up, the animal that is sucking his blood must drop from under his wing.

But that the intellect will be most successfully cultivated through the moral powers, appears, secondly, because it is lower than those powers, and subordinate to them; and because, in securing a higher good, we best secure that which is subordinate and lower.

That the intellect is lower than the moral powers appears, because it is conditional for their activity. And here we find a criterion which may be universally applied in determining, both in matter and in mind, what agencies and powers are higher, and what are lower. Always that which is conditional for another thing, and so serves it, is lower than that thing. The foundation of a house is conditional for a house, and is lower, in more senses than one. It is indispensable, but of no value without something beyond itself. So of all the powers and agencies of inanimate matter. They are conditional for vegetable life, and are lower. So, again, vegetable is conditional for animal life, and it is lower; so with the heart and the brain; so with the body and the mind; and so with the intellect and the moral powers. The intellect is conditional for choice and activity, in which are the end of man, but it does not choose. It does not even know ends, as such. It can judge of their attainability, and of the fitness of means; but the apprehension and choice of an end, and especially, that highest act of the mind, the choice of an ultimate end, belongs to a higher power.

The inferiority of the intellect is also manifest,

because it is an instrumental and not a governing power.

We cannot too carefully discriminate those powers in us, by which we choose ends, from those that are merely instruments in their attainment. In the one is wisdom, in the other talent; in the one is character, in the other capacity; in the one, the man himself acts in his whole being, and very personality; in the other, the faculties play on the surface. The end is already chosen, and the whole work is simply executive. But, as has been said, the intellect does not choose. It is an axe, a saw, a hammer, a piece of machinery to be worked by a power back of itself. It is a Swiss mercenary, that may be enlisted in any cause, good or bad, and, as such, is inferior to the employing and directing power.

It appearing thus that the intellect is lower than the moral powers, it remains to show that the well-being of that which is lower can be best attained only as we secure that of the higher.

This was illustrated at length the last year, on an occasion similar to this. It was shown to be true of health, and pleasure, and wealth, and reputation, and fame; and also that the principle implied is incorporated into all the works of God. It is a great law of nature, with as few exceptions as there are to most of her laws; and we may fairly presume, till the contrary shall be shown, that the intellect is no exception.

But again, that the intellect will be best cultivated through the moral powers will appear, if we compare those powers with any other force by which it can be worked.

As has been said, the intellect must be worked by something back of it. It is as the muscle, that is nothing without the nerve; and its efficiency will depend partly on original structure and on training, and partly on the power that lies behind. That power must be some instinct, tendency, appetite, passion, taste, feeling, some capacity of emotion or enjoyment; and if we make a comparison among these, we shall find that the moral powers have the advantage, both in strength and continuance, and also in the unity and harmony that result from their working.

Man's nature is not a hive of faculties without a queen bee. It is not a mob. It is rather a commonwealth where each has its place, and where there can be strength and continuance and harmony of action only as the moral nature is made central, and as all move and cluster about that.

If any force can compare favorably with the moral nature, it must be ambition. But ambition refers, for its standard, to the opinions and attainments of others; when it has gained its end, or become hopeless of gaining it, its efforts cease. Let that end be but gained, and it does not require the improvement of time; it knows nothing of working in harmony with God, and so nothing of healthy, symmetrical, beautiful growth and development, as good in themselves. It has no power of self-regulation, and so is often consuming and self-destructive. It puts the mind in conflict with itself, and makes it anxious for the result. It is selfish, repellant, and tends to isolation. That follows here which follows always when the lower faculty is disengaged from the higher, and ceases to act in its light. That which was intended to walk erect by holding on to something above it, becomes a serpent going upon its belly and eating dust.

But the moral nature is stronger than ambition. It underlies all true heroism, all martyrdom, and, by uniting us to God, was intended to be the paramount and immortal force of our nature. Let this, then, lie back of intellectual effort, and we have a permanent, constant, self-regulating principle, that will always bring the faculties up to the full glow of a healthful activity, and forbid them to go beyond. Now, the standard will be fixed, not with reference to others, but by capacity and opportunity. The mind will act in its unity, with no conflict of its higher and lower faculties, and with no fear of the result. Hence there will be, not only strength, but balance and completeness and order and beauty. Not only will there be harmony among the faculties themselves, with no tendency to a repellency of others, or to isolation; but it will be felt that the activity is with all, and for all. It will be felt to be a struggling towards that absolute perfection of one which is necessary to the perfection of all.

But whatever may be said of individuals, of communities there can be no doubt. The spiritual and moral elevation of a people would certainly secure their general enlightenment. It would not make every individual intellectual, but it would create a summer atmosphere for the quickening and growth of intellect, that would rest alike upon the hill-top and in the valley, and would solicit every latent capacity. The higher faculties would so strike down, and stimulate and appropriate the lower, that there would be, if not technical intellectualism, yet a broad, balanced, directive intelligence which would, as by instinct, bear society on to its right ends; and in the light and under the stimulus of which, individual growth, whether humble or gigantic, would be most favored. Then would the necessity of toil be no longer a blessing to man by keeping him from mischief. Leisure would be a blessing. A community let loose into that, would rise like a bird. Under the power of moral motives, leisure—the power to do what we please—would be equivalent to a college education, and the works of God would be to every man a university. Without these motives, even a college education becomes, within the limits of possible graduation, a systematic evasion of study, the works of God are a blank, and this furnished world becomes a pig-stye or a pandemonium. It is in the use to be made of its leisure, that the problem of the race lies. Who shall drain this bog?—hitherto a bog bearing weeds and sending up miasm—who shall drain it, and make it healthful and fruitful? Tell me what is to be done with the leisure that a machinery, gigantic and tiny, myriad-handed and half-reasoning, is beginning to give, and will yet give more fully to the race, and I will tell you what the destiny of the race will be. To the opportunities and facilities it will furnish, for intellectual and social elevation, there is scarcely a limit; there is none to the sensuality and degradation which may grow from its abuse. But intellect in the service of the passions tends downwards. Only from the sense of obligation and the free play of those spiritual affinities by which we are united to God, will there be the broad light of an intellectual day.

We conclude, then, that the higher intellectual power, whether of the individual or of the community, can be reached only by waiting on God, and by the culture, through that, of the spiritual and moral powers.

If, now, it be inquired how the impression of intellectual power has come to be associated with skepticism and wickedness, an answer may be found, first, in the fields of literature and speculation commonly entered by the skeptical and licentious. These are those of imagination, wit, ridicule, and transcendental metaphysics. Often, pervaded by a sneer, and quietly assuming the falseness of religion and the weakness or hypocrisy of those who profess it, we have, in novels, in poetry, in essays, a combination of all these. Their object, the last excepted, is not truth, but impression; and this last is as yet so overrun with strange terms, so the common ground of truth, falsehood, and nonsense, each aping the profound, that it is difficult to say whether it is better as a hunting-ground for truth, or a stalking-ground for vanity, or a hiding-place for falsehood. That there is power in this literature, is not denied; but the power of imagination, wit, assumption, and even of bathos, is not distinguished from that of fair and searching investigation.

A second answer we find in the effect upon the

mind of all irregular action, especially when combined with daring, or fool-hardiness. The utmost power of a horse, exerted in the true line of draft, will excite no attention. Half the power put forth in rearing and plunging, will draw a crowd about him. A cheap method of notoriety, the world over, is this rearing and plunging. Sam. Patch, leaping over Genessee Falls, could gather a greater crowd than Daniel Webster. The great powers of nature, those by which she wheels up her sun, and navigates her planets, and lifts vegetation, and circulates her waters, by which she holds herself in her unity and manifests her diversity, are regular, quiet, within the traces of law, and excite no attention. Here and there the quiet eye of a philosopher expands in permanent wonder, but from the very fact, the greatest wonder of all, that these forces are so clothed in order and tempered with gentleness, they are to the multitude nothing. Not so with volcanoes and earthquakes, with hurricanes and thunder-storms, with water-spouts and cataracts. These are irregular manifestations of the great forces that lie back of them. Compared with those forces, they are only as the eddy to the river; only as the opening of the side-valve and the hiss of the steam compared with the force of the engine that is bearing on the long train; and yet these are the wonders of the world. So with the mind. When it respects order and law, when it seeks the ends and moves in the channels appointed by God, its mightiest and most beneficent movements excite comparatively little attention. But combine now irregularity with audacity;

open a side valve ; assail the foundations of belief ; make it impossible for God to work a miracle, or to prove it if he should ; turn history into a myth ; show your consciousness of power by setting yourself against the race ; flatter the nineteenth century ; dethrone God ; if you make the universe God, yourself being a part of it, so much the better,—do thus, and there will not be wanting those who will despise the plodders, and hail you as " the coming man."

I have thus endeavored to show, first, that moral goodness is the only exception, on this earth, to the law of decay ; and, secondly, that it is the condition of the highest intellectual power, both for the individual and the race.

In the light of these propositions we may see, first, what must be the essential elements in the promised kingdom of our Lord Jesus Christ.

They must be righteousness and knowledge. So says the prophet. "The people shall be all righteous: they shall inherit the land forever." "And the work of righteousness shall be peace, and the effect of righteousness, quietness and assurance forever." "And wisdom and knowledge shall be the stability of thy times, and strength of salvation." This gives the line and order of effort for all who would labor for Christ. Not for an unintelligent piety—well-meaning, but blundering—are they to labor; not for a superstition without knowledge, calling itself righteousness, but weak, sentimental and showy—bolstered up by the fine arts and wire-pulled by a hierarchy ; not for knowledge without righteousness, sensualized, self-conceited and presumptuous ; but for a combination of righteousness and knowledge working together like the warmth and the light, every where pervading society in its free, oceanic, and multitudinous action, and building it up into the order and beauty of heaven.

In the second place you, my Beloved Friends of the Graduating Class, will see what you are to do in carrying out your own education.

That education you have, I trust, entered upon not wholly from worldly ends, but with some reference to the state of your permanent being, and to an immortal progress. For it, many of you have made sacrifices, and have applied yourselves laboriously and faithfully. That education is but begun. Probably you have never felt more painfully than now the limitations, the inadequacy, the relative nothingness of your knowledge. If you have any thing of the spirit of the instructions you have received, of the spirit of a scholar and of a true man, whatever profession or business you may follow, you will give a portion of your time to the cultivation of learning, and the acquisition of mental power. Grow, my friends ; seek to grow. But as a condition of a growth that shall be permanent, healthful, symmetrical, do not ignore that interaction of the higher and lower powers which is like that of the leaves and the trunk of the tree. As in that, elaboration, assimilation and ultimate growth are from above, so it is only through the higher moral nature that the sap of knowledge is converted into wisdom. If your chief sphere of study were to be the abstract sciences, cold, and passionless, where, as in mathematics, the relations depend on no will, your moral state would be of less moment; but your chief sphere is to be nature and man, where every thing is constituted by design, and where the key to the whole structure and to each particular department is to be found in ends and uses. Here love, trust, sympathy, will be stimulants of thought and elements of moral power. Nature is from God no less than mind. It was made for mind. It reflects the thoughts and feelings of God. It is understood only as the thoughts of God in it are reached, and it must be that, as we are in a right moral state, and in sympathy with God, we shall have a finer sense and a quicker sympathy on the side of nature. She will open herself to us more fully, and become, in a far higher sense, a companion and an educating power. But let now a man study nature with a scoffing spirit, and he must fail of insight. His standpoint will be wrong. Movements that are onward and beautiful when seen from the centre, will seem to him retrograde and perplexing. The sweetest voices of nature, her hymns, he cannot hear; her highest beauties he cannot see, her profoundest teachings are to him mere babble. Jeers, sarcasm, fault-finding, exciting no enthusiasm, with no reaction on thought, with no element of satisfaction except as they minister to notoriety, will take the place of admiration, love, adoration, by which thought is naturally quickened and rewarded. Would you study the works of God, and yourselves as a part of those works, be in harmony with yourselves, and in sympathy with God.

But thirdly. Not only are you to educate yourselves, opening your minds to all light, and putting forth all effort, but directly and indirectly you will have much to do in educating the community, and you will see, in the light of this subject, your duty in that regard.

You will neither form, nor encourage, any extravagant expectations from what is commonly called education. Not so will society grow up into its true life. If there be that above the intellect to which it ought to be subservient, but is not, then there will be a law of degradation even in its own activity. Education will become, either simply an accomplishment, or a drudge. It will do nothing towards removing the follies and weaknesses of society; so that you will find, as we now do, communities claiming to be the most highly educated, pervaded, even more than others, with a credulity and a superstition that would have disgraced the days of witchcraft, but without the earnestness which saved those from being contemptible. This we may satirize and deplore, but, under the system, it cannot be helped. The only true method is that of our Saviour. Nothing now on the earth, or that ever has been, can compare with Christianity in its educating power. Wherever it has been in its purity, the standard of general education has always been highest. It is so now. You cannot have a pure Christianity without general education, while yet education, as such, is not the object of Christianity at all. Its educating power results solely from its reaching and controlling that which is highest, and from the necessary stimulus and rectification through that, according to the principle laid down, of all that is lower. So has it wrought from the beginning; so will it work, and only in and through this can you work effectually. Hence one great blessing of those revivals of religion with which God has blessed our colleges—of that revival with which he has blessed us the past year, and for which we thank and adore him. Hence you will make, simply as educators, a capital mistake, if you do not seek to enthrone Christianity in all our seats of learning, and to extend and deepen its influence in every possible way. Hence no institution, not pervaded by Christianity, can do much in really educating and elevating the community.

Finally, we see from this subject where lies the permanent strength and the true good of man.

It is much to know, that there is any one thing on this earth that does not decay; that while the body is constant only by change, and its identity is only similarity, there is in the mind a central point that is unchangeable, and an identity that is absolute. It is more to know that in this we find our true selves, that by this we are allied to God. This takes us out of the sphere of that law of uniformities, in the light of which we have hitherto chiefly regarded this subject, and brings us into that of free personalities. Made in the image of God, allied to him as personal and free, we have faculties, call them moral, call them spiritual, by which we apprehend him, and through which we become receptive of influences from him. These influences imply no inspiration of particular truths as to prophets and seers, but are open to the race. They come as the tide to the stranded vessel that gradually surrounds it, and lifts it up, and bears it into the depths and boundlessness of its appropriate element. By these influences, respecting the laws of our freedom, and the bounds of our individuality, the Spirit of God enlightens, sustains, purifies, exalts us, and makes us partakers of his own blessedness. This is the Scripture doctrine of the indwelling of the Holy Spirit, that last link in the work of human salvation, by which, all incompatibilities of justice and mercy having been removed, the law becomes written in the heart, and we are brought to rest in the activity of a full and unceasing complacency in a holy and infinite God. Thus God himself becomes the portion of the soul. Thus do we enter into the " fullness of him that filleth all in all." Beyond this, nothing of good can be conceived of. This is our rest — our ultimate goal. This it is that we yearn after; in the congruity of this to the mind, and in the deep, conscious want of it, it is that we find the solution of those enthusiasms, and extravagancies, and distortions of the religious nature, which have made religion a by-word. These suppose a capacity and need of communion with God just as insanity supposes reason, and they will cease only when that communion returns.

Do you, my friends, accept this doctrine? Will you accept it practically? Will you open the way for the coming into your own souls of divine light and divine help? Will you put away sin? This is the one condition of a pure light and a true elevation. You must begin with the heart, for only the pure in heart can see God, and only as we see him, and in his light, can we see all other things in their true proportions. Will you then open yourselves fully to the light of the divine teachings, and to the intimacy of a divine communion? Not only morally, but intellectually, will the answer to this question be the turning point in your destiny. The question involved in this doctrine of a divine communion and help, is the cardinal one for the race. At every point this doctrine meets not only our weaknesses and wants, but also our *sinfulness*, and so transcends all transcendentalism, and all possible philosophies and devices of man. It is not merely a philosophy, but a redemption and a remedy, a companionship and a portion. Without this doctrine, man is but a waif upon the waters, a severed branch that must perish. With it, he is united to God, and so there is nothing too great for him to hope. With it, the figure of the text—"they shall mount up with wings as eagles"—is fully justified. See the eagle as he leaves his perch. He flaps his broad wings, and moves heavily. Slowly he lifts himself above the horizon, till the inspiration of a freer air quickens him. Now there is new lightning in his eye, and new strength in his pinions. See—how he mounts! Now he is midway in the heavens. Higher he rises—still higher. Now his broad circles are narrowing to a point—he is fading away in the deep blue. Now he is but a speck. Now he is gone. To the eye of sense, and for the purpose of the figure, it is an endless, upward flight.

Such a flight, my dear friends, may be yours; but only as you yield yourselves to be upborne by an all-encompassing and an omnipotent Love. You are, indeed, youths, the very youths spoken of in the text; for this word is for all ages; but in the dusty and thronged ways of life you will faint and be weary. Yes, the hours will come when you will be, O, how weary! You are young men; but the strength of nature will depart, and, relying only on this, you shall utterly fall. Only " the Everlasting God, the Lord, the Creator of the ends of the earth," who " fainteth not, neither is weary," can gird you for the coming conflict and sustain you. Wait upon Him, and you " shall mount up with wings as eagles; you shall run, and not be weary; and you shall walk, and not faint."

In addressing to you this parting counsel, in which all is thus seen to depend upon God, I am permitted to address, as one of you, my own son. I rejoice that he has been one of you. And now, with the most pleasing recollections of the past, cherishing for you all the spirit of a father, commending you all to that God who alone is able to keep and to guide you, I close by addressing to him and to you the words of one of old, who was also a father. " And thou, Solomon, my son, know thou the God of thy father, and serve him with a perfect heart and with a willing mind: for the Lord searcheth all hearts, and understandeth all the imaginations of the thoughts: if thou seek him, he will be found of thee; but if thou forsake him, he will cast thee off forever."

THE MANIFOLDNESS OF MAN.

A

BACCALAUREATE SERMON,

DELIVERED AT

WILLIAMSTOWN, MS.

JULY 31, 1859.

BY MARK HOPKINS, D. D.

President of Williams College.

PUBLISHED BY REQUEST OF THE CLASS.

BOSTON:
PRESS OF T. R. MARVIN & SON, 42 CONGRESS STREET.
1859.

Entered according to Act of Congress, in the year 1859,
BY T. R. MARVIN,
In the Clerk's Office of the District Court of the District of Massachusetts.

SERMON.

LUKE i. 66.

WHAT MANNER OF CHILD SHALL THIS BE?

The circumstances preceding and attending the birth of John the Baptist, were extraordinary. As his father, Zacharias, then "well stricken in years," "executed the priest's office before God in the order of his course," "there appeared unto him an angel of the Lord standing on the right hand of the altar of incense," and foretold the birth of the child. When Zacharias did not believe him, "the angel answering said unto him, I am Gabriel, that stand in the presence of God, and am sent to speak unto thee, and to show thee these glad tidings. And behold, thou shalt be dumb, and not able to speak, until the day that these things shall be performed." Accordingly Zacharias was dumb until the time came for naming the child. Then, after he had written the name given by the angel, "his mouth was opened immediately, and his tongue loosed, and he spake and praised God." These things "were noised abroad throughout all the hill-country of Judea;" and it is not strange that "all they that heard them laid them up in their hearts," or that they said, "What manner of child shall this be?" Of a child whose birth was thus heralded and signalized, something extraordinary could not fail to be expected.

But while this inquiry was thus naturally made respecting John, may it not also be appropriately made respecting every child that is born? There may be nothing extraordinary, either in connection with the birth of the child, or with the child itself, and yet that child shall be different from every other child that ever was born, or ever shall be; and its capacities of development, and the possibilities of its future, shall run in lines of such divergency from those of every other, that we may well ask respecting it, "What manner of child shall this be?"

There is nothing in the works of God more striking than the differences there are of things that are similar, and the similarities of things that are different. In the perception of these two we have the element of science on the one hand, and of practical skill on the other. So far as beings or things are similar, they may be named alike, and treated alike, and so a knowledge of one becomes the knowledge of all. This is science. Through this the individuals which God has made, vast as they are in number and variety, are marshaled, and ranged in regiments, and battalions, and companies. In this, and so far as it goes, exceptions and individualities disappear; what seemed promiscuous and irregular falls into order, and the universe assumes the appearance of troops marching and countermarching in a grand review. But so far as things are different, each individual must be studied by itself, and treated by itself; and as differences constantly appear, they furnish the occasion of constant study. Thus it is that through similarities the dictionary of human knowledge is greatly abridged, while, through diversities, the faculties are kept constantly awake. At the point where we cease to discriminate differences, all interest ceases from uniformity and monotony. At the point where we cease to discern similarities, interest again ceases from diversity and confusion.

But while these elements pervade the works of God, while our scientific interest in those works and practical power over them are from these, yet are they nowhere more striking, and nowhere as interesting to us, as in man. Every man has, and as a man must have, the great features and characteristics which make him a man, and yet how infinite the diversity! No two are there that look alike, no two that think alike, no two that act alike; and doubtless this diversity will become greater and greater, so long as they shall exist. Here, and here only, in this diversity ever increasing yet not divorced from unity, do we find the basis of a harmony that shall also ever increase.

This diversity it was which was implied in the question of the text. That referred not merely to the childhood, but to the whole career of John. What manner of man should he become? What part should he perform in the great drama of human affairs? Should he be a monarch, a conqueror, a sage, a lawgiver? Should he play over again the old games of ambition, and pleasure, and gain? or should he be something new and fresh in the world's history?

The question supposes a great difference between the child then, and what he would become. And how great was that difference! Now he is an infant of eight days, with no visible distinction from other infants; just as helpless and dependent. A Pharisee might have taken him under the enlarged border of his garments, and have borne him through the streets of Jerusalem, and no one have known it. But pass on now thirty years, and what is he? He is "the voice of one crying in the wilderness, Prepare ye the way of the Lord, make his paths straight." He cries, and all Judea, and Jerusalem, and the region round about Jordan are stirred, and go out to him. He is the fulfillment of prophecies made centuries before, the forerunner of the Messiah, a bright and shining light, one of whom it could truly be said, that of those born of women, there had been none greater than he.

But great as this change was, there was nothing in it so unusual as to attract attention. The man attracted attention, but not the change. This was so gradual, that wonder was superseded by familiarity. It was but a single exemplification of a general law. Hence I observe, in the first place,

That there is a great difference in all organic beings, between what they are at first, and what we see them become.

We might ask of any seed just germinating, What manner of plant shall this be? See; here is a point of green just visible. Look again. It has become a violet, with its eye on the sun, suffused with beauty, and throbbing with the pulses of the universal life. Here is a filmy substance; it lies upon the palm of your hand, and a breath will blow it away. From this, too, emerges a point of green no larger than the other, and with no perceptible difference between them. But this shall become the elm with its pendent branches, towering and spreading, the pride of the meadow. We may ask the egg, 'What manner of creature shall this be?' Now there is in it a beating speck—a mere point that pulsates. The philosopher is peering at it through his microscope, searching for the principle of life, as the child chases the foot of the rainbow. That principle he finds not, he shall not find it, but it embodies and perfects itself, and from points undistinguishable, it becomes now a wren, chattering and vivacious; now a golden oriole, warbling and weaving its pendent nest; now a solemn owl; a peacock, with its "goodly wings;" an ostrich, with its "wings and feathers," fleet and powerful; an eagle, screaming and breasting the storm-cloud far in the sky. It is indeed now said, that every plant, from the lichen to the oak, and every animal, from the insect to man, has its beginning in a single cell. It is in these cells, undistinguishable by us, that Omniscience can see the future, and from them that Omnipotence can call "the things that are not, as though they were."

This capacity of transformation and growth, by which beings seem to us to pass from the very verge of nonentity to great perfection and magnitude and power, is among the most striking characteristics of the present state. It is also one which we think of, and Revelation confirms the impression, as belonging to this state alone. There are not wanting those who believe that this world is the nursery for peopling this planetary system at least, if not the worlds scattered through all space.

The individuals thus starting from what seems a common point, are different in rank, and fall into different classes; and we next inquire what the rank of each will be.

The rank of each will be determined, first, by its rank in its own class; and, secondly, by the rank of the class.

The rank of an individual in its own class will be determined by its capacity of development, and by its actual development in one direction. The California pine may reach a circumference of thirty feet, and a height of three hundred and fifty, and so be the first of its class; but it is by a repetition always of the same processes, an extension and increase in one line. Between the greatest and the least of them there is no difference, except that of development in a particular direction. Among men, a man will be really first, who possesses most perfectly what is distinctively human; and in general, whatever individual of a class shall manifest most fully its distinctive characteristic, will be the first in that class.

But while rank *in* a class is determined by development in one direction, the rank *of* a class is determined by the capacity of individuals in it for development in different directions; thus giving wide scope to the imagination in answering the question, 'What manner of being shall this be?' The power in a tree of varying from a given line is as nothing. So it can grow, so only. In animals, this power is greater; in man, greater still—and the more things it is possible for him to become, the more complex must be his nature, and the higher his rank. As the scheme of the creation is, that that which is above takes up into itself all that is below, the more complex the nature is, the higher it must be, the more directions it may take, and the greater is the uncertainty that must hang about its final destiny.

And here I observe, in the third place, that, in sensitive and moral beings, a capacity of development in one direction involves its opposite, and that in an equal degree. In this we find startling indications respecting the possibilities of our future. In creatures merely sensitive, perhaps a different constitution was possible, but we know of no instance of it. A capacity for pleasure always involves that of pain, and, so far as we can judge, in a degree precisely correspondent. But whatever may be possible in the region of simple enjoyment, in a moral being the capacity of development in one direction must imply that in the other. He who is capable of moral elevation, must also be of moral degradation. He, and he only, who is capable of great moral excellence, is capable of great sin. This is the basis of the maxim, universally true, that the best things, corrupted, become the worst. The better, the higher, the purer, the nobler any being is capable of becoming, the more utter and awful may be its downfall and ruin. It requires an angel to make a devil.

From what has been said, it appears that the rank of man will be determined by the range of his possible development in different directions. And how wide is that range! How different in this is man from any other being on the earth! Let us look at the breadth of this range, first, in respect to *belief*. An animal cannot be said to believe at all, but for an infant how wide is the range of possible belief! Wonderful is it, that with the same faculties, thrown into the same world, with the same phenomena, and orders of succession, and similarities and differences, such a range should be possible. Especially is this true of religious belief, where the range is the widest conceivable.

Here are two infants just opening their eyes upon the light, and beginning to gather those materials which are to be the basis of their belief. What manner of men shall they be? They seem alike; but when manhood comes, one of them shall stand upon this earth so full of the goodness of God, under these heavens which declare his glory, he shall see all there is in them of order, and beauty, and beneficence, and yet be an atheist.

Causeless, aimless, fatherless, hopeless, with nothing to respond to his deepest wants, for him the universe shall be whirled in the eddies of chance, or swept on by the current of a blind and remorseless fate. The other shall believe that there is one God, infinite, eternal and unchangeable, omnipotent and omnipresent, holy, just and merciful, the Creator and Governor of all things, to whom he may look up and say, My Father. For him, compared with this God, the universe is as nothing. In Him it has its being. It is irradiated with his glory, as the evening cloud with the glory of the setting sun. Except as expressing his attributes and indicating his purposes, it had no grandeur and no significance.

One of these again shall look forward to death, and see in it the end of man. For him, the sullen sound sent back from his coffin when the sod falls upon it, is the last which the conscious universe is to know of each individual man, unless, indeed, the geologist of some future era may find in the impression of his bones, a record of this. For him, man has, in death, no pre-eminence over the beast. By the other, death shall be welcomed as a friend. It shall be for him the beginning of a higher life, of clearer insight, of purer joys, of a greater nearness to God, and of an unending progression. He shall

> " The darkening universe defy,
> To quench his immortality."

He shall believe with a certainty that shall enable him to say with one of old, that he *knows* ' that if this earthly house of his tabernacle were dissolved, he has a building of God, a house not made with hands, eternal in the heavens,' and so his great hope shall lie beyond the tomb. One of these, again, shall believe in no accountability after death; the other shall believe, that " every idle word that men shall speak, they shall give account thereof in the day of judgment."

So these two may come to believe, and yet be men. These three great doctrines—of God, of a future life, and of accountability—without which there can be neither religion nor morality, one shall receive, and the other shall reject. Side by side they may stand, separated by scarcely a point in space; but in that whole interior life which is most intimate and essential to them, they are as wide asunder as the poles.

But here it is to be noticed, that while the possibility of this divergence in belief indicates elevation in rank, yet the fact of such divergence indicates for some a low position in that rank. A perfect instinct is uniform. So is perfect reason, and these would coincide. These are the extremes, and between these, imperfection and diversity lie. Truth is one, and a failure to see it is always the result either of feebleness or of sin. Hence, diversity of belief is not among those needed for harmony, but the reverse. A measure of it is compatible with harmony, that is, such as this world admits of, but the harmony of the universe will be perfect only when all rational creatures, so far as they see at all, shall see eye to eye.

But if the divergence of men in religious belief, and in all belief, is great, it is not less, and is even more striking, in their objects of worship.

One " planteth an ash, and the rain doth nourish it. Then shall it be for a man to burn. He burneth part thereof in the fire, and the residue thereof he maketh a god, even his graven image; he falleth down and worshipeth it; he prayeth unto it and saith, Deliver me, for thou art my god." He may worship, as men have done, flies, and serpents, and crocodiles, and oxen, and the sun, and moon, and stars, and heroes, and devils; and worshiping these, he becomes, so far as is possible, assimilated to them. How different these from Him who is 'the Lord, the true God, the living God, and an everlasting King;—who hath made the earth by his power, who hath established the world by his wisdom, and hath stretched out the heavens by his discretion.' And can the intelligent worshiper of this God, the holy prophet, or apostle, rapt in vision, or swallowed up in adoration, be of the same race with the idolater casting himself beneath the car of Juggernaut, or with the cannibal savage eating his victim, and dancing before a carved, besmeared, and hideous log? Can it be that those who do thus, might have changed places?

Here, again, diversity is not the basis of harmony. If harmony requires diversity, it has its root in unity, the unity of truth and of God; and so, of belief and of worship.

We may further ask what any child shall be in

position, in attainments, and in the extent of his influence. Shall he be a miner, thousands of feet beneath the earth's surface, untaught, unknown, unthanked, uncared for, with a mind as narrow and as dark as the sphere of his labors? Shall he be a slave, whose range is the plantation, and to whom cupidity and fear forbid the knowledge of letters? Shall he be a misanthrope, self-exiled from society, who dies alone, and whose body is found by accident? Shall he be, as probably he will, neither rich nor poor, neither learned nor ignorant, neither widely known nor wholly obscure—one of the countless throng on life's thoroughfare of whom the casual observer would take no note? Or, shall he tread the high places of art, of learning, and of power? Shall the canvas or the marble wait for his touch to become immortal? Shall he be a poet, "soaring in the high region of his fancy, with his garland and singing robes about him?" Shall he govern nations, command armies, sway senates, wrest from nature her secrets, lead the van of progress, and make his thought and will felt over the globe?

But chiefly may we ask concerning any infant, What manner of child shall this be in character, and in the *kind* of influence he shall exert. Upon character every thing depends, and from this, influence flows. And shall these be in the line, and on the level of sensuality and of sense? or of a selfish and all-absorbing ambition? or of a pure philanthropy? or of a whole-hearted consecration to the will of God? Shall the child be an apostle of righteousness? a martyr missionary? a preacher like Whitfield, whose eloquence and zeal shall set a continent on fire? Shall he be a fashionable exquisite, admiring himself, and supposing himself admired by others? Shall he be a political intriguer? an adroit depredator upon society? Shall he be a drunkard, and die in a ditch? Shall he be a thief? a murderer? a pirate? Can it be that he who sails under the black flag of death, and whose motto is, that "dead men tell no tales," once drew his life from the breast of a human mother, returned her caress, and answered to her smile? Who is this upon whom every eye in the vast multitude is fixed? Over his face the fatal cap is drawn, and he stands upon the drop just ready to fall. It is but a few years, and his tiny hand held the finger of his mother, and in him were garnered up her fond hopes and high expectations.

At this point the import of the question is deepest, because the dread issues involved in our immortality are here at stake. Here are harnessed the forces that are to move on the plains of eternity. Every thing indicates that in the mind, as well as in the body, there is a possibility of RUIN; that there are there also processes that are cancerous and leprous; and that they may gradually pervade, and at length utterly pervert and corrupt the whole being. Awful and significant it is, to see such a disease spreading itself over the body, tainting the fluids more widely, and implicating more tissues, till deformity becomes only the more obtrusive, and hideous, and persistent, as the forces of nature were originally greater and more beneficent. And so it may be in mind. Whatever the fact may be, no one can doubt the fearful capacity for this. It belongs to our conception of spiritual forces that they are indefinite, or without limit in their capacities, in whatever direction they may move. It is the natural pledge of their immortality, that whatever point they may reach in knowledge or affection, in virtue or in vice, it will always be possible for them to advance still further. This point, whatever it be, must be reached under the law of habit, and under that still more general law that "to him that hath shall be given," and thus the time must come when there can be no return. For the same reason that the path of the just shall be as the shining light, that shines more and more, the gloom of to-day shall become the darkness of to-morrow, and the deep midnight of the day following. Selfishness, passion, hate, shall gain a permanent ascendency, and the reign of retribution begin. The immutability of law is the rock to which the sinner shall be bound; the ceaseless action of the spiritual powers is the immortal liver that shall grow as it is consumed, and the diseased action is the vulture that shall prey upon it. The worm shall gnaw till it shall become undying, the fire shall burn till it "cannot be quenched." This, not crumbling arches, not mouldering cities, but this, this is ruin.

What a contrast between this and the possibilities we see before us and in us, when we look at the *man* Christ Jesus. In him, in him alone, can we form a right estimate of our nature; and that he has enabled us to do this, is no small ground of our indebtedness to him. So far as he was man only, there was in him no excellence or perfection which we may not attain; and the perfections in him were not only an example to us, but were a pledge to his followers that they shall attain the same. The disciple shall be as his Master. They shall be like him, for they shall see him as he is. Christ was the Son of God as Adam was not; and in him humanity was glorified as it could have been in no other way. There was stamped upon it the seal of an infinite value. It was so taken into union with God as to show that God can dwell with it, and that the highest divine perfections may be manifested through it. Christ was the " brightness of his glory," as manifested on the earth, " the express image of his person," and whoever would see the capacities there are in man for elevation and excellence must look to him. " Looking unto Jesus," is the motto of the Christian. He is the only type of normal development for the race. I point you to no heroes or sages, but to Him; to no abstract conception, but to embodied excellence, living, walking, speaking, sympathizing, suffering among men. The divine image, marred in Adam, was restored in Christ, and is so held in him that it can be lost never more. The gem is now set forever. It will belong to the riches of eternity. *This image we may attain.* Between the attainment of this and any thing else, the difference is infinite. This is the true good. And O how great, how infinite is this good! In view of it, how forcible the question of our Saviour, 'What shall it profit a man if he shall gain the whole world and lose his soul? Or what shall a man give in exchange for his soul?' Fully attained, this good is heaven. Whatever outward circumstances may be, potentially, substantially, ultimately, this is heaven. He that is like God shall dwell with God. The son shall be in his father's house. He shall abide forever. For this we bless thee, O our Father. Cease, my friends, your disputes about religion. He that is like God shall dwell with God, and he that is not like God, shall not dwell with him.

We thus see that man must be in the highest rank of created beings, and how it is that his manifoldness is a proof of his greatness. Touching the extremes of being, he is capable of development on the level of any nature of which he is partaker, and at any point along a line that reaches from the instinct of the animal up to God himself. He may become an animal, or simply human, or devilish, or divine. . Made in the image of God, capable of indefinite progress, of falling to a depth profound in proportion to the height to which he can rise, no wider scope could be given to the imagination than is now given, when the question is asked concerning any child, "What manner of child shall this be?"

My beloved Friends of the Graduating Class, this discussion is especially for you, and in applying its principles, I address myself directly to you. You are no longer children, but men, and in view of the wide range of possibilities now presented before you, I ask you, What manner of men will you be? I come to you individually, and with affectionate earnestness and deep solicitude, ask each one of you, What manner of man will *you* be?

The question, observe, is not, What will you *get?* but, What will you *be?* The first is the paramount question with selfishness; the second, with reason and religion. In asking the first, you are not necessarily selfish; in making it paramount, you are. In seeking, on the other hand, to be great, good, noble, like God, you are indeed consulting your own good most wisely, but are not selfish, for how can a man be selfish, when his very object is to *be* benevolent. How be selfish in seeking to be like God, for God is love. This question, then, I ask with emphasis, for under the government of God your all must depend upon it. And not only do I ask it, this College that has watched over you, and will follow you with an abiding interest, and which you will either honor or disgrace, asks it. Your parents and near friends, to whom you owe every thing, ask it. Your country asks it. The church of God asks it. The nations that are in ignorance, and under oppression, ask it. And I doubt not there is, at this solemn moment in your own hearts, a " still small voice," in which God is, that asks it. What manner of men will you be?

This question, as put to you, I desire to limit as I have not done in the general discussion. That was in view of two kinds of diversity that must be discriminated. There is one having its root in repugnance and opposition, involving elements that can never be brought into harmony, and that can have no unity even, except as there is fixed between them a great and impassable gulf. For this gulf there is provision in the essential difference of moral good and evil; and while these may be embraced in the unity of one government of eternal righteousness, yet this can be only on the condition that that gulf shall be *fixed*.

But there is also a diversity which springs from unity, and is the basis of harmony; and within this limit diversity is a good. Only through this can we have the riches and beauty, as well as the harmony of the universe. In this we have the one light refracted into its seven colors, making the earth green, and the sky blue, and the clouds gorgeous. In this is the one sound now parting itself into its seven notes for music, now articulating itself in speech, now becoming the chirp of the cricket, and now the roar of the thunder. In this is the one water seen in mist, in dew, in steam, in ice, in snow, in the green heaving ocean, and in the rainbow that spans it. In this is the one body with its organs, the one tree with its branches, the one universe with its suns, and planets, and satellites, and comets. Within this limit, the wider the diversity, the richer are the fields opened to us in science, in beauty, and in character.

And now, when I put this question to you, I would have all your diversity within this limit. I wish to speak with you of no other. This will involve no restriction, no monotony, or tameness, or repression of any manly energy, no abatement of the zest and foam and sparkle of life. It will only lift you above obstructions, and enable you to move calmly and freely, as the balloon that floats in the long upper currents, instead of being whirled in the lower tempests, and wrecked among the branches. O, could I but know that all your diversity would range within this limit, that you would all be Christians, true followers of the Lord Jesus, almost would I say to you, Be what you please. Certainly I should prefer, since one star differs from another star in glory, that you should not be among those less bright. But only be a star. Shine, and choose your own shade of light. Be Paul, or Peter, or John, or James, or even Thomas; any of them but Judas. Be a Luther, or Melancthon; be Jonathan Edwards, or Harlan Page; be—but I will go no further; I will rather recall what I have said, and say to you, *Be yourselves.* Bring out your own individuality. It is your own. As such, respect and cherish it, only avoiding all affected singularity. You will, I think, allow that that individuality has been respected in your course of instruction here; that the object has been, not to put upon you the ear-mark of any system, but to bring your individuality out under the inspiration of a love of truth. If it be different from that of others, do not be troubled. It ought to be. Bring it out in its simplicity, any where within the broad light and expanse of the one perfect example. Christ was peculiar, but not singular, except as Mont Blanc and the Ocean are singular. So be you, and you shall polish a gem for its setting in the diadem of Him who weareth many crowns, that shall have in it shades and lines that no other can have.

And while I thus call upon you to bring out your own individuality, let me say to you also, Respect that of others; and not only so, appreciate it, and rejoice in its manifestation. Nothing is more needed among men than the power and readiness to do this, and to accept, in religion, in politics, and in social life, those diversities of belief and of forms which spring from this, but which yet have their root in essential unity, and no more cease to be of it than men of different colors cease to be of the race. To do this, is liberality, in distinction from laxness and indifference to the truth. This God intended should be. It is not for nothing, that the notes of birds, and the colors of flowers, and the outlines of mountains differ, yet are all pleasing. It is not for nothing, that we are told that the foundations of the New Jerusalem are of twelve manner of precious stones; and the jasper is not better than the sapphire, nor the sapphire than the emerald, nor the emerald than the amethyst, and all are better than any one would be, and all are one in their common nature as gems, and in their common office of adorning and supporting the heavenly city. How to draw the line rightly, in particular cases, no rules can be given; but you see the general principle, and I beseech you to do this wisely and liberally, remembering that it is the tendency of egotism and selfishness to fall into clannishness, and into a party and sectarian spirit, and to magnify non-essentials.

In the light of what has been said, let me turn your thoughts to the provision God has made for the growth and enjoyment of his creatures as intelligent, and aside from the affections. For these the great conditions, in the construction of his works, are, first, unity. By this is not meant an indivisible unit of which there may be any member without either unity or harmony, and which must remain unfruitful; but a unity like those spoken of above, capable of being parted into diversity, and of returning to itself again. The second condition is diversity—not merely numerical, but that which is implied in parts having relation to a common whole. The third condition is harmony, that is, such a relation of parts to each other and to the whole, as to realize and complete our conception of that whole. For intellectual growth and enjoyment, a perception of these is all that is needed; and how inexhaustible these are, and how wonderfully blended in this universe, I need not say. In this view of it, the universe is an organ that constantly discourses music to angels and to God. The relations of its parts at a given moment, in their adjustment to each other and to ends, are its harmony, and the succession of its events are its melody. Its harmony we can begin to study. Of the melody we can know comparatively nothing, for our time is too brief; but we may be sure that both will forever increase.

In view of what has been said, you will also be able, not only to estimate the place and value of diversity in the universe, but also of what has been called many-sidedness, in the individual. Plainly this is a proof of greatness. At times the admiration for this has been overdone, and there has been about it, in certain quarters, something of cant. On the other hand, there are those who say that a man can excel in but one thing, and should attend to but one. Doubtless the greatest effect requires concentration, and there should be no attempt at varied excellence that would diminish this; but there are few occupations in which all that a man can do may not be done with less than his whole energies; the use of the powers in different directions gives diversion and strength, and there seems no good reason why a man may not gain excellence in all the directions in which he is capable of development. Why may not a man cultivate both muscle and mind, both mathematics and music, both poetry and philosophy? I trust you will shrink into no one channel, but as you have begun, so you will continue to advance in a liberal culture.

Once more, if the rank of man be so high and his capacities so great, then is this world a fit theatre for that great redemption which the Scriptures reveal. Between him and that redemption there is no want of congruity or proportion. Some there are who speak of this world as a mere speck in the universe, and of man as too inconsiderable to be the object of such regard as is implied in the coming and death, for him, of the Son of God. But so far as is possible for any creature, man takes hold on infinity. He is a *child* of God, and in the dealings of God with him there may be involved all those principles of wisdom and righteousness and mercy which can be involved in the divine government any where, and so the whole universe, mighty as it is, may be brought, through man, to the "light of the knowledge of the glory of God." Little can they who think thus, have meditated upon those sublime and consoling words of the Apostle, " Beloved, now are we the sons of God, and it doth not yet appear what we shall be; but we know that, when he shall appear, we shall be like him; for we shall see him as he is." This redemption, O let us magnify, for in it is all our hope. This redemption I commend to you renewedly, earnestly, affectionately, in this solemn and parting hour.

Finally, my beloved friends, if there is, in the *capacities* of man, a fit occasion and ground for the redemption revealed in the Scriptures, so is there in his *diversities* a fit occasion and ground for that future and final Judgment which they also reveal. How could these diversities be greater? How is every thing respecting God and his government, even to his very being, denied, questioned, challenged, ridiculed, mocked? Taken by itself, how tangled, perplexed, and insoluble by reason, is the present state? What shades of character! What modifications of responsibility! What wrongs unredressed! What questions cut short by death! And in connection with these, what scope for the application, in every delicate adjustment, of every principle of moral government! Probably in no other way than by such a Judgment, could these diversities be reduced to the comprehension of finite minds, and the ways of God to man be vindicated. Here, as elsewhere, the reality of what God does, and proposes to do, transcends all that man could have imagined to be possible, and hence many deny this also. They say, "Where is the promise of his coming?" "But the day of the Lord will come as a thief in the night." "The Son of man shall sit on the throne of his glory, and before him shall be gathered all nations." This, we believe, will be the next great epoch in this world's history. And in view of it, I ask the question no longer in regard to this world, What manner of men will you be? This world and its scenes, now so bright before you, will be nothing then. I ask this question in view of that day when there will be but one alternative. What manner of men will you then be? Will you be among the righteous? Will you be on the right hand? Will you *all* be there? May you all hear the music of that voice which shall say, "Come, ye blessed of my Father, inherit the Kingdom prepared for you from the foundation of the world."

A

BACCALAUREATE SERMON,

DELIVERED AT

WILLIAMSTOWN, MS.

JULY 29, 1860.

BY MARK HOPKINS, D. D.
President of Williams College.

PUBLISHED BY REQUEST OF THE CLASS.

BOSTON:
PRESS OF T. R. MARVIN & SON, 42 CONGRESS STREET.
1860.

Entered according to Act of Congress, in the year 1860,

By T. R. MARVIN,

In the Clerk's Office of the District Court of the District of Massachusetts.

SERMON.

JOHN vi. 12.

GATHER UP THE FRAGMENTS THAT REMAIN, THAT NOTHING BE LOST.

Among the more striking miracles wrought by our Saviour, was that of feeding five thousand men from five barley loaves and two small fishes. But, striking as it was, it was simply a reproduction, in a different form, of the great miracle of nature that is constantly going on around us. The miracle was not at all in the things made, but wholly in the manner of making them. Bread had been made before, and as good bread; and there had been fish before; but never before had they been formed at once, by the energy of will, from their original and simple elements. In both cases the elements existed. There was no new creation; but in the miracle they were brought together in a manner entirely different.

When the sower sows the seed in which is the nucleus, the possibility, and the promise of all the bread that is to be eaten the succeeding year, where are the materials out of which that bread is to be made? They exist, but are dispersed hither and thither, and are held in different affinities. No human eye can see, and no skill can detect them. They are like an army in ambush, ready to come at the appointed signal, but answering only to that.

And now the earth receives the seed. It is buried, but not forgotten. Small as it is, the ocean knows of it and offers it moisture; and the atmosphere knows of it, and is ready with its invisible fingers to lift the mist, and fashion the cloud-car, and transport the moisture to it. The sun, too, distant as it is, remembers it, and sends it heat and light. These provoke its hidden life, and the roots shoot downwards, and the stem upwards. But in those roots, and in that stem, there is no particle that will make bread. There must first be a blossom, and then a receptacle formed, and then the stalk of grain must set itself at work, and the earth, and the air, and the sun, electricity and magnetism, agents, visible and invisible, must give their aid; and then the particles of oxygen and hydrogen, and nitrogen and carbon, will come from their hiding places and marshal themselves into starch and gluten, and the full seed will be formed. The yellow harvest shall lift itself towards heaven, and wave and toss itself in the wind, a gift from all the elements and agencies of nature to man. So do they all serve him. Then comes the harvesting, and threshing, and winnowing, and grinding, and leavening; and then the fire does its work, and it is bread. Through the processes of a year, through changes so slow and minute as to escape observation at the time, by the combined agencies of the earth, and air, and ocean, of the sun and the fire, the materials that were scattered and hidden, have heard the call that was made for them, and have come forth; they have entered into their new combinations, and have become the " bread that strengtheneth man's heart."

But in all this there is no miracle. There is nothing strange. Oh, no. We have seen it all, and have eaten such bread all our lives. It is nature that does all this; or nature and art; though in reality, art, human art and skill, can do nothing but to give the opportunity, and provide the conditions for nature to work. Nature it is, and there is nothing strange about it.

But now, instead of this complicated and mighty agency extending over months of time, and reaching millions of miles into space, implicating, indeed, the whole planetary system, instead of sympathies and interactions between materials where there is no direct evidence of personality, and so, of anything above what we call nature, there comes One who claims to be the Lord of nature, and as quietly as the sun shines, without even indicating that he is working a miracle, he calls for the elements to come from their hiding places, and enter into their new combinations, and they obey. The materials were all around him, and he controlled their affinities at once, as nature controls the same affinities in her long processes. The simple record is, that " Jesus took the loaves; and when he had given thanks, he distributed to the disciples, and the disciples to them that were set down; and likewise of the fishes as much as they would." There was no seeming effort, no ostentation, no production of anything but barley bread, just such bread as was made by the people, and of fish such as were caught in their waters. But this was a miracle, a strange thing, so strange that many cannot believe it. But obviously, if we had been accustomed to this, and then had seen the other for the first time, it would have been accounted by far the greater miracle.

And here we may remark what a testimony the miracles of our Saviour, generally, were to the perfection of the works of God in nature, and so to his own oneness with God. As the bread which he made by a miracle was no better than that made by the ordinary processes, so when he raised men to life, it was to the same life that they had before, and that other men have. When he restored a palsied limb, or a blind eye, it only became as it was before, or like other limbs and eyes. A miracle could make them no better. In this consists the simplicity and grandeur of our Saviour's miracles, and in this the force of their internal evidence for his divine mission. He honored nature, while he showed that he was her Lord.

Thus calling the materials together without effort, the Saviour provided for the wants of five thousand men. Nor was the provision scanty; it was ample and bountiful. They took as much as they would, and the fragments left were more than the original loaves and fishes.

And what the Saviour did at that time, he was able to do at any time. To his power in this respect there was no restriction. Always he could provide for himself and for his disciples in the same free and magnificent manner. And now, when he had just made such a provision, and had it in his power to do so at any time, shall he care for the remnants, the fragments that remain? Not so should we have done. But, and this is not the least remarkable part of the transaction, the Saviour did thus care. "When they were filled, he said unto his disciples, Gather up the fragments that remain, that nothing be lost." The same thing also he did on another occasion, when he had fed a multitude in a similar manner.

What then have we here? Something of penuriousness and smallness? of an undue desire of saving? That can hardly be in Him who never owned property, and who had just dispensed his bounties so freely. Have we then a command appropriate only to that time and place? or have we, as in so many other instances of the sayings of our Saviour, clothed in a particular and individual form, a universal maxim, a great principle of the government of God, and one that should regulate the conduct of men? Are these words as the index of a partial and local force? or are they as the magnetic needle that indicates the polar forces of this planet, and, so far as we may conjecture, of all planets and systems? Are they the word of the individual speaking for that time and place, or of the Lawgiver, speaking for all times and for all places? "Gather up the fragments that remain, that nothing be lost." Why should *anything* be *lost?*

Anything once possessed is said to be lost, when it is so concealed or removed from us that we do not know where it is. The piece of silver in search of which the woman swept the house, was lost.

The sheep which had wandered away, and which the owner brought back rejoicing, had been lost.

Anything is also said to be lost, when it fails to accomplish the end for which it was made or given. A journey is lost, when the end for which it was undertaken is not accomplished. A day is lost, when in it, no good is done; an education is lost when no use is made of it; a man is lost, when he becomes hopelessly a drunkard, or is given over to any vice. We know where to find him, but he is lost.

That a thing should be lost in the first sense is accidental, and incident to us from the limitation of our faculties. Not so with God. To the Omniscient, nothing can be hidden, or obscure, or remote; and if in his agency he shall fail to cause any past event to be brought to its bearings, or any existing thing to accomplish its end, it will not be because he does not know what it is, or where to find it. In our agency a thing may be, and often is lost in the second sense, because it is in the first. We fail to put a thing to its use because we do not know where to find it.

It is plainly in the second sense, that the term "lost" was used by our Saviour in the text. It was not that there was danger of concealment, but of waste. It is in this sense that God would have nothing lost.

The principle involved in the text manifests itself in two forms, both in human affairs and in the divine administration. In the one it respects economy of force when any thing is to be done; and in the other the waste of material or of means when any thing is possessed. Let us look at the Divine administration with reference to both of these.

And first, of the economy of force.

If we consider those forces that operate in free space, by which the planets and planetary systems are moved with such velocity, and guided with such precision, we have no means of measuring any thing except by the results. But these will suffice for us. When the earth comes round to a given star at the appointed and predicted moment, we must know that not one iota of the force that brought it there could have been spared. It is just brought there, and no more. When gravitation draws the earth to the sun, it is by a force that just retains it in its orbit, and no more; and the opposite force that would drive it into lawlessness and seclusion, is but just sufficient to prevent it from falling into the sun. As the avalanche is suspended by a balance of forces so delicate that the traveler who walks beneath fears even to whisper, lest it should be launched upon him, so hang the heavens. The slightest difference of adjustment, the least diminution of force, in any direction, would ultimately bring the system rushing together to the centre, or scatter it hopelessly.

And what is true of the forces that act at such vast distances, is equally true of those that are acting around us, and at distances that are inappreciable. The affinities by which solid bodies and gases are held together are so balanced that a less amount in any direction would unchain their elements, and the atmosphere would be decomposed, and the earth would effervesce and boil like lime when it is slacking.

We may notice, also, not only a balance of forces, implying a minimum in both directions, but also the different and apparently opposite offices which the same agents and forces subserve. Under precisely the same outward conditions, acted upon by the same outward agents—the same atmosphere, and storms, and sunshine—a tree that is growing shall be carried up to its perfection, and one that is decaying shall be resolved into its original elements. It is in this way that the constant circuit, and interdependent succession of life and death is kept up.

But perhaps the economy of force is best illustrated in the structure of animals, where there is not, in the same way, a balance of forces, but simply mechanism. Take the skeleton of any animal, and let the problem be to cause it to perform the same variety of motions that the animal can perform, and with the same rapidity, and the forces can be applied only as they are in the animal. In every animal, regarding its structure, and its position and surroundings relative to that, in the bird that flies, the fish that swims, the worm that crawls, the insect that creeps, in the four-footed animal, and in man, the economy of force is absolutely perfect. In no instance has any mechanician been able to show how this economy could be greater. On the contrary, mechanicians have borrowed many hints from the structure of animals for the economy of force, and might borrow more; for her motors are all perfect, both in their principle and in the mode of its application. Guided by the principle that nature does nothing in vain, Harvey discovered the circulation of the blood; and guided by the principle that she does every thing in the simplest and best way, the mechanician, if he will but allow for the difference of circumstances, may safely adopt any of her models and methods.

But on this point there is no need of detail. The principle contended for is involved in one of those broad inductions of Newton, which has been universally accepted as a law of philosophizing. The law is, "That no more, and no other causes are to be allowed, than are sufficient to explain the appearances."

Having thus considered the economy of force, we next look at that of material and of means. Between these, the relation is intimate, since all material used, and all means put in operation, require force.

As an illustration of economy in both, as thus related, but especially of material, we may take the stems of grasses and of grain. Contrive, if you can, a support for an ear of wheat that shall be adequate, and yet have in it less of material than that now provided. It is hollow and jointed, because, with a given amount of material, it is thus stronger. The same principle applies to the bones of animals, and to the quills of feathers. How perfectly discriminating, how illustrative of the principle involved, is the difference here between a stem of wheat and the trunk of a tree! As intended but for a season, the one, though adequate, is hollow and fragile ; but the other, as solid, has not too much material for the support of its top, and to withstand the storms ; and then it is needed, and was intended, as a supply for the permanent wants of man. The provision that surrounds the germ of a seed is just enough to support the young plant till it can strike its roots into the earth, and no more. The same is true of that about the vital point in an egg. The quantity of the atmosphere is just sufficient for the density needed to bear up clouds and birds, to give force to winds, that they may waft ships, and for the pressure needed upon animal bodies. The amount of heat and of light are in exact accordance with the demands of vitality and of vision. Vast as it is, the ocean is not too large for the evaporation needed to supply vegetation, and wells and springs ; and certain it is that the earth, as a whole, is not a particle too large in its relation to other bodies to hold its place firmly, and exert its due influence amidst the perturbations and actions and reactions of the system.

Another form of this economy may be noticed in the use of the same structure or substance to subserve different purposes, and those independent of each other. The lungs have an adequate end in the oxygenation of the blood, a function wholly within us, and so vital that a very brief suspension of it is death. They might seem to have sole reference to that. But see these same lungs in their connection with the voice, circulating fresh thought and sentiment through society, a function wholly without us, and not less vital to it than the renovation of the blood is to the body. The one substance, oxygen, is a main constituent of water, of the atmosphere, of all acids, of all vegetable products, and of most mineral substances and rocks as found in nature. It gives its heat to fire, its acidity to vinegar, and to potash its caustic power. It is the vital element of the atmosphere, and its destructive element. Water! How common it is, yet how manifold in its uses! It becomes ice, and so a reservoir of cold for the summer; it becomes steam, and so a power in locomotion and in manufacturing; it becomes vapor, and so fits the air to be breathed, and descends in dew; it becomes clouds, and so transports the rain; it becomes snow, and so gives the earth its winter robe. It is the element and home of all fish, and of the monsters of the deep; it is the chief constituent of all fluids of plants and of animals; it quenches thirst; it is the great cleanser and purifier; it is an element of beauty. With no running water, with no tossing ocean, with no cataracts, no dew, no changing clouds, now dark and seamed with lightning, now fleecy and mottled with the blue beyond, and now gorgeous in the sunset, with no showers, and no rainbow, where would the beauty of the earth be? And all this from the one substance, water! What economy of material! It would seem as if no property or capacity of usefulness in this substance could be lost.

The same principle also appears in the results of all decomposition. This seems a destruction; but in the sense of annihilation there is no destruction. In this sense nothing has ever been lost. The materials merely change their forms, and enter into new combinations. The servants retire, and reappear in a different garb. The partners are changed; and so, like a star in the heavens, each changing particle of matter walks its appointed round. Of this economy in connection with apparent destruction, we find large evidence in geology. There have, it seems, been creations and epochs long since that have come to an end; but when they did so, the command was given to the earth, " Gather up the fragments that remain, that nothing be lost," and the earth heard and obeyed. And now we have these fragments in the form of soil and drift; in granite and marble; in mines and coal-beds; in foot-prints and fossils, for the profit and instruction of those who now live; and probably much more, of those who shall live hereafter.

But while these instances are sufficient to establish the principle, there are objections and difficulties. There is apparent waste. Large portions of the earth are mere sandy plains, deserts, or inaccessible mountains; and upon these the sunshine and rain and dews descend. There is also an apparent and great waste of the germs of life.

In reply, it may be said that deserts and mountains are of use physically. "Were it not," says Maury, " for the Great Desert of Sahara, and other arid plains of Africa, the western shores of that continent, within the trade-wind region, would be almost, if not altogether, as rainless and sterile as the desert itself. We are to regard the sandy deserts, and arid plains, and the inland basins of the earth, as compensations in the great system of atmospherical circulation." The inaccessible and snow-capped mountains condense the moisture and form water-sheds. They are as a hand lifted up to compress the distended atmosphere, and to return to the ocean in long, and fertilizing, and navigable rivers, the tribute it had given.

But aside from this, if we admit, as we must, moral considerations and reasons, these difficulties vanish! Those deserts are not too large, or sterile, to be a mirror in which the man who receives the blessings of God and makes no return, may see his own features reflected. Those mountains of rock are not too hard and unimpressible to represent that adamant that can resist a Saviour's love. Those germs of life destroyed are not too many, or too precious, to show what is possible in regard to those powers and capabilities which every man has, and which he may dwarf and ruin. Without a correspondence between external nature and the character of man, the end of probation here could not be reached; and without these and similar features and facts in nature, that correspondence could not exist.

To many, the above would be a sufficient solution of the difficulties. It is so to me. But the text suggests another. It implies that to the accomplishment of any great work, fragments may be incidental, nay, that they may be required, for the completeness of the work itself. There are cases in which a provision is not enough, if it be not more than enough. So it was here. If no fragments had remained, it would not have been in accordance with the liberality of a bountiful provider, and something, yea, much, of the moral effect of the miracle would have been lost.

Now it is plain that there is, in this world, a great work carried on through, or in accordance with, what we call general laws. It is thus that the rain and the sunshine descend, and that the current of life, broad and deep, is kept in its even flow. To this the earth as a whole and the elements minister. In this great work it could not be expected that the sun should withhold his beams from every barren spot, or that the rain should skip and shun every stone and sand-bank. This would be petty, not in accordance with the nature of general laws, or with the dignity of the divine government. The great work is done. The current of life flows on, and no more. The nations are fed; and if there are outlying facts, the bearing of which upon the result we do not see, we may well class them with fragments that remain, which will be used at another time, or are used in other connections.

On the whole, then, we conclude that the economy of God, both with respect to force and to material, is perfect. In so wide a reach, where we confessedly know so little, it is not reasonable that a conclusion so borne out by the great mass and current of facts should be held in abeyance out of respect to mere exceptional eddies. Sustained, therefore, by the science of the nineteenth century, we venture with the fullest confidence, in regard to every particle of this universe, the assertion implied in the sublime interrogatories of the prophet: "Who hath measured the waters in the hollow of his hand, and meted out heaven with the span, and comprehended the dust of the earth in a measure, and weighed the mountains in scales, and the hills in a balance?"

The principle of economy thus regarded in the divine administration, ought to be equally regarded by man in the conduct of life. It ought to be thus regarded, but is not. Not only is there indolence, and so dormancy of capacity, but there is great misdirection of force, and waste of material. Who is there that gathers what he might? that becomes what he might? that achieves what he might? In doing each and all of these, and in that only, would be the highest success; and to this, economy is no less necessary than energy. The monarch who conquers a country provides for retaining it; without this his victories would be fruitless, and they become available only as he can incorporate it into his own dominions, and, if need be, make it the means of still further conquests. So it is with us. The two elements or factors of success in life, mental capacity being given, are the energy, the will, needed for getting, and for achievement; and the economy needed for so keeping what is thus gained, that nothing shall be lost. Of these elements the first is more exciting, more naturally attractive of sympathy, and has received, by far, greater attention. Young men are constantly exhorted to energy and enterprise, to perseverance and force of will, while the power of a wise economy and husbandry of resources is disregarded.

This general principle needs to be applied, first,

in regard to health and physical energy. In the management of these there has been, and still is, unspeakable loss. Let the pressure of necessity be removed, and men have not sufficient resolution and self-control to comply with the conditions of physical vigor. Civilization, the accumulation of wealth, refinement, leisure, bring facilities for various forms of indulgence incompatible with this vigor in its highest form; and so uniform is this, that no nation, highly civilized, has escaped physical deterioration. They have not learned the secret of gaining in refinement, without losing in a robust manhood. The population of cities, it is said, requires to be renovated by men fresh from the country every third generation, and that it is such men, or their descendants of the second generation, who hold the wealth and places of influence there. Of course there are exceptions, but this is the general rule. The third generation are inferior, both physically and mentally. They are second or third-rate men. Instead of being judges of soils and of oxen, they are judges of actors, and singers, and neck-ties; instead of being leaders in a town meeting, they are leaders of fashion. They become *dilettanti*. They drink, they gamble, they give themselves up to pleasure, they are of no particular use in the world, and not seldom either they or their children are beggars in the streets where their fathers were merchant princes. Meantime, everywhere, in the city and in the country, in the counting house and in the college, men are drawn into " the old way," or rather, ways " which wicked men have trodden." They become victims of licentiousness, or of some form of artificial stimulation; and with various alternations of hope and fear on the part of their friends, and of successful struggle and defeat, they become a curse to society, and go down to dishonored graves. The promises of early life are not met. The parental hand is pierced by the reed that it leans upon. Instead of fruit, awakened hope finds ashes in her grasp.

Of this loss something is due to ignorance, but there is scarcely any one whose knowledge is not in advance of his practice; and where that is the case, the root of the evil, and generally of the ignorance itself, lies deeper. It lies in the insane purpose to secure present enjoyment, regardless of consequences. From this no mere regard to self-culture, to the laws of health, to enjoyment on the whole, will hold the masses back when solicitation stands at every corner, and addresses every sense. Restraint will be spurned, and caution mocked at, and a pure and efficient manhood will disappear. This, a pervasive Christianity can prevent, and nothing else can. Nothing but the cross of Christ can so startle the spiritual nature from its torpor, as to make it an effectual counterpoise to the debasing and sensual tendencies of the race. Favored by temperament and education, individuals may measurably escape, but if the race is to triumph in the conflict between the flesh and the spirit, between the lower propensities and the higher nature, they must, as Constantine is said to have done, see the cross, and on it the motto, "*In hoc signo vinces.*" By this sign you shall conquer.

But, secondly, this principle is peculiarly applicable in its relation to time.

There is a low philosophy which says that time is money. It is more; it is the interval between two eternities; it is life; it is opportunity; it is salvation. It is that which, once past, comes not again. It fixes the past. It moulds the future. Money cannot buy it. A dying queen may exclaim, "Millions of money for an inch of time," but the millions will not buy the inch. Money has no relation to it. To waste it costs no effort. We have only to wrap our talent in a napkin and sit still; but to improve it requires both effort and wisdom, for it may be, and most often is, laboriously wasted.

"Gather up the fragments" of time, "that nothing be lost." This can be addressed only to those who are employing the greater portion of their time in some earnest work. He who floats loosely and aimlessly in society has no fragments of time, as related to a whole. It is all fragments. He himself is a fragment, lying useless, and his whole life requires to be recast. But whatever the great business of a man may be, however engrossing, there will always be some fragments of time that will remain; and with most men these are so considerable, that the disposition made of them will greatly modify the results of life. The secret of doing much is to do a little at a time, but to persevere in doing it. A half an hour a day, in the service of an earnest purpose, has been sufficient for the acquisition of languages and the writing of books, and for laying the foundation of a lasting fame. Even the minute fragment required for drawing his waxed ends, was employed by Roger Sherman in looking on his book open before him ; and it was thus that he became a sage, and a signer of the Declaration of Independence. Let a professional man, or any man, when he starts in life, have a side study, be it History, or a Language, or Poetry, or any branch of Natural History, as Geology, and let him give to it the fragments of his time, and he will be surprised at his own acquisitions ; the whole tone of his thoughts and life will be elevated, and the change of subject will be his best recreation. Of such a pursuit of Mineralogy and Geology, we have a striking instance in this vicinity. And what is thus true in literature and science, is still more so in religion, and in all that relates to duty. There is no time too brief for an ejaculatory prayer. When the countenance of Nehemiah was sad for the desolations of Jerusalem, and the king asked him, "What is thy request?" there was time between the question and the answer for him to pray "to the God of heaven." If the object of this world had been to furnish opportunities for doing good, it could hardly have been arranged better than it is ; and whoever has a heart set upon that, will have no need that any fragments of time he may gather up, should be lost.

But, once more, you will expect me to say that this principle applies also to property.

Owing to the undue estimate of wealth, this has indeed been supposed to be the special field and domain of economy, and there are those who make it their chief business to practice and to inculcate a small economy in this department. Certainly the principle applies here as elsewhere. Why should *any* property be lost? If it is worth the getting, why not the keeping? It is by saving, no less than by getting, that accumulation comes; and failure in this is oftener from a want of economy than of enterprise. Should there then be accumulation? Certainly. The right of property is given by God. Property itself, that is, something accumulated and kept, is a necessity for society. It not only confers comfort and independence, but is a great and desirable power for good. It is a duty to give; we are commanded to give; but he who has nothing can give nothing. This is commonly thought a sufficient excuse. It may, or may not be. It is so, just as it is a sufficient excuse for begging, that a man has nothing to eat. But how came he to have nothing to eat? How came the man to have nothing to give? If there has been a want, either of industry, or of the strictest economy, it is not a sufficient excuse. Of the extent of this accumulation, with its temptations and dangers, I am not now to speak. Of that every man must judge for himself. But be it greater or less, there need be no hesitation in saying that any loss of property, any want of economy in spending it, any failure to save any portion of it, must be the result either of human imperfection or of sin.

But in this attention to minute things, this regard to fragments, is there not something of smallness and narrowness; of a carefulness and painstaking not compatible with enjoyment? Is there not something alien from the tone and temper of a high and free and generous spirit? That there are such associations, in connection with what is called economy, cannot be denied. But we must here make distinctions. There is that, if we call it economy at all, which must be called a wicked economy. It is that of the miser. He saves for the sake of saving, and so loses by his very keeping. The fragments were to be gathered up, not that they should be carried about in baskets and kept till they should be mouldy, for then they would have been lost by being kept; but that, subsequently, and on the first fit occasion, they should be put to the use for which they were made.

There is, also, as I have said, a small economy— a careful parsimoniousness, not exactly miserliness, but bordering upon it. It is born of fear, has reference to self, and does not contemplate use, except for low and personal ends.

There is, again, an honorable economy, having for its end the gratification of the natural affections, opportunities for mental improvement, position in society, and all these in connection with the highest manhood and most perfect personal independence. For a parent to be economical, to the point of severe self-denial, for the education of a child; for a young man to be thus economical for his own education; for one accustomed or seeking to associate with the wealthy and the fashionable, to conform to no habit of expense that would require dishonesty or meanness in any direction, implies high qualities; and the economy thus practiced is an honorable economy.

But besides these, there is what may be called a sublime economy. This is not confined to money, or property, but is in imitation of the method of God, and from a perception of its connection with beneficence. It includes the employment and expenditure of whatever would bear on human wellbeing, and its principle is, "*That nothing be lost.*" It sees that the water must be gathered in clouds before it can be poured out in rain; that the reservoir must be filled before the city can be supplied; that every where God gathers by little and little what he dispenses with a liberal hand, and thus, instead of being connected with smallness or narrowness, this economy becomes the very spring and fountain-head of generosity and liberality and beneficence. He who adopts this principle looks around him, and over the earth, and sees hunger to be fed, and nakedness to be clothed, and ignorance to be instructed, and vice to be reclaimed, and talent and worth to be encouraged, and institutions to be aided; he hears the cry of heathen nations calling for the gospel; and now a regard for the least thing that can work towards either, or all of these for which God is working, is dignified and consecrated by the principle that gave it birth. Now, nothing that can thus work is small to him. Of the cold water that he is bearing to the wounded and perishing on the battle-field of life, and which he knows to be far short of their necessities, he would not lose a drop. Now he works for God, and with God; and he finds enlargement both of mind and of heart just in proportion as he is able to comprehend in his working plans, as God does in his, every instrumentality and means, however apparently insignificant and minute.

In these parting words of instruction to you, My Beloved Friends of the Graduating Class, with whom I have been so long and so pleasantly associated, it has been my wish to place before you one great element of all success, whether it be of that outward but delusive success, that belongs only to time, or of that inward and true success, that lays up its treasures in heaven. In connection with both, the principle applies, that nothing should be lost. This element of success is not the primitive, or the greatest. I have no wish to magnify it at the expense of the power of attainment and acquisition, but call your attention to it as equally indispensable with that, and because its character is often misapprehended, and its value not appreciated.

Between the two elements of success just mentioned, as between the great forces of nature, there is a tendency to opposition, and you will need to balance them carefully, if you would preserve the true course and orbit of life. With some, the constitutional tendency is towards energy, attainment, acquisition; and as the consciousness of power in this direction is greater, it is natural there should be a certain profusion and recklessness in expenditure. To the young and self-confident, their resources of time, of health, of energy, if not of money, seem exhaustless; and why should they care for loss? With others, the tendency is towards caution. They gain by saving. They never either pay, or give, too much for any thing. They are in danger of withholding more than is meet, even when it tendeth to poverty. Of these elements, if there must be a preponderance of either, let it be of the first. But, rightly viewed, these are not conflicting, but complementary elements. If there were no gathering, there could be neither saving nor giving; if there were no saving, there could be no systematic, far-sighted, effective use or distribution. Here, as everywhere, the example of our Saviour is perfect. How grand the energy by which he controlled the elements! How adequate, and more than adequate, the provision for all that use required! And yet how perfect the economy—an economy, you will be careful to observe, that in no degree restricted use, but simply provided against loss. Here we have the whole principle. *Everything for use, nothing to be lost.* Why should any thing, that can be used, be lost? How can it be, but from recklessness, or weakness, or wickedness?

You, my Beloved Friends, have rich endowments, a rich inheritance, a capital of priceless worth, no part of which ought to be lost. You have youth, and health, and education, and freedom, personal, civil, and religious. You inherit the past, and stand on the threshold of a future that must be richer in thronging events and in opportunities for good, than any past has been. Your fathers inherited a continent that required to be subdued. You, one that requires to be cultivated; they inherited the printing press worked by hand, and the stage coach, and the sailing vessel; you inherit the cylinder press worked by steam, and the railroad car, and the steamship, and the electric telegraph. It was for them to lift up their eyes upon the varied forms of destitution and crime in our land, and upon the darkness and woes of heathendom, and to form the associations, and gain the knowledge necessary for effective working. It is for you to take these instrumentalities and work them. Work them with accelerated speed, and with mightier power. Meliorate the physical condition of man. Bring back a revolted world to its allegiance to God. And when you look at the magnitude of this work, is there anything, whether of time, or health, or money, or influence, or of capability in any direction, which you can afford to lose? No. Oh, no. In such a work every resource is needed; "Hold fast what thou hast;" for such a work, "Gather up the fragments, that nothing be lost."

But, my friends, if it be the will of God that you should lose nothing of time, or health, or even of money, how much more must it be his will that you should not lose yourselves. This you can do. You can lose yourselves; and such a loss, you will observe, implies not merely deprivation, but all there is of suffering and of penalty under the moral laws of God. As the loss of health is sickness, and of light, darkness, so is the loss of hope, despair, and the loss of heaven is hell. You can throw yourselves away. You can become of no use in this universe except for a warning. You can lose your souls. Oh, what a loss is that! The perversion and degradation of every high and immortal power for an eternity! And shall this be true of any one of you? Will you be lost when One has come from heaven, traveling in the greatness of his strength, and with garments dyed in blood, on purpose to guide you home—home to a Father's house—to an eternal home? Will you not rather, on this day of interest, it may be of final decision, when all the world, and all choices are open before you, hear his voice saying, "Follow me." "For what shall it profit a man, if he shall gain the whole world, and *lose* his own soul?"

THE LIVING HOUSE,
OR
GOD'S METHOD OF SOCIAL UNITY.

A

BACCALAUREATE SERMON,

DELIVERED AT

WILLIAMSTOWN, MS.

AUGUST 3, 1862.

BY MARK HOPKINS, D. D.
President of Williams College.

BOSTON:
PRESS OF T. R. MARVIN & SON, 42 CONGRESS STREET.
1862.

SERMON.

1 PETER II. 4, 5.

TO WHOM COMING, AS UNTO A LIVING STONE, DISALLOWED INDEED OF MEN, BUT CHOSEN OF GOD, AND PRECIOUS, YE ALSO, AS LIVELY STONES, ARE BUILT UP A SPIRITUAL HOUSE.

In building a house, materials of great diversity are brought into unity. They are placed in such relations as to be mutually subservient, and become one thing. This is what is done in all construction. It is what God has done in building this material universe. The process of this, as conducted by him, is expressly compared to the building of a house by man. "For," says the Apostle, "every house is builded by some man, but he that built all things is God."

As thus constructed, the universe is no multitudinous mass of unrelated units baffling all comprehension. The separate beings and facts are, indeed, without number, and are infinitely diversified; but they may yet be partitioned off into divisions, assorted into groups, the ligament which binds each of these into unity may be distinctly traced, and each group, thus assorted and bound together, becomes the field of a separate science. And not only are the facts within each group related to each other, but the groups themselves. Not, as the ancients supposed, are the heavens, and the earth, and the regions beneath, constituted and governed, each on different principles. The light from the farthest star is the same as that which comes from the sun, and which is struck from the flint; the particle of dust that floats in the air is governed by the same laws as the earth that floats in space and is enveloped by that air; the spire of grass at our feet requires not only the sun and the rain, but all those laws of electricity, and magnetism, and cohesion, and affinity, by which the globe itself, and the solar system, and the far vaster stellar systems cohere and stand up together. Not only, therefore, is there a unity of each science, but a unity of the sciences. The farther we investigate the more do we find of unity in the works of God, and nothing seems left to science but to accept that instinctive and universal conviction which has recorded itself in language, and which calls these works of God, so varied and so vast, a *uni-verse*.

With this constitution of the external universe, that of the mind is in harmony. It is a necessity for it to seek to reduce its knowledge to unity. Before science can begin, we must observe separate facts; but as soon as these are observed, there is an effort to bring them into system, that is, into unity; and when this is fully done, there is a completed science. No man can observe a new and strange fact, without seeking to bring it into relation with facts already known and classified.

But it is not solely as speculative that man desires, and is required, to reduce all things to unity. As a practical being, it is his great business to do this. As the beings and facts of nature are given to him, as speculative, that he may find their mutual relations, and thus their unity, so are the substances of nature given to him, as a practical being, that he may find their capabilities, and bring them into such relations of convergence and unity as shall subserve his purposes. Like the facts and phenomena, these substances are given separately. The air is given by itself, and the iron, and the fuel, and the fire, and the water, and all these are to be brought into such convergence and unity of action as to cause the locomotive and the steam-ship to be, and to speed them on their wondrous way. In all contrivances, from the simple lever to those marvelous combinations of machinery that seem endowed not only with hands, but with thought, there is always to be found a unity in the subservience of every part to the purpose of the designer, and it is this unity which he designs to produce. As a creature made in the image of God, man not only finds in his works unity with reference to an end, but he wishes to produce such unity.

But this is not all. If we pass from matter to mind we find another, a spiritual universe, to which the first is subservient. We can scarcely avoid the conclusion, favored as it is by the Scriptures and by all analogy, that there is a spiritual universe corresponding in vastness and variety to the material one; and if so, the great object of God, in the whole, must be such an arrangement and government of this as shall secure for it the highest social and spiritual unity. This, too, is favored by the Scriptures. Christians are to be built up a spiritual house. Christ prayed that they might all be one; and the Apostle, glancing, it would seem, at that wider range of which we have spoken, says: " That in the dispensation of the fullness of times he might gather together in *one* all things in Christ, both which are in heaven, and which are on earth; even in him."

And here, also, in this spiritual universe, man is not merely to find a unity produced by God; he is also, and in this chiefly, to seek to produce unity.

In doing this, the first sphere of action for every man is his own spirit. Blessed is he who can bring into that, that unity which is at once peace and power. This is the first condition of all true rest, and of all healthful activity. The more complex man is; the more incompatible are his desires; the more deeply opposed are the flesh and the spirit; the more needful, and the more beautiful is that unity which belongs to the original design of God, and which is brought in by one overmastering purpose subordinating all things to itself. In this is singleness of eye; in this consistency, efficiency, a ground for self-respect, and for the respect of others.

But this unity of the individual spirit is not only a condition of individual peace and joy, but also of those bonds of peace by which individuals are united to each other. This brings us to a wider and more complex field, to that social and spiritual unity which we now propose to consider.

In this field the first and most perfect unity is to be found in the marriage union. In marriage, according to its original idea, there is the most perfect social unity known on earth. They twain become one flesh. It is based on a diversity in the whole being,—a diversity, not of opposition, but of correspondence, by which each supplements the other, and in which there is always the basis for the truest and deepest unity.

It is from such a unity that society springs, branching out into families, communities, and nations. Here, again, unity is needed not only within each family, community and nation, but also between families, communities and nations. This is possible. Despite the isolations, the alienations, the enmities there are, it is the law, it is the only condition of social good, and it is the production of this that is the end of all constitutions, and legislation, and government. A solution of all social problems, those which have taxed the powers of man from the beginning, can end in nothing better than this. That the race of man should recognize its own unity in a spirit of brotherhood, overlooking no one having the attributes of man, and thus, under the government of God, become fitted for a unity with other races, trained in other planets, in other systems, related to us by the correspondence of diversity, they fitted to supplement us, as we them, gives us the grandest conception of a social system which it is possible for us to form. It is towards this that all true reformers look ; as they approximate this, their end is attained ; as they find the principle of this, they find the principle of all real reforms.

It is of this complex social unity that the text speaks under the figure of a house built up of separate stones. "Ye are built up a spiritual house." And this unity men have sought, and still seek to secure, chiefly in two ways.

The first is by the balance of mutual interests and selfishnesses.

Interest and selfishness are not, like malignity, necessarily repellent. So far as two selfish persons are either necessary to each other from the conditions of their being, or can make use of each other, they can go on together ; and, by a skillful adjustment of checks and balances, much may be done to make it for the immediate interest of all to go on thus. Selfishness may do good to others, that others may do good to it ; it may lend to others, "hoping to receive as much again." It may, for its own sake, do much for the upbuilding and perfection of society ; and with this as its controlling principle, together with the gregariousness common to man with the animals, society may exist and have a degree of unity. But with a governing selfishness, held in check, and known to be, solely by expediency, there must be constant distrust. Thus governed, men will overstep the limits of right when they dare, and the individuals of society will resolve themselves into an armed neutrality, with a constant outlook for opportunities of safe aggression. Outward peace there may be, but it will be from mutual dread, as when two prize-fighters survey each other, and each prefers to decline the contest. It will be on the principle that a certain gun, supposed to be very destructive, was named "the peacemaker." There will be sought a balance of power like that so long made the object of European politicians. Such a political balance required for its maintenance standing armies, and navies, and fortifications, and constant watchfulness. And such a balance in society will require the division of powers, and a police, and courts, and prisons, and written contracts, and securities. Such a unity may be better than none. It is far better; but there must be something better than this.

A second mode of producing unity among men is by power, or pressure from without.

This involves the first, to some extent, and is superinduced upon it. It is the method adopted by all despotisms, whether of one man, of a few, or of many. The great object of ambition has been to exercise the power of a despotic will over masses of men organized as armies, and through these to hold in subjection, as one empire, vast regions, peopled, it may be, by nations the most discordant. Such was the empire of Nebuchadnezzar, who sent forth his decree 'to every people, and nation, and language.' Such was the Persian empire under Ahasuerus, whose letters were sent 'to the rulers of the provinces which were from India to Ethiopia, a hundred and twenty and seven provinces, unto every province according to the writing thereof, and unto every people after their language.' Such was the empire of Alexander, that fell in pieces by its own weight, as soon as his strong grasp upon it was relaxed. Such, emphatically, was the Roman empire. Extending from the African deserts to Britain, and from India to the pillars of Hercules, it held in a forced unity nations utterly diverse in language, and habits, and interests. It was a mere aggregation, a conglomerate, whose parts were held in position by Roman legions. Such, indeed, were the *republics* of antiquity, when they became extensive. Of the rights of man as such, they knew nothing; they did not extend citizenship with their conquests, but held their provinces in subjection, and so preserved unity by power. Such has been, and still is, to a great extent, the condition of Europe; much more of countries less enlightened. Different nationalities are forced together. Every where there is the pressure of power as an external force. The free play of affinities, whether laterally, or vertically, is checked; and the spirit, if not the laws of caste, is rigidly maintained. Hence the unity, such as there is, being enforced, is unquiet; not peaceful, spontaneous and fruitful.

In opposition to these methods, now tried so long that the world is weary, is that adopted by God, and beautifully indicated in the text. The figure in this passage is remarkable, as bringing into coalescence objects and qualities seemingly the most incompatible. A stone is passive. You may lift it, toss it, hurl it, smite it, lay it in a wall, and it will resist only in virtue of its inertia and cohesion. A stone is dead—so dead, that when we would speak of the perfection and intensity of death in other things, we say of them that they are stone-dead. A stone is solid, permanent, a fit material to enter into structures that are to endure for ages. How opposite is all this to that vitality, and sensibility, and self-assertion, and transient character that belong to all organic and living things! How opposite, especially, is it to spirituality. Nothing could be more opposite, and yet it is precisely in the blending of these opposites that the power and beauty of the figure are found. That the building should be of stone, was required to indicate its perpetuity; for its turrets are to gleam forever in the light of eternity. That the stones should be living, was required to indicate their union, each in its place; not by mechanical means, or outward pressure, but by *vital affinity.*

Here it is that we reach the peculiarity of this structure. It is that the materials are living, and are united by a vital affinity. If now we suppose this affinity to spring from that which is deepest and most essential in the materials, we shall have the whole method of God in producing social unity; we shall have that which *we* must adopt in seeking to produce it, if we are ever to succeed.

Of this method of union by vital affinity, there are two conditions. The first and indispensable one is, that the materials should be vitalized, or be alive. The second is, that they should be free to move in accordance with the laws of vitality.

What it is to be vitalized in mere matter, and how this is done, we know. It is to have life communicated to that which was dead; and this is done by bringing the materials, not in masses, but particle by particle, into contact with that which already has vitality. It is done as by a leavening power, a kind of sacred contagion; and when it is done, the materials are ready to be marshaled into their places, and to perform their functions under the vital laws.

So far the process is beautiful and typical, but the marshaling is perhaps more so. Here the second condition, that of freedom, comes in. In matter, fluidity is freedom. It is the freedom of the individual particle to move in any direction; and strange as it may seem, that a fluid should be alive, yet it is, and the Scripture doctrine, that the blood "is the life thereof," is a philosophical necessity. Having then materials for the upbuilding of every part of the body, vitalized, and free, as held in solution, what is to be done? There are to be formed bone, muscle, tendon, brain, nerves, skin, hair, nails, the transparent humors of the eye, and its dark pigment. The materials are undistinguishable, and mixed in utter confusion. But now the affinity shows itself, and the miracle of bringing order out of chaos, as seen in the first creation, is repeated. Each particle goes to its own place, stands in its own lot, performs just the office it is fitted to perform; and thus, to a body constantly changing in its matter, there is given permanence, and strength, and beauty.

Of the process now mentioned all materials are not capable, but only food. It is the capability of this that makes them food. But whether capable of it or not, any substance not actually vitalized, or in a position to be so, is a foreign substance. As such it is either an encumbrance or an irritant, and is expelled by the vital force. This power of rejection and expulsion is no less essential than that of assimilation.

All this perfectly represents what occurs, or should occur, in that higher social region of which the text speaks. Every particle thus vitalized becomes a living stone to build up a living house, and in thus helping to build the whole, its own place is found, and its appetency satisfied.

In passing to the higher spiritual region, if we find differences, it is only those required by the nature of the subject. We have here the same indispensable conditions of vitality and freedom, and the same expulsive power. But life here, in accordance with the usage of the Scriptures, and with all usage, is something more than life, and death is not merely its absence. Life here is consciousness, sensibility, sympathy, affection. It is consent and harmony, and the more intense the life in one direction, the more perfect the death in another. To be alive to God is to have every faculty active and quick in apprehending his perfections, and in doing his will; and one wholly in this state would be dead to sin. Its allurements would awaken no more response than an appeal to the senses of the dead. They would be viands set at the mouth of a tomb. On the other hand, no life is more intense than that of him who is "dead in trespasses and sins." He is so engrossed in his own selfish plans that no voice of the word, or providence, or Spirit of God, makes any impression upon him. Call as you may, there is no response. There is no voice, nor any that answers or regards. He is dead. In the same way men may be alive to the beauties of nature, or of art, to the behests of duty, the calls of compassion, the voice of their country; and they may be dead to all these. They may be wholly engrossed in business, or in pleasure. Men may be so alive to the wages of unrighteousness as to become, as the Apostle says, "trees twice dead, plucked up by the roots."

We say, then, that for a social structure, he is a living stone who is capable of being so inwrought into it as to add, and only add, to its strength and symmetry. This will imply that he be permeated by those ideas which are the life of the system, that he be plastic to its forces, and responsive to its instinctive wants. He must be an agent, and not an instrument. It is the characteristic of vital methods, as opposed to mechanical, that the movement is from within. The moment the interior appetency, and impulse, and choice, cease to be respected, there is social death; the idea of mutual subserviency through vital action, which is God's idea, is lost, and society, instead of moving like the heavens, becomes a crazy mechanism, whirling and crashing on with the blindness and unsteadiness of human passion and power.

Such is the idea of vitality in a social system. It implies a sympathy, a rational consent and harmony of the individual with the movements and ends of the system, that will lead him to seek and to keep, not office, but just that place for which he is best fitted.

The idea of freedom, figurative in matter, is literal here. It implies both the immediate absence of arbitrary power, and security against it. The lion must not only be sated for the moment, or accidentally sluggish, he must be caged. There must be no intervention of mere will, seeking, for a side and selfish purpose, to wield the masses as instruments, or to prevent any living stone from finding its true place. The idea of freedom also implies the absence of any horizontal and petrified strata in society, as caste, or fixed classes, which would prevent a free movement, upwards or downwards, horizontally or obliquely. Such strata *may* exist without arbitrary power; *it* may exist without them, but they naturally go together and mutually aid each other. Established orders are a frame-work to support the throne, and the throne concentrates power to guard these orders from the encroachments of each other, and of the people.

Of such a combination of concentrated power and established orders, great public works, and high civilization and refinement in the favored classes, are the natural result, while the lower classes are degraded. In such a form of society there may be much of beauty, and power, and beneficence. Once originated, it readily perpetuates itself, and becomes venerable. From this, with the vast wealth accumulated, public and private, though in few hands, and from the consequent magnificence, it appeals strongly to the imagination and tends to control the associations. Being born into it, children are overshadowed by it, and their associations are conformed to its order as they are to that of nature. Both seem to come from a power above them, and to belong almost equally to an order of things over which they have no control. Institutions, just those established, with their settled order, are everything; the individual is nothing. There is no longer room for an appeal to original rights and fitnesses. The sphere of choice and of action provided by God, and needed for the best development of the life of all, becomes limited. There is no fluidity, and for a man to pass up through the orders of society by merit, is a marvel. If he choose to fall in with the prescribed course, well; but if Buonaparte is to rise from the lower strata of society to its top, it can be only as the metallic vein is shot up through the earthy strata by an underlying force that would convulse a continent.

Of the two great elements of social order now spoken of, vitality and freedom, freedom has been most prominent in the thoughts and in the speech of men. Freedom has been the battle-cry of the race. For this heroes have fought. Men seek scope, that is freedom, for the action of vitality, but do not so readily feel the deficiency of that or seek its increase. This is natural, because the absence of freedom is a restraint that is instantly felt, and naturally resisted; but the absence of vitality is insensibility, and the less life a man has, of any kind, physical, intellectual, spiritual, the less inclined will he be to struggle for more.

But while freedom is thus more prominent than vitality, it is not at all in the same rank. All good is from vitality. Freedom is only the condition of its best exercise. For a good man, freedom is a good; for a bad man, it is an evil. Without vitality in the sense of the text, freedom becomes anarchy. With it, pervading the whole social system, there will be essential freedom, whatever the outward form of society may be. If every stone in the house be living, there will be nothing to originate mechanical methods and obstructions; vital laws will rule, and the rule of these is freedom.

All that has now been said will apply to social unity of any kind; but that spoken of in the text is spiritual. "Ye are built up a spiritual house." Let there be vitality and freedom, and there may be unity after God's method; but its strength and value will be as the life from which it springs. Spiritual unity must be from spiritual life, and in these we find the sphere and method of God in his grandest work.

Of spiritual unity the peculiarities are two. The first is, that it springs from that life which is deepest.

Surely, if man is made in the image of God, that by which he is thus made must be that which makes him man, and so is his very being. If so, his natural affinities—using the word natural in its highest sense—will be for God and those who are like him. If so, as union with God and those who are like him is essential to this life, it must expel every interest, or life, or love incompatible with it. No love of father or mother may compete with it. It will move on as the river towards the ocean. Not to do this, would be to deny its own nature.

The second peculiarity of spiritual life, at least in man, is, that Christ is, for him, both the source of vitality and the centre of unity.

Without Christ, men are destitute of spiritual life. They are "without God, and without hope." This is the cardinal fact in the moral history of the world. The recognition or non-recognition of this, will determine the character of all speculative theologies, and also the character and results of all efforts for the good of man. This fact the world do not admit; and hence they disallow Christ, both as a source of life and as the centre of unity. He is "disallowed indeed of men, but chosen of God and precious." It is on this that the whole method of God in the restoration of man is based, and it is for the recognition of this by men, and their adoption of God's method of vitality and unity, that the tardy and laboring and distracted times wait. No partial reform will do; no "coming man." Every where men are divergent, repellent. The bond of a common humanity has been found to be but a bond of tow to bind the Samson of human selfishness and passion. There must be a divine life, a divine centre, a more than human bond. This life is in Christ. He is "the life." This bond is from him. In him are condensed all human relationships, as of "brother and sister and mother;" and to these—higher and holier—that of Saviour is added. In him, as the second Adam; in his matchless character, human, yet divine; in his all-embracing and self-sacrificing love; in him, as the champion of humanity in its weakness and guilt, able and willing to bring succor in the hour of its direst need, and to raise it up from the darkness and the dust of death, there is every requisite for a centre of unity for the race, so that "all things which are on earth," as well as "those which are in heaven, may be gathered together in one, even in him." In this, in this only, is there an object worthy of God. He has created worlds, and families of worlds, of mere matter, and given them a unity of unspeakable beauty and grandeur; but without sensation or recognition, without enjoyment or praise, what would they be worth? Nothing. No, the only work worthy of God is one crowned by creatures made in his image, with their vitality from him, and himself the centre of their unity—unity in love, fitly represented by the marriage union. This work, we believe, will correspond in its vastness to that of the stellar hosts, and as far transcend them in glory as mind transcends the inanimate clod. It will embrace all orders of rational intelligences, in all worlds; sin and its consequences will be eliminated, and it shall stand in its glorious order forever. The promised new heavens and earth do not so much respect any new combinations and unity of matter, as of conscious agents; and they will be such that all that has gone before in the works of God will be as nothing. " For behold," says God, " I create new heavens and a new earth; and the former shall not be remembered, nor come into mind. But be ye glad and rejoice forever in that which I create; for, behold, I create Jerusalem a rejoicing and her people a joy."

It is of such a social system, my beloved friends of the Graduating Class, that you are to fit yourselves to form a part; it is into such a system that you are to seek to bring others. This will comprehend your whole duty. It is the focal point to which our efforts for you have converged, and if your education here has not fitted you for this, it is a failure. This you will best do, not by ignoring or disregarding those lower social systems on earth which God has ordained, but by filling your places as living stones in them all. That you may do this rightly, I have wished, in these parting words, to furnish you both with a test of systems, and with guiding principles.

First, then, it will follow, from what has been said, that if you are either to fit yourselves for such a system, or to aid in fitting others, an indispensable condition must be, that you should be *alive.*

What can a dead man do ? In the first place, death can enjoy nothing. And then, what place has a cold, unconscious, apathetic stone, where everything is vital, and responsive, and eager to meet the wants of the whole ? It is an obstruction not merely, but an offense, and cannot be permanently suffered. So is it in the family; so in the college—what is the use of a dead student ? so in the state; so in the church; so, emphatically, must it be in heaven. With little vitality, such offenses may be endured, but the more intense the life, the more does it array itself against all death, and seek to free itself from its contact. The very pavement of heaven would rise against the foot of the wicked; it would cast them out. "Without are dogs." And what, again, can a dead man do in communicating life ? Life comes from life. God is its author; but, having originated it, it spreads from centres according to laws, and those centres must be alive. In the spiritual, as in the natural world, there is no spontaneous generation. Would you communicate knowledge ? You must have it. So of life. Christianity does not spring up of itself; it must be borne by the living preacher. Yes, by a *living* preacher, and not by one that is dead.

If, then, you would enjoy any thing; if you would not be an offense; if you would communicate any thing, you must be alive.

You will also find, in what has been said, a test of all social organizations. Of these, the present emergency requires that I should refer especially to those that are national, and to your duty to the government in which you are to have a part.

Organizations express life, and react upon it. Of these, some are better than others. It is not true, that "that is the best government which is best administered." That government is the best, and is likely to be best administered, which is constructed most nearly after God's method, as indicated in the text. That, accordingly, is the best government which combines most perfectly vitality, freedom, and unity. We are wont to think of the excellence of our government as from freedom. Not so, except as there is vitality back of the freedom, and as it leads to unity. Its excellence is that its *method* is vital, and not mechanical. It is self-government, working out, as by an instinct of life, the common good. It is a common-wealth. It casts the character in the mould of freedom, and becomes a great educating and formative power. It makes a radical difference whether the people have a government distinct from themselves and exercised over them, or whether they *are* the government, expressing their will through constitutional forms. In the one case the people will be recipients and instruments, receiving a provision made for them by those whose business it is to take care of them; in the other, they will be vital, and will perform a high function of vitality by which, if they perform it well, they must grow into a larger manhood. *If they perform it well!* Just here it is that the voice of patriotism, of oppressed humanity every where, that the voice of God reaches every young man, and especially every educated young man. You inherit a government more conformed to the methods of God than any other. There is in it more of freedom in all directions; we trust there is also more of vitality, of unity, and of power to expel what would be destructive of its life. But this is yet to be tested, and the result will depend on the present generation of young men. If our national life shall come out triumphant in its struggle with that internal and cancerous malady to which it has at times seemed to succumb, it will be the most glorious triumph of free principles the world has ever seen. Will it thus come out? We think so. The government has a power, and the nation a life and a conscious unity, that we did not know of till the present struggle. Let but the demon of slavery be cast out, and though it leave the nation rent, and torn, and prostrate, we shall yet rise to a strength and greatness unknown before. There is no strength like that of unity from vitality and freedom. There is no beauty like it. Go forth, then, and do what you can in giving to the nation this strength and beauty. Be true to God's methods; be true to the interests of freedom, and to the rights of man.

Again, as we have seen that vitality is the chief thing in order to social unity, it will follow that your highest aim will be to communicate that.

This was done by our Saviour. He had life in himself. He was the Life, and his great object was to give life to the world. For this he gave himself. This principle was original with him. It is distinctive. It is this, and this only, that has made his religion a power in the world, working like leaven. Overlooked by the world, "disallowed of men," it is yet demonstrably the only true principle of reform. If a living house is to be built, there must be living stones. *The difficulty in social structures is in the material.* If this nation is to fail, it will be from that. Ambition, selfishness, human wisdom, take such materials as they find and use them as they may, often skillfully, for their own ends. Christ says, begin with the materials. "*Make the tree good.*" Go to the ignorant, the vicious, the proud, the sensual, the selfish in every form, and teach them that wisdom of God which consists, not in getting any thing, or in achieving any thing, but in *becoming* as little children before him. Thus shall they enter, by love, into his kingdom, and into the heirship of all things. This is totally different from any achievement for admiration, or from any exercise of power, as by the great ones of the earth. It is wholly alien from the spirit of the world, and yet from this only can there be renovation in society, or fruit unto life everlasting. This will preclude all monkish seclusion, it will bring you heart to heart with your fellow-men, no matter who, so they be men, and will call for all you may have of life to communicate. Your usefulness will not be as your talents, but as you may communicate vitality. I rejoice, my dear friends, in the confidence that so many of you have adopted this principle. Apply it in your lives, unmoved by the sneers of skepticism, or by the success and self-complacency of the worldly wise.

Once more, in view of the discordance and divisions in the world, it will readily occur to you, from what has been said, how important it is that your centres of unity should be rightly chosen.

Both your influence and peace will depend much upon this. Here your wisdom will be to choose only those which God has established. God has established the family, and not communism; the state, and not party; the church, the one living, spiritual church, and not sects; Christ, and not popes, or theological doctors and teachers. The true ground of union is vitality with reference to a common centre; and distant as it may seem, we hope and believe the time will come when men will every where swing away from centres false, artificial, divisive, and revolve only, with mutual attraction, around those that are God-appointed.

Finally, while I exhort you to enter, as a vital part, into every social unity instituted by God, the great question with you, as with us all, is whether you have come to Christ. "Unto whom coming." Have you come to him as unto a living stone, and so been made yourselves living as to be fit to become a part of that spiritual house which God is building? Christ, my dear friends, is still "disallowed of men." The builders refuse him. So do not you. You are building for eternity; look well to your foundation. Christ is "chosen of God," and other foundation can no man lay. He is precious to him as "the Head-stone of the corner." "He is precious to them that believe." If you have not done so, come to him now, in this hour of transition, and of out-look upon the future, and he will be precious to you. Is it to be to any of you that your strength will be weakened in the way, and that death will claim you early? Christ will be precious, O how precious! Are any of you, as some are, in seeking to sustain those powers that be, and that are ordained of God, to encounter the temptations of a camp, the exposure of a southern climate, the hazards of the battle-field? How precious will be the presence and succor of One that sticketh closer than a brother! Are you to bear the responsibilities of life, and wage its battles till old age? Little do you know of your own weakness, and of the besetments and fierce struggles of the long way, if a divine Helper would not be precious to you. He will be precious to you in the final hour. When you shall walk through the valley of the shadow of death, his rod and his staff, they shall comfort you. And when the present order shall come to an end, and that building of God, whose stones are now preparing, shall go up without the sound of the axe or the hammer, till "the head-stone thereof shall be brought forth with shoutings," you shall be there, and cry, "Grace, grace, unto it."

' The Lord bless you and keep you: the Lord make his face shine upon you, and be gracious unto you: the Lord lift up his countenance upon you, and give you peace.'

ENLARGEMENT.

A BACCALAUREATE SERMON,

DELIVERED AT

WILLIAMSTOWN, MS.

AUGUST 2, 1863.

BY MARK HOPKINS, D. D.
President of Williams College.

BOSTON:
PRESS OF T. R. MARVIN & SON, 42 CONGRESS STREET.
1863.

Entered according to Act of Congress, in the year 1863, by

T. R. MARVIN,

In the Clerk's Office of the District Court of the District of Massachusetts.

SERMON.

2 CORINTHIANS vi. 13.

NOW FOR A RECOMPENSE IN THE SAME, (I SPEAK AS UNTO MY CHILDREN,) BE YE ALSO ENLARGED.

That is a slow process by which enlargement comes to man in his apprehension of himself, and of his wider relations. At his birth he is often spoken of as a stranger. He is a stranger in a strange world — how strange! — but to no one is he a greater stranger than to himself. How little does the infant know or suspect of the capacities that are in him for apprehension, for joy and suffering, for varied emotion and passion, for action, and for an eternal duration. He is a point that is to enlarge into a capacity to reflect the universe, but that capacity is revealed only as he is brought face to face with that which is to act upon him, and upon which he is to act, and few men, if any, learn, during a life-time, their own capacities. Among the last things that a man comes to know thoroughly, is himself.

Then of the past, of the future, of things around him, what does he know? Of that endless duration that is back of him, he knows nothing. He does not know that there has been such a duration, much less what has taken place during its countless ages. Whether he is the first child of the first man, or the last in a succession of myriads of generations, he knows not. So of the space around him, and what is in it. To him, the walls that his eyes rest upon are the limit of the universe, and those around him are all the beings it contains. Of wide plains, and high mountains, and broad oceans, of an infinite space with its countless suns and systems, of the multitudes of men, and the myriads of the heavenly hosts, he has no apprehension or suspicion. So also of the great future. Shall all things continue as they are forever? Shall the earth and the things that are therein be burnt up? When will the millennium begin? Where will he be after myriads of ages? These, and such as these, are questions that do not as yet disturb him.

Now the business of education for this incipient being, certainly its first business, is simply enlargement — enlargement in the apprehension of things past, and future, and around him; and the comprehension of them so as to bring them all into unity.

But to this enlargement there are great natural obstacles; and if man be left to himself, it must, whether we regard the individual or the race, be slow. In part, it is indeed spontaneous. The child, let alone, will grow up to such apprehension and enlargement as will enable him to meet his animal wants, and something more. But in its relation to the human faculties, this universe is so constituted that enlargement soon ceases, unless there be voluntary, rational, persistent, and organized effort. From the great number of objects around us, their complexity, the magnitude of some and the minuteness of others; from the subtlety of natural agents, the interaction of laws and the long cycles of nature; and from the necessity of labor and the brevity of life, it is clear that one individual, or one generation, could do but little. How could the first man, or the first generations of men, have known that the earth is round, or that it revolves round the sun, or that its surface lies in strata, or have calculated an eclipse? How could they have known the composition of bodies, and the subtle agents of chemistry? Clearly man was placed here as in a school, and both the individual and the race were to be gradually educated into such an enlargement as to comprehend and use wisely the substances and forces around him, and to know something of his position, among the stars, and as related to other worlds.

Owing to the obstacles just mentioned, this process of enlargement could not have been rapid, but it might have been more so than it has been. Men are sluggish, and gravitate towards sensuality; they fall into habits and routine, and run in ruts; they carry the grain on one side of the horse, and a stone on the other, because their fathers did. Notions indolently taken up gather about them a crust of antiquity, that no one dares to break through. There is nothing that men have been so reluctant to do as to think. They would go on pilgrimages, hang on hooks, accept dogmas, bow down to power, but they have been slow to put forth their powers in an earnest effort after comprehension and enlargement.

And not indolence only, but pride and selfishness have arrayed and organized themselves against this enlargement. Once accepted, a dogma links itself with modes of thought and habits of association; it becomes a part of the systems of the schools, or of religious teaching. Then pride comes in, and the will is up, and men contend, not for truth, but for victory. Often also a dogma is so inwoven with the structure of society, that if you overthrow it, men's occupation will be gone. Then interest takes the lead, and pride and passion fall in, and the whole guild of silversmiths, with whatever rabble they can collect, are full of wrath, and cry out, saying, "Great is Diana of the Ephesians." Again, knowledge is power. Ignorant men may be held in subjection, and used as instruments; and whole classes, nay, the mass of mankind, have been so held, of set purpose, and by law, that those thus holding them might rule over them, and avail themselves of their labor.

From these causes there has been little zeal for truth; and men zealous for it, and especially those in advance of their age, have been persecuted. Leaders of the race, and those set for the advancement of truth, have been its worst enemies. Holding the key of knowledge, they have not entered in themselves, and them that were entering in, they have hindered. Seats of learning, the very fortresses erected to guard and advance truth, have turned their guns against her.

But now there is a change. The bonds are relaxed. Henceforth no coming Galileo shall need to smite with his foot the floor of a dungeon when he says the earth moves. If not the summer, yet the spring-time of truth is come. The few are greatly enlarged, and the mass of humanity is quickened. A feeling that gropes for the light, is pervading it, a dim thought that it is coming out into enlargement. Always there has been a voice from every thing that could supply want, or gratify curiosity, or enlarge science, or adorn life; from the flower on the earth and the star in the heavens, saying, Be ye enlarged; but now that voice is heard by the alert sense of very many. Now, too, it begins to be felt that truth is one. The different angles and walls of her temple are seen to belong to one building, and instead of scowls and reproaches, the workmen more often send greetings to each other, and feel that they are working together.

To this wide enlargement there are, as has been said, natural obstacles; but there is also a tendency to it, and with right affection progress would be indefinite. From the first, the affections are complicated with the intellect, they react upon it as the brain upon the stomach, and when these are disordered and dwarfed, it is not possible that the general intellectual level should be high. Society will soon reach a point where it will become stationary, and will begin to go back. Hence the great thing needed is enlargement of the affections, and it is accordingly of this that the Apostle speaks in the text. "O, ye Corinthians," says he, "our mouth is open unto you, our *heart* is enlarged. Ye are not straitened in us, but ye are straitened in your own bowels. Now for a recompense in the same, (I speak as unto my children,) be ye also enlarged." Be enlarged in your affections. Give as you receive; love as you are loved.

For the Apostle Paul to say this to the Corinthians, was a great thing—how great, we can understand only by going back to his position. Socially, the world was in a state of disintegration. Men were divided into clans, tribes, nationalities, with diversities of language, customs, interests, that were constant grounds of alienation and of settled antipathies; and, to human view, any common ground or centre of unity for the race was hopeless. Except in dreams of conquest and subjugation, the very idea of such unity did not exist. But of nations thus diverse and hostile, the Jews were the most exclusive, and the Apostle was not only a Jew, but had belonged to their straitest religious sect. As a Jew, his pride, and self-complacency, and zeal for Judaism, were boundless, and he looked upon Gentiles with contempt and aversion. Yet we here find him offering his fraternal regards, and warmest love, and intimate fellowship to Gentiles, and seeking theirs in return, and this without regard to the previous rank, or cultivation, or character of those

Gentiles. Of some we know that their origin was low, and that their character had been vile. This too he did on a principle that would include all, for we hear him saying to other Gentiles, "There is neither Jew nor Greek, there is neither bond nor free, there is neither male nor female; for ye are all one in Christ Jesus. And if ye be Christ's, then are ye Abraham's seed, and heirs according to the promise."

Now here was a moral miracle. I do not hesitate to say it. To one who has observed the tenacity of national pride and hate, and the virulence of religious bigotry, and who knows the state of feeling at that time in regard to women and slaves and barbarians, this transition from the extreme of narrowness to enlargement and absolute universality of affection, and to the recognition of all as entitled to common privileges, is as unaccountable on merely natural principles as any miracle of the New Testament. Now, the sympathies of this former bigot embraced the race. He knew no man after the flesh. To him every man was a *man*, made in the image of God, redeemed by Christ, exposed to the second death, but capable of being saved, and so he preached Christianity to all men alike, and received all men alike, for so must it be preached, and so must men be received, if it is to have its full power.

In adopting the above principle, the Apostle was simply faithful to the system he had espoused, which stood self-vindicated as from God by its recognition of man as man, and through that, by its fitness and tendency to become universal. Hence its leavening power. Did the Apostle preach at Rome? Why not in Spain also? If in Spain, why not in Britain and to our barbarous ancestors there? By ignoring every thing incidental, and seizing, as the material of its system and the ground of its regards upon humanity itself as it must exist under all modifications, it passed at once through all barriers of nationality, and clanship, and caste, and condition, and showed itself to have an assimilating and organizing power that was capable of bringing all people into unity. This was the wonderful fact about it. As related to ultimate success it was the cardinal fact, and one not to be compromised. It is the fact that has made Christianity revolutionary from that day to this. If at times the giant has seemed to be quiet, as if pressed down by the mountains of human wickedness, it has only been to gather strength for the upheaval, and the earthquake. And so it will be, for in this fact is the principle of all true progress.

Marvellous then as this enlargement of the Apostle would appear on any other ground, it is yet perfectly natural when we look at him as a disciple of Christ both comprehending his system, and in sympathy with him. As in sympathy with Christ he could not do otherwise. The example of Christ was the great miracle of love, both in its intensity and in its enlargement. In its intensity it was unto death, in its enlargement it was for the whole world. Receiving such a spirit of enlargement as this from the Master, how could there be in the disciple any thing of restriction or limitation? How could he refuse to preach Christ's gospel to any for whom He died? How could he refuse to receive any whom Christ received? No longer do we wonder when we find this former bigot and persecutor exulting in this universality, and saying so freely, and fully, and grandly, "Where there is neither Greek nor Jew, circumcision nor uncircumcision, Barbarian, Scythian, bond nor free; but Christ is all, and in all."

From this example of the Apostle, we readily see what that enlargement is of which he speaks. It is a coming out from all narrowness and restriction of nationality, or clanship, or sect, or caste, or local prejudice, or prejudice from color, and so apprehending the rights of man as God-given, and his dignity and destiny as made in the image of God, that we shall always feel towards every man, and treat him as a man. This is no glittering generality, barren and impracticable. It is the great want and claim of this age in which we live. It is the law of God. It is the claim of humanity.

This enlargement, which is that of Christianity, some, especially French writers, have sought to identify with democracy; but while Christianity is the only foundation of a quiet and permanent democracy, they are yet rather in contrast. Democracy respects political rights and relations; Christianity respects all relations, and may exist under all forms of government. Democracy looks chiefly at rights; Christianity at duties. Democracy respects this world; Christianity includes both worlds, but looks chiefly at ultimate destiny. Democracy concedes rights, but requires no enlargement of the affections; Christianity is, itself, in its very essence, an enlargement of the affections. Democracy is compatible with great individual corruption within a nation, and with hostility and boundless ambition in the relations of nations to each other; Christianity involves individual integrity and good-will to all. Democracy may be atheistic — men have sought to make it so; the very principle and foundation of Christianity and the enlargement it implies, is from the relation of each to all as in the image of God, and so from their common relation to him.

To the enlargement now spoken of there is not, as to that of apprehension, any natural obstacle. Enlargement of affection might, and should accompany that of the intellect as naturally as the heat of the sun accompanies its light. But in this world it is not thus, and it is both sad and amazing — if it were not so sad it would be amusing — to trace the history of the world as it is related to this want of enlargement. There is no conceivable difference by which men are separated from each other that has not been made a ground of alienation in affection, and often of positive hostility.

"Lands intersected by a narrow frith
Abhor each other. Mountains interposed
Make enemies of nations."

A difference in name, nation, color, language, clan, occupation, residence, as in different towns, or even at different ends of the same street, and especially a difference of belief and opinion, become the ground of alienations, divisions, and of settled, hereditary and unreasoning hate. Passions thus excited have been strong enough to override both humanity and self-interest. Often, as in families and clans, these passions have been intense and persistent in proportion as their range has been narrow; often too as the point of difference has been frivolous, and as the opponents resembled each other the more, except in the one point of difference.

Such differences must, of course, respect points that are capable of drawing in by association the deep feelings of our nature, and will have more power as those feelings are deeper.

Hence it is that, in this respect, religion has furnished so sad a chapter in the history of the world. When its grand beliefs, tending only to enlargement, are displaced by superstition, and those deep feelings in which true religion chiefly consists, concentrate themselves about trifles and forms, we might expect a narrowness more intense than any other, and a bigotry more unscrupulous and cruel. And so it has been, and is now. So great has been this narrowness that it has been impossible to caricature it, because the imagination could conceive of nothing more narrow. The Little-Endians and the Big-Endians of Swift, whose difference was on the question whether they should break their eggs at Easter at the little or the big end, were not a whit beyond the four-year-olds and the five-year-olds in Ireland of whom we have seen accounts the present year, whose feuds have often led to murder, and between whom it became necessary for the bishop to interpose his authority. But more wonderful than this, we have seen, in our own country, large and intelligent bodies of Christians whose differences touched, and were conceded to touch, no vital point of Christianity, withholding all tokens of Christian communion and fellowship, and holding each other as heathen men and publicans; and we have even heard prescribed, as the way of peace, the putting up of high fences and keeping them in good repair. What a work for the followers of Him who "broke down the middle wall of partition" between the Jews and the Gentiles, "having abolished in his flesh the enmity, even the law of commandments contained in ordinances"—that is in external rites and things unessential—"for to make in *himself* of twain, *one* new man, *so* making peace!"

It is also impossible to conceive of bigotry more unscrupulous and cruel than there has been. In connection with no one of its elements, save that of religion, could human nature have either originated or endured such an institution as the Inquisition; and the imagination may be drawn on in vain to exceed in its conceptions the horrid enginery that has been devised to do professedly the work of Christian love.

But as much ground as there is for discouragement in regard to this form of enlargement, yet here, too, the bonds are relaxed. Not alone is there light on the mountain tops, there is more of quickening warmth in the valleys, and here and there a deeper verdure. That the perfection of the world requires that the two forms of enlargement should go on together, we can see. But as there are in the way of this no natural obstacles, so neither is there for it any law of progress, except as love naturally follows light, which all experience shows that in this world it does not in fact do. Hence, for such a training of the race as shall effect this enlargement, we must rely wholly on the special providence and grace of God.

The two points to be reached are — the one, that every man shall so respect manhood as to treat every other man as a man — the other, that every Christian shall so respect Christianhood, as to treat every Christian as a Christian. Manhood in man; Christ in the Christian — these are to be the objects of our regard, and nothing selfish or sectarian, nothing local or accidental may prevent our enlargement to the full recognition of every right and claim which these would involve. It is not that the claims of self-interest rightly viewed, and of nearer relationship are to be disregarded. These have their place, primary, imperative, sacred; but these claims are met with the broadest wisdom only when they are met in full compatibility with the claims of the widest enlargement. Towards these two points the movement has been slow. It is wonderful with what difficulty men have broken away from the narrowness of family, and clan, and tribe, and party, and caste, and sect, and nationality. But there has been movement. Feudalism melted into nationalities, often ill-assorted, and mere aggregates, but always with some increase of enlargement. Clanship, as in Scotland, that seemed to inhere as by some special mordant, has faded out. The Thugism of Ireland has well-nigh passed away. The French Emperor has kissed the English Queen, and the English and French have fought side by side. A new continent, this American continent, has been opened, where men might stand and see in the distance, and in a way to cause enlargement, arbitrary distinctions and conventionalities that had become chronic and hopeless, and where they might begin anew on a broader basis. To this continent and to this country have been swept, as by a vast diluvial current, English, and Irish, and Scotch, and French, and Germans, and Hollanders, and Swedes, and Jews; and in the surging of free institutions they have been rolled together, and rounded, and smoothed. No experiment devised for the purpose could have been better adapted to promote enlargement.

And if we turn from nationalities and political relations to the church and to sects, there too there is movement. The cave whence Giant Pope formerly came out to seize pilgrims on the King's highway, has become his prison, where he is guarded by foreign soldiers, and must needs be defended from his own subjects. The Inquisition cannot be reproduced. In Spain, though by great effort and special grace, instead of imprisonment for nine years, those who read the Bible are only spoiled of their goods, and banished. Even Turks are converted to Christ, and avow it, and their heads remain on their shoulders. Nay, Turkey may well put Spain to the blush, for there the Bible may be freely sold and read. In England there is progress. The intolerance of the Established Church is waning, and, both politically and socially, Dissenters are less under ban. And then there is one country where there is no alliance of church and state, and no civil disability, or liability, to taxation, or social ban with a court to sanction it, on account of religious belief, or form of worship. If, to some of these things, there are tendencies here; if we are in danger, as we are, from ecclesiasticism; if the old aristocratic leaven, driven from politics, tends to pass into the church; there are also opposite tendencies, and we hope the spirit of enlargement will gain the mastery. It must gain it in the end.

Having thus seen what that whole enlargement would be that is involved in the text, I observe in the first place, that the Bible method of reaching this is the reverse of that adopted by the world. The world seeks first intellectual enlargement. Its education is for that, and the ends secured through that. For enlargement of the heart it cares little, and supposes that will follow of course. But not thus can even a general enlightenment be reached. The interworkings and counteractions of selfishness would prevent that. Those who would gain such enlightenment must first seek a higher end, as he who would have all other things added must first seek the kingdom of God. Hence the method of the Bible is to begin with the heart. Any enlargement of the intellect without this it reckons as nothing. For the guidance of a moral being it is nothing. The doctrine of the Bible is, that "he that loveth his brother walketh in the light," but that *"he that hateth his brother is in darkness, and walketh in darkness, and knoweth not whither he goeth, because that darkness hath blinded his eyes."* This doctrine the world has yet to learn. A general enlargement of intellect in any community can be reached only by bringing to bear upon the heart of that community the great motives of Christ's Gospel.

I observe again, that we may learn from the doctrine of this discourse what must be the solution of that problem which is now convulsing this country, and steeping its soil in the blood of civil war.

In speaking of the elements of that experiment, if I may so call it, that grand providential movement which God is now making in this country for the enlargement of men, I purposely omitted to mention what may ultimately appear to be the most effective element of all, that is, not the people who have come, but those who have been brought here. Under our declaration of independence, asserting for every man the right to life, liberty, and the pursuit of happiness, and under institutions practically, as never before, maintaining that right, all, with the exception of the negro, have been thrown together, if not without fear, yet without favor, to work out as they might their personal ends; and though we have had cast upon us nationalities so diverse, and have had sent to us the vicious and abandoned products of other institutions and forms of civilization, and then been reproached with the results, yet, under the beneficent agencies of freedom, with the exception above mentioned, the processes of elevation and assimilation were working well. But in the face of our public and solemn declaration, a declaration that in our own case we had maintained with blood, here were men endowed by God with every natural right, having in their veins that " one blood of which God made all nations for to dwell on the face of the whole earth," who were deprived by statute and organic law of every natural right. Thus aloof from the legitimate working of our institutions, the negro element became, first an irreducible, and then a disturbing element. It did nothing positively, but was an obstruction that showed itself at every point. It was marvelous how inevitable it became in every political, in every religious meeting. Every body wished it out of the way, or said they did, and nobody knew what to do with it. Here was a call for enlargement, and it was not fairly met. The nation failed signally, and before the world, to apply impartially its own avowed principles; and every man knows that this is *that cause*, without which the present civil war could not have been.

And now it has not escaped the observation of many, that the point of enlargement to which the providence of God is pressing us in this war, is the full recognition of the manhood of the negro in all his rights as a man. This point, as fully as the laws of the Union would allow, was reached in this State, immediately after the Revolution. In the eye of the law the negro was placed on an equality with other men. From this no harm came, and if this point could be reached throughout the whole country to-morrow, our troubles would cease. When the black man shall be permitted to go where he pleases, to earn his own honest living in his own way, to enjoy all the natural rights of a man, and such civil rights as he is fitted for, the country will be quiet. We may not wish this; probably we should not have ordered it so; we may struggle against it. But this distinction of color and of race is from God; these people are here by his appointment, and we are not to narrow ourselves by prejudice, and fear that the heavens will fall, if we apply impartially and fully those great principles of natural right which are surely from God, and which we have avowed before the world. It is these principles that are now in question, and it is the struggle between these and their opposites that is convulsing, and is yet to convulse the nations.

It is into that double enlargement of the intellect and the heart, which has been presented in this Discourse, that I now invite you, my dear

Friends of the Graduating Class, to enter more fully. With the enlargement of your sphere of action, be *ye* also enlarged. As liberally educated, you are under obligation to intellectual enlargement. You owe it to yourselves, and to the community, not to lay aside your liberal studies. You ought to do something " for the increase of knowledge among men." Especially ought you to have that wide and liberal spirit which will appreciate knowledge of every kind, and encourage its advancement.

But, as you will have inferred already, my chief desire is that you should be enlarged in your hearts. There has been enlargement of heart towards you. You little know how you have been loved and cared for by parents and friends. There has been enlargement on the part of the public in providing for your education; there has been enlargement towards you in the hearts of your teachers—there has been in my heart—as I have known you more, you have grown upon me—and now what we ask you is, " For a recompense in the same." The best recompense of love is love in return, and the deeds which love prompts. What a recompense that is which you can make to your parents and friends! How will your parents rejoice, how will your friends, how shall I rejoice, to see you giving back love for love, care for care, and filling every enlarged sphere with an enlargement of intellect and of heart like that of the Apostle himself.

For this enlargement there is ample scope in this world; but in that which is to come, O the illimitable enlargement of which you are capable! O the wealth which God has provided! The wealth of this universe is not in the things that may be possessed, though they be gold and gems, though they were suns and systems; nor yet in the sciences that may be known, though they branch out into infinity; but it is in the beings that may be loved—God himself and his holy kingdom. Possessions, knowledge, are but the pedestal to be crowned with love. It is because there is excellence to be loved that heaven is possible, and the possibilities of heaven itself are to be measured by the possible enlargement of love. My dear friends, I speak as unto my children—have not I a right so to speak? Be ye also enlarged.

At this point, however, perhaps a caution is needed. The enlargement to which I call you is not to be confounded with what is sometimes called liberality. This is a term under which, with the pretence of enlargement, men often cover indifference to the truth, and, if the truth be pressed, essential narrowness and even bitterness. With such liberality, the enlargement to which I call you has no affinity. It is its opposite. The more enlargement there is, the more vivid the apprehension will be of the beauty of truth, and of the dignity and excellence and unutterable value of righteousness. You are called to an enlargement of comprehension and of love like that of Paul, with a corresponding opposition to all fundamental error and essential wickedness. The enlargement to which I call you is that of Christianity itself, which is at once the most universal and catholic, and the most exclusive of all systems. If it had not been broad and catholic, it would not have been fitted to include all nations; if it had not been exclusive, it would not have revolutionized the world — it would not have had martyrs. Christ himself would not have died, if there had not been something to stand up for, and to hold on to, with the whole energy of our being. What this is we may know. God has not shut men up to the alternative of the frigidity and imbecility of indifference on the one hand, or to a narrow and fierce bigotry on the other. No; there is an open way of enlargement in comprehension, and in the love of God and of man, and in hating nothing that love and righteousness do not compel us to hate.

With this caution, the word that I would leave with you, that I ask you to carry with you through life, is *enlargement* — enlargement of intellect, enlargement of the heart, enlargement of the intellect through that of the heart.

From this combination there will naturally, but not necessarily follow, an enlargement of personal influence. To insure this there must be added, energy of will. With that added, your preparation for the work of life will be complete. Then, not only will you yourselves grow by the exertion of your own activities in the right direction — grow to be more like God, and so more truly human — but in the same proportion you will have an influence for good over others. Influence for good over others! This is the object of a legitimate ambition; and in this you will find, what so few have found, the point of coincidence between the highest ambition and the highest duty.

And now, my dear friends, in view of what has been done for you, of what is expected of you; in view of the wants of your distracted and imperiled country, of the wants of a lost world; in view of your capacities, and of the scope there is for them in the infinities that surround you; in view of the call of God himself, and of Redeeming Love, I speak to you as unto my children, and I say to you, "Be ye also enlarged."

CHOICE AND SERVICE.

A BACCALAUREATE SERMON,

DELIVERED AT

WILLIAMSTOWN, MS.

JULY 31, 1864.

BY MARK HOPKINS, D. D.
President of Williams College.

𝔓ublished by 𝔑equest of the 𝔒lass.

BOSTON:
PRESS OF T. R. MARVIN & SON, 42 CONGRESS STREET.
NEW YORK: SHELDON & COMPANY.
1864.

Entered according to Act of Congress, in the year 1864, by

T. R. MARVIN,

In the Clerk's Office of the District Court of the District of Massachusetts.

SERMON.

JOSHUA xxiv. 15.

CHOOSE YOU THIS DAY WHOM YE WILL SERVE.

Probably Joshua is the most illustrious example on record of a great warrior who was also a thoroughly religious man. Chosen by God to bring Israel into the promised land, he had under him a people trained as no other had ever been. With the exception of Caleb the son of Jephunneh, not a man of them was over sixty years old. The faint-hearted and the murmurers of a former generation had perished, every one of them, from among them, and the nation, instinct with one life and one purpose, were ready to follow their leader. The faith of that leader never faltered, and with the single exception when there was an Achan in the camp, he led them to uniform victory. Having conquered the country, he divided to each tribe its inheritance, and for a time the land rested in quiet.

In this quiet the Israelites did not relapse into idolatry. They remained steadfast in their allegiance to God. That generation and the succeeding one received a higher testimony than any other that has been on the face of the earth. It is said, "And Israel served the Lord all the days of Joshua, and all the days of the elders that overlived Joshua, and which had known all the works of the Lord that he had done for Israel." Still, the heathen were not entirely expelled; the Israelites were the descendants of those who had made the golden calf at the foot of Sinai, and as the time for his death drew near, Joshua desired to do something to guard the people against that departure from the living God which was the only thing they had to fear.

Accordingly he "gathered all the tribes of Israel to Shechem, and called for the elders of Israel, and for their heads, and for their officers; and they presented themselves before God." Then was seen one of the most solemn and imposing spectacles in the history of the nation. This leader, whose success had been so great, whose authority had never, like that of Moses, been questioned, now more than a hundred years old, stood before the assembled nation, and surrounded by its chief men, recounted to them what God had done for them, and required them to choose deliberately and solemnly the service of the God of their fathers; or, if they would reject that, to choose whom they would serve. The question was to whom they would render supreme allegiance, and that question they were then to decide. This decision Joshua was careful should be made only with the fullest light. He not only told them what God had done, but also that he was a holy God, and the difficulty of his service on that account. They heard, they understood, and decided that they would serve the Lord. " And the people said unto Joshua, Nay, but we will serve the Lord." That was decisive of the history of that generation. So far as the choice was from the heart, it decided the influence and destiny of every individual during the whole course of his being.

In this transaction with the Israelites one thing was required and another implied. It was required that they should choose their supreme object of affection and worship ; it was implied, that, having chosen, they would serve him. The choice was to be made once and forever ; the service was to be perpetual, involving volitions and acts constantly repeated. In this choice and these volitions the radical character of the Israelites found expression ; in a similar choice and the consequent volitions our character will do the same, and on these our destiny will depend. Let us therefore look a little at these acts of choice and of volition, as they are in themselves ; as related to each other ; and to human character and well-being.

Taking then the act of choice, I observe, in the first place, that we *must* choose.

There are certain original and necessary forms of activity through which man knows himself. These are commonly said to be three—thinking, feeling, willing. In reality there are four, thinking, feeling, *choosing*, willing. These were never taught us. They are not the product of will. We do not think because we will to think, or choose because we will to choose, any more than we will because we will to will. We think and choose and will by a necessity of our nature immediately and directly when the occasion arises. These forms of activity we find originally in us, and a part of us; they go back with us to our first remembrance and conception of ourselves. If man did not find in himself each of these he would not be man. Free we may be in choosing, but not whether we will choose. This is so a condition of our being, that the very refusal to choose is itself choice.

And not only must man choose, he must also choose an object of supreme affection. A supreme object of worship, an object of worship at all, he need not choose, but of affection he must.

This belongs to the constitution of our nature. If a man were compelled to part with the objects of his affection one by one, as the master of a vessel is sometimes obliged to throw overboard his cargo, it must be that there would be a last thing to which he would cling. Without this our nature could have neither consistency nor dignity. In this the great masters of thought agree, and through it they account for the apparent anomalies of human conduct.

"Search then the master passion—there alone;
The wild are constant and the cunning known."

As a river, if it be a river, despite backwater and eddies, must flow some whither, and as those eddies and the backwater are caused by the very current they seem to contradict, so must there be in man some current of affection, bearing within its sweep all others, and that would, if known, reconcile all seeming contradictions. In this too the Scriptures agree. It is only a statement in another form of the great doctrine announced by our Saviour, that in the moral sphere there can be no neutrality and no double service. "He that is not with me is against me." "Ye cannot serve God and mammon."

How far God so reveals himself to each man as he did to the Israelites that there must be a distinct acceptance or rejection of him, he only can know, but every being having a moral constitution must be either in harmony with, or in opposition to the great principles of his moral government, and thus virtually either choose or reject him.

To know what the supreme object thus chosen and the master passion is, is the capital point in that most difficult and valuable of all knowledge, the knowledge of ourselves. Not our capacities alone do we need to know, but the set and force of that current within us which is deepest. But what the object thus chosen is, or even that he does thus choose, a man may not distinctly state to himself, and it may come out into clear consciousness only as he is brought to a test. The covetous man may go on for years amassing property; the upas tree of avarice may grow till every generous affection is withered beneath it, and yet no test may have been so applied as to compel him to say to himself, "I am a miser." He may not even suspect it. If told the truth he may honestly, in one sense honestly, as well as indignantly and reproachfully deny it, and say with one of old, "Is thy servant a dog that he should do this thing?" A Christian may be in doubt whether he loves God supremely. But let persecution come and demand his property, and that will be one test; let it demand his liberty, that will be another; let it demand his life to be given up through reproach and torture, and that will be a third and a final test. Then will there be a felt ground of consistency and of dignity. The ship will right itself in the storm, and with its prow towards its haven, the fiercer the winds the faster will it be driven thither.

But while we are thus necessitated to choose, and to choose an object of supreme affection, the choice itself is *free*. There is always in it an alternative. In this it differs from all that precedes it either in nature or in ourselves. Here it is indeed that we find the birth-place and citadel of that great element and royal prerogative, Freedom, which underlies all moral action and accountability. This it is which brings us into a moral and spiritual sphere wholly out of and above that of mere nature. The sphere of nature has for its characteristics uniformity and necessity, but here is freedom. This element is typified indeed, and foreshadowed in nature through all her forms of unconscious life. Very beautiful it is to see a multiform life working spontaneously towards its ends. Wonderful is that selective power by which the root and leaf of each vegetable, and the sense and digestive apparatus of each animal, appropriate that which will build up the life of each and reject all else. But here is no freedom. And the same may be said of all that precedes choice in our own life. We must previously have knowledge, but we know by necessity. No man can help knowing his own existence and acts of consciousness. We must previously have desire. Hunger and thirst, the desire for food and drink, are necessary; and there are hungerings and thirstings, appetencies and cravings so running through our whole nature that if we do not hunger and thirst after righteousness even, we cannot be filled. But here too the congruities are pre-arranged, and the desire is necessary. As such it has a wider range than choice. We desire many things which we do not and cannot choose. We desire wealth, position, power; we may desire the possession of the stars, or of universal dominion, but we can choose only that which is offered to our acceptance. There is in choice appropriation, and the thing chosen must be in such a relation to us that it may, in some sense, become our own.

But the peculiarity of an act of choice is that there is in it an alternative. This belongs to its definition. There is an overlooking of the whole ground, a comparison, and a felt power of turning either way. We must indeed choose, but we are under no necessity of choosing any one thing. When but a single object is offered us we may choose or reject it; when two are offered both of which we cannot have, as learning and ease, power and quiet, pleasure and virtue, we may choose between them. Thus, through the whole range of faculties which God has given us, we may choose which shall be brought into predominant activity; and through the whole range of objects which he has set before us, including himself, we may choose which we will appropriate as the source of nutriment to our inmost life.

In this act of choice, having thus an alternative, every man so stands forth to his own consciousness as free, that a conviction of his freedom must cling to that consciousness forevermore. The freedom is so a part of the act, and enters into the very conception of it, that men generally would as soon think of denying the act itself as of denying its freedom. No man can honestly deny it. Hence, as being known at once, and certainly, just as is the act itself, freedom can neither be proved nor disproved, but must be accepted on the immediate testimony of consciousness. A man might as well deny the fact that he exists, as to deny those characteristics of his being which enter into his conception of himself; and of these, freedom of choice is one. "We lay it down," says Dr. Archibald Alexander,* "as a first principle—from which we can no more depart than from the consciousness of existence—that MAN IS FREE; and therefore stand ready to embrace whatever is fairly included in the definition of freedom." Let the few then impugn as they may this great element and fact of freedom, they can never lead the mass of men to disbelieve it. They can never really disbelieve it themselves, they can never practically discard it.

---

* Moral Science, page 111.

And this leads me to observe that as freedom finds in an act of choice its cradle, so does it also its citadel.

Interfere with a man in his outward acts, restrain him from passing the limits of a town, shut him up in a prison, fetter his limbs, and you are said to deprive him of his freedom. You do invade it in its outer sphere, and in the sense in which it is generally understood, but there is still a freedom which you do not and cannot touch. There is in choice an activity of the spirit that abides wholly within itself. It neither requires nor admits of means, or instrumentalities, or outward agencies. Hence no power, human or divine, that does not change the essential nature of the spirit itself, can reach the prerogatives of this power. Here is the inner circle of freedom, its impregnable fortress. Within this, man is a crowned king. Here, though but a beggar, he may retire, and without his own consent, no man can take his diadem. Retaining the powers which make it what it is, nothing can prevent the spirit from choosing and willing, from loving and hating, and so nothing out of itself can prevent it from being loyal to duty and to God. But while we thus claim for man full powers of free agency, we also assert the power of God to govern free agents; and the necessity of the Divine Spirit to quicken and regenerate those whose choice of evil is so exclusive and intense that they are " dead in trespasses and sins."

We thus see what choice is. But the Israelites were not only to choose, they were to serve. By distinct and separate acts of volition, or of will, they were to cause the choice thus made to find expression in all their outward life. Let us then, as was proposed, look at these acts of volition, and their relations to choice.

Almost universally, and by the leading philosophers, as Kant and Hamilton, choice and volition have been confounded under the common name of Will. As more immediately connected with action, volition has been made the more prominent, and obscurity and sad misapprehension have been the result. But not only are choice and volition, or an act of the will, not the same, they are totally different. To this I ask special attention.

And first, choice must precede volition. No man can intelligently will an act except with reference to some object previously chosen.

Secondly, choice, and not volition, is the primary seat of freedom. In a sense we are free in our volitions. They are wholly within ourselves, they require no means or instrumentalities, and no earthly power can interfere with them; but yet they must be in accordance with some choice that predominates at the time, and can be changed only by a change of the choice. But are not men compelled to will what they do not choose? Not strictly. By force unjustly used they are said to be compelled to will what they would not but for that, and this is slavery; still the will will be in accordance with the choice on the whole, else a man could not become a martyr. A patriot, having chosen as his end, and with his whole heart, the good of his country, and while thus choosing, cannot will acts in known opposition to that good. He may die, but he cannot do that.

Again, choice and will respect different objects. In strictness, we never choose what we will, or will what we choose. The objects of choice are persons, things, ends. The object of volition is an act; always an act. We choose God, we choose a friend, a house, a profession, an ultimate end, but we do not will these. To say that we will a house would be absurd. We choose health, we will exercise; we choose learning, we will study; we choose an apple that hangs with its fellows upon the bending bough, we will the act by which we pluck it.

And as the objects of choice are different from those of volition, so are its grounds. We choose the apple because it is good; we choose a friend for his intrinsic qualities; we choose an end as good in itself; we choose God as infinitely excellent in himself, and as meeting through that excellency every capacity of our rational being.

Always we choose an object for something in itself—some beauty, some utility, some grace, some excellence, by which it awakens emotion or desire, and comes into some relation to our well-being. But an action we never will for any thing in itself, but only as it is related to an end. An action tending to no end would be a folly, and one abstractly right without reference to an end, is inconceivable. We do indeed will actions as right, but we mean by that, sometimes simply their fitness to gain an end, and sometimes, also, that the end is good. If the end be good, and be chosen because it is good, the action will be morally right; if not, it will be right simply from its relation to the end. An act of choice is itself right when the true end for man is chosen, and the choice is made, not merely because it is right, but, as all choice must be, in view of some good in the end. Universally, then, it is true that we choose objects and ends because they are good, and will actions because they tend to secure such objects and ends.

Once more, in choice man is not executive, in volition he is.

We think, feel, choose, and though active in these, are not conscious of putting forth energy. Every one knows the difference between a mere choice, or even purpose, and that putting forth of energy, by which we attempt to realize our purpose. This gives a new element. Before, the man was contemplative, choosing an end, maturing plans; now he is executive, working for an end. Choice and purpose are known in themselves, volition by its effects, and what these may be, experience only can reveal.

Thus at all points do we find a difference between choosing and serving, that is, of willing. Choice is primary—volition secondary; choice is directly free—volition indirectly; choice respects persons, objects, ends—volition acts; choice is not executive—volition is; choice too has the common relation of source to both willing and loving; volition is not a source at all; choice fixes on ultimate ends and absolute value, which is a good and not a utility. The very idea of utility is excluded from this sphere. A System of Morals based on the choice of a supreme end as good in itself, cannot be one of utility. In choosing the supreme end appointed by God for the good there is in it, there can be no undue reference to self. If this had been seen, much misapprehension would have been saved. Ultimate ends we choose for the sake of an absolute value; a utility is a relative value. It belongs to means and instrumentalities, to volitions and acts as related to ends.

We have now considered choice and volition as they are in themselves, and as related to each other. If any one should say that these points are too elementary, or, if you please, metaphysical, for an occasion like this, I should agree with him if their connection were less vital with human character and well being. That connection it remains for us to consider.

And first, I observe that choice, free as we have seen it to be, is the radical element in rational love. In this is the difference between rational and instinctive love. I know that mere emotion has stolen the name of love, and that the impulsive affections have been made identical with the heart. I know that there are affinities, and attractions, and a magnetism between persons as well as things, that there are subtle and inexplicable influences by which individuals are strangely drawn together, and that under the domination of these they think they love. And so they may; but not from these alone. So long as attractions are balanced by defects of character, or incongruities of temper, so long as there is a parleying between the better judgment and the feelings, and while as yet there is no ratifying choice, there is no rational love. Let this choice be withheld, and however emotion may eddy and surge, it is not love, and in time it will die away. But when the deliberate and full choice is made, the *heart* is given. Then objections become impertinent, imperfections disappear, and the full tide of emotion flows on, tranquil, it may be, but deepening and widening. Choice is not emotion, nor a part of it, but it opens and shuts the gate for its flow. It is the personality determining where it shall bestow those affections that are its life. It is the nucleus of a train that sets the spiritual heavens aglow. Emotion fluctuates; it comes and goes with times and moods and health, but love is constant, and this is the constant part of love. It is principle as opposed to emotion. In these two—choice and emotion—it is that we find what is called in Scripture "the heart." "His heart is fixed," says the Psalmist. There is the choice and the principle. "Trusting in the Lord;" there is the emotion. The heart is not the affections regarded simply as emotion; it is not the will except as will and choice are confounded. It is the affections, including choice; born of choice and nurtured by it. Hence, under moral government the heart may be rightly subjected, not only as emotion, to indirect regulation, but as choice, to direct and positive command. For God to say, "My son, give me thy heart," is wholly within his prerogative as a righteous moral Governor. This is a point of the utmost moment, and often but imperfectly apprehended.

Again, if choice be thus an element of love, I need hardly say that it must determine character.

This follows because the character is as the paramount love. If this be of money, the man is a miser, if of power, he is ambitious, if of God, he is a religious man. It is said by some that character depends on the governing purpose. It does proximately, but purpose depends upon choice. We first choose, then purpose. On this too depends disposition, so far as it is moral. A supreme choice is the permanent disposing by a man of himself, in a given direction. This is the trunk of that tree spoken of by our Saviour, when he said, " Make the tree good, and his fruit will be good." From this will flow a sap that will reach the remotest twig and leaf of outward expression, and give its flavor to every particle of the fruit. Such a choice will determine not only the disposition, but the subjects of thought, the habits of association, the whole furniture of the mind. Hence those expressions of the Bible, " the thoughts of the heart," " the imaginations of the heart," are perfectly philosophical. Thoughts, imaginations, fancies, castle-buildings, take their whole body and form from those choices and affections which *are* the heart. These come and go, but they swarm out as bees from the home of the affections, and there they settle again. So it is that " out of the heart proceed evil thoughts, murders, adulteries, fornications, thefts, false witness, blasphemies ; " and so it is that " out of *it* are the issues of life." But it is in these, as thus springing from the heart, that character is expressed, and hence it is that the heart, having its nucleus and salient point in choice, *is* the character.

But if character thus depends upon choice, then the connection of choice with human well being opens at once upon us. Under a moral government—and if we are not under that we can have no hope of any thing—if we are not under that there is no God—under a moral government character and destiny must correspond. Whatever apparent and temporary discrepancies there may be, ultimately they must correspond. That they should do this enters into the very conception of moral government. Settle it therefore, I pray you, my hearers, once and forever, that as your character is, so will your destiny be. Whatever capacities there may be for enjoyment or for suffering in this strange being of ours, and God only knows what they are, they will be drawn out wholly in accordance with character. There shall be no inheritance of possessions, or felicity of outward condition, no river of life, or gate of pearl, or street of gold, there shall be no serenity of peace, or fullness of joy, or height of rapture, or ecstacy of love; there shall be no hostile and vengeful element, no lake of fire, no gnawing worm, no remorse or despair, that will not depend upon character. It is by their bearing upon this that we are to test every claim made upon us in the name of religion for outward observance and self-denial; and we are to sweep away as superstitions all forms and observances that do not tend to the purification and elevation of character, because it is this alone that bears upon destiny. This is destiny.

We thus see the amazing import and reponsibility attached to this prerogative of choice. As we are active and practical it is the one distinguishing prerogative of our being. Entering into it, not as that which we *may* do, but as that which we *must* do, it is so a part of our being that it cannot be separated from us, and that its responsibility cannot be shared by another. It is that by which we make ourselves known for what we are. It is by choice only that our proper personality, our self, acts back upon the forces that act upon us. As an original primitive act, admitting no use of means, it requires no one to teach us how to choose; no one can teach us. If I am required to kindle a fire I can be taught how, because means must be used, and there must be a process; but I must think and choose before I can be taught how.

As a moral act the results of choice are immediate and inevitable because it is in that that morality is. Outward results and general consequences will depend on powers and agencies out of ourselves, but this is wholly between man and his God, and reacts upon the soul leaving its own impress forever. To that impress all things outward will come to correspond, and thus it is that man decides his own destiny. His destiny is as his choice, and his choice is his own. In this, not alone in immortality—immortality without this would be but the duration of a thing—in this, crowned by immortality, is the grandeur of our being. All below us is driven to an end which it did not choose, by forces which it cannot control. But for us there are moments, O, how solemn, when destiny trembles in the balance, and the preponderance of either scale is by our own choice. Do you deny this, ye who speak of the littleness and weakness of man, and of the power of circumstances? Ye who scoff at freedom, and sneer at human dignity, and mock at the strivings of a poor insect limited on all sides, and swept on by infinite forces, do ye deny this? Then do you deny that man is made in the image of God. You deny that he can serve him. You destroy the paternal relation of the Godhead, you blot out a brighter sun than that which rules these visible heavens. If God is to be served it must be by a free choice; by a free choice it must be if his service is to be rejected. Other service would do him no honor, other rejection would involve no guilt. Feeble as man is, and we admit his feebleness; limited as he is, and we admit the limitation, it has yet pleased God to endow him with the prerogative of choosing or rejecting Him and his service. Therefore do I call upon you, my hearers, every one of you, to choose this day whom you will serve. I call upon you to choose God, the God in whom you live and move and have your being, the God who has made you, and redeemed you, and would sanctify you. Him I call upon you to choose and to serve as that service is revealed in the Gospel of his Son. "If the Lord be God, follow Him, and if Baal, then follow him."

Upon all who hear me the call now made is most urgent; but for you, my Beloved Friends of the Graduating Class, the words "this day" have a peculiar emphasis. You have now reached the point towards which the thoughts, the plans, the efforts of long years have converged, and from which your influence is to radiate into the future. To bring you to this point parents have labored and prayed; as you have moved towards it you have been followed by the hopes and inquiries of friends. For this, and scenes like this, Colleges have been built, the wisdom of the past has been garnered, and instructors have toiled. Nor have you been wanting. Without your co-operation all else had been vain, and it gives me pleasure to testify to the heartiness and kindly spirit with which you have so given yourselves to the work that the labors of your instructors have not been simply *for* you, but *with* you. Nor, in looking at the past as preparatory for this hour, can we fail to remember the special favor of Him without whose blessing nothing can prosper. You will go out from sacred scenes which you can never forget. God has come to you by his Spirit, and led many, we trust the most of you, to choose Him and his service. For this we render everlasting thanks. In this respect you are before him to-day as the Israelites of old, who had chosen God, but were called on to renew and ratify their choice. And standing where you do it is fitting that you should be called upon this day, all of you, whoever, or whatever you have chosen, solemnly to review your choice. If any of you have chosen God and his service, I call upon you to renew and ratify that choice. If any of you have not chosen Him, I call upon you as my last instruction and advice, and in view of eternal sanctions, to choose Him this day.

Choice and *service*—these were demanded of the Israelites, these are demanded of you; these only. Choice and service—in these are the whole of life, and heeding practically the characteristics belonging to each, your life must be a success.

To choice belongs wisdom. Here, indeed, and in the choice of ends rather than of means, is the chief sphere of wisdom. The whole of wisdom is in the choice and pursuit of the best ends by the best methods and means. But in the choice of methods and means to secure their ends " the children of this world are often wiser in their generation than the children of light." The difference is in their choice of ends. The ends of the children of this world are madness, and this, in the eye and language of the Bible stamps them as fools.

But while wisdom belongs to choice, to service belong energy and firmness tempered by skill. You will be careful here not to mistake for energy a prevalent reckless and boastful tendency to " go ahead," or for firmness, a dogged obstinacy without candor. Indiscriminate antagonism is easy. Denunciation, indignant or sarcastic, coarse denunciation mistaking elegance for sin, is easy. By these a reputation as a reformer may be cheaply gained. But to be energetic and firm where principle demands it, and tolerant in all else, is not easy. It is not easy to abhor wickedness and oppose it with every energy, and at the same time to have the meekness and gentleness of Christ, becoming all things to all men for the truth's sake. The energy of patience, the most godlike of all, is not easy.

But while energy is to be tempered, it must still

be *energy*, and, service being wisely chosen, failure in this is your chief danger. It is one thing to make a choice and adopt a principle, another to carry it out fully, wholly, entirely, giving it all its scope. It is one thing to say, and to believe that "all men are born free and equal," and another to give to four millions of slaves all their rights. Here, I repeat it, is your danger. Here it was that the Israelites failed. Their choice was right; their resolution was good; they promised well, but they failed to take full possession of the promised land. Will you fail "after the same example"? Before you, as there was before them, there is a promised land; shall I not say there are promised lands, to be possessed? There is outward prosperity and honor; there is the inward peace that comes from well-doing; there is a country to be made united, peaceful, prosperous, free, wholly free; there is that better time coming for which the whole world waits; there is, above all, a promised land beyond the dark river. All these are a promised land to you, and wait with more or less of dependence on your wisdom and energy. They are no illusions. Bright as any or all of them, except the first; may seem to you to-day, if you do your part, the reality will be brighter. Always the realities of God transcend the imaginations of man. "Eye hath not seen, nor ear heard, neither have entered into the heart of man the things that God hath prepared for them that love him."

For these things you go forth to labor. *You* go, but not all who began the year with you. Once there was, beloved of us, a child of many prayers and hopes, who heard the call of his country, and felt that these peaceful scenes were no longer for him. He went hoping to return when the war should be over, and complete his course. He went offering himself freely on the altar of patriotism, of human rights, of universal liberty. We followed him; we saw his form enter into the smoke of battle. We saw him fall, the paleness of seeming death spreading over his countenance; and then the vail was dropped that has not been lifted. He, and the cause for which he fell, are in the hands of God, and if it be his will that the name of Lieutenant EDWARD PAYSON HOPKINS be added to those of the victims of this rebellion, his will be done.

But for the cause for which he fell, and for all good causes, you remain on the earth to labor. For you there remains the opportunity of choice and of service, of wisdom, and of energy. *Wisdom and energy*—this is the watch-word that I would give you as you go down into the battle. Do any of you say, we have not wisdom? I say to you, "If any man lack wisdom let him ask of God that giveth to all men liberally and upbraideth not, and it shall be given him." Do you say, we have not strength? I say to you, "Lo He is strong," and "underneath are the everlasting arms." Guided by his wisdom, strong in his strength, there may yet be for you struggle and suffering, the darkness and the storm. "The disciple is not above his Master." There may be weeping that shall endure for a night, but joy shall come in the morning. If the night cometh, so also the morning, "a morning without clouds," the morning of an eternal day.

AN

ADDRESS,

DELIVERED IN BOSTON, MAY 26, 1852,

BEFORE THE

Society for the Promotion of Collegiate and Theological Education at the West.

BY MARK HOPKINS, D. D.

BOSTON:
PRESS OF T. R. MARVIN, 42 CONGRESS STREET.
1852.

BOSTON, MAY 27, 1852.

DEAR SIR,

I am instructed by the Boston Directors of the Society for the Promotion of Collegiate and Theological Education at the West,—acting in behalf of the whole Board,—to present to you their thanks for your very able, eloquent and acceptable Address delivered before the Society which they represent, at their meeting in this city yesterday,—and to request of you a copy for publication.

Very respectfully and truly,

Your friend and servant,

S. H. WALLEY.

Rev. M. HOPKINS, D. D.

WILLIAMS COLLEGE, MAY 29, 1852.

DEAR SIR,

It gives me pleasure to know that the Address before the Society for the Promotion of Collegiate and Theological Education at the West, was acceptable to the Directors. If they think its publication will promote the good work in which they are engaged, it is at their service.

With great respect and regard, yours,

MARK HOPKINS.

Hon. S. H. WALLEY.

ADDRESS.

CHRISTIANITY is God's method of restoring man to his lost manhood. This consists chiefly, indeed, in the image of God, for "in the image of God created he him;" but there is no attribute of a true humanity which Christianity will not quicken and ultimately make perfect. It is an evidence of the truth of our religion, that no man can become more of a Christian, without, at the same time, becoming more of a man. The Author and first Minister of this religion was a perfect man. He was perfect, not merely as sinless, but in his sympathy with all God's works, and in the perfection and balance of his faculties; and what the church needs, what she is to labor and pray for, is a ministry as nearly as possible like him.

Such a ministry it is the object of this Society to furnish. It is not a College Society, for the sake of Colleges as a means of general education. Not for that, important as it is, does it occupy the pulpit on the Sabbath. It would, indeed, strengthen all those affiliated influences, from the common school upwards, in connection with which the church is best sustained; but it has to do with Colleges only as it can inscribe upon them, as our fathers did upon Harvard, "Christo et Ecclesiæ;" only as they can be made the most efficient instruments in raising up such men as the church needs.

But what men the church needs, and of course the education they should receive, will depend on the functions they are to perform, and the relations they are to sustain to the people. If they are to be a hierarchy, separated from the people by dress, by manner, by the prerogatives of a transmitted sanctity, with subordinate ranks, so constituted as to furnish within itself objects of cupidity and ambition, and, either by itself or in connection with the temporal power, seeking its own wealth and aggrandizement, then there will be needed, and will be among them, some men of high talent and the most finished education. These will generally do, in substance, under the garb of religion, just what is done by the leaders in civil and military affairs; but the mass will receive, as in the papal church, but a narrow, technical, monkish education, fitting them for subordinate places in the order. They will be educated as ecclesiastics, and not as men; for the good of the order, and not of mankind. They will become both agents and instruments in a system of education, which will be at once an engine of a selfish ambition and of popular degradation. If such is to be the general type and attitude of the ministry, it is clear that clerical and popular education can never coalesce.

But such is not the ministry which the church needs. She needs an order of men who will devote themselves, in sympathy with Christ, to the elevation and salvation of the race. They are to have no separate interests, as a class. They are to be of the people, and with them, and for them. Adopting no narrow sectarianism, but Christianity, as God's method, and the only one, of elevating men, they must seek to apply that as teachers and leaders. As the method reaches that which is deepest and most peculiarly human in man, it may and ought to embrace, and subordinate to itself, every legitimate form of human culture.

If ministers are to make the people in the highest sense men, they must themselves be such men ; and the education best fitted to make a minister, will be that which is best fitted to make such a man ; it will be that which will bring him most fully into sympathy with God, as revealed not only in his word, but in all his works, and also with a true humanity. He will need no culture which will separate him, by refinement and fastidiousness, from the humblest and most ignorant ; he will need one which will put him in sympathy with the most refined and intelligent. He will, in short, need, not so much an education that is technical and professional, as one that is broad and liberal, an education for man as man.

Perhaps our Fathers did not state this in terms, but it was a perception of it that led them, in founding what they called "Schools of the Prophets," to found institutions, furnishing for all the most generous and liberal culture which the times could afford. Surprise has been expressed that an institution, adapted as Harvard was, to all, should have been founded with primary reference to the education of the ministry ; and that it should have been called, for more than a century, the "School of the Prophets." But we may here find an explanation of that fact. It arose from a comprehension, by men who have been sometimes called narrow and bigoted, of the true position of the ministry, and of the relation of Christianity to every thing that can exalt and ennoble man. The Fathers of the Puritan church said, that those who were to teach them, should themselves be taught ; that the church should have, for the education of her ministers primarily, but also for all her sons, institutions at once Christian and liberal. Such institutions she founded and has sustained. And what the Fathers said, we say. We say that the church must and will have, for her sons, institutions of the highest order, which she can feel to be Christian institutions, and to which she can give her sympathies and her prayers. We insist, too, that the union of religion with all knowledge is as essential to the healthy life of a free state as to that of the church; and hence, that the founding and sustaining of such institutions is the duty of both.

But what the Fathers did for New England, this Society would do for the West. With such modifications as a sound discretion would dictate, it would transplant the New England College to the western prairie, for the purpose of raising up there a Christian ministry. This the church might do from her own resources. If it were the only way of obtaining a suitable ministry, she ought to do it. But if in doing this, she will provide an indispensable link in that chain of educational instrumentalities, which are at once the strength and glory of a free people, then patriotism may be appealed to as well as piety, and the object is one in which the whole country is directly interested.

The question then arises, whether the New England College, transplanted, and perhaps modified, would be, in its place, the best agency that could be devised, in such a system of general education as a great and free people ought to have. This opens a field so wide that we can scarcely enter upon it; but it is clear that this Society can legitimate itself most fully, and find its most triumphant vindication, only in the establishment of this general position.

It was said by Dr. Johnson, that education was as well known in his day, and had long been as well known, as it ever could be; and in this country the same self-complacent opinion formerly prevailed. But now, the waters have come up into these channels of discussion that were dry; and it is only the most solid structures that are not afloat. In some of the States, the whole system of Common Schools has been revised, and an attempt made, we hope a successful one, to introduce new methods of instruction, and to place them on higher ground. In the opinion of some, the whole system of Academies is wrong, and should be displaced by High Schools for towns; and there are those who think that the College system should be abandoned. They regard it, if not positively injurious, yet as antiquated and narrow, and not furnishing the education demanded by the times. In this diversity of opinion, and especially where the foundations are to be laid in new States, it may be well to inquire whether there are any points respecting a collegiate education concerning which we may hope for a general agreement, and also, incidentally, where the points of divergence will arise.

And first, I think it will be generally agreed, that the country needs provision for a system of liberal education. By a liberal education, I mean that which has for its object the symmetrical expansion, and the discipline of the human powers,—the cultivation of man as man. By the expansion of the powers, we give them strength; by their symmetrical expansion, we give them balance; and by discipline, we give the man control over them. If we can do these three things, we shall have such men as are needed,—strong men, with well-balanced powers, fully subject to their own control. Such an education is distinguished from a professional, and what some would call a practical one, by the fact that knowledge and power are gained without reference to any specific end to which they are to be applied.

That provision for such an education is needed is obvious, because it meets one of the higher wants of our nature. Man was not made to be wholly a slave to the interests of the present life. There is in him an element that lifts him above them, and gives him a delight in beauty, and in truth, as well as in goodness, for their own sake. The humblest individual, who cultivates a flower for the sake of its beauty, wears the badge of a nature not wholly of earth and of time. The artisan, who spends an hour, when his toil is done, in solving a mathematical problem; the clerk, or the farmer's boy, whose mind turns spontaneously to some department of literature or of science, where, without thought of fame or of gain, he finds delight in his own activity, as the swallow finds it in flying, shows a capacity and a want that can only be met by a liberal culture. It is the mind working in its own proper sphere, for the pleasure of the work. This tendency may be encouraged where it shows itself, may be quickened where it lies dormant. It often exists strongly, not with reference to any particular department, but to knowledge generally; and we need institutions that shall draw out and give scope to whatever there may be of this ennobling element among a people.

Moreover, man is by nature an artist; in the fine arts, beauty and completeness are his sole ends, and all the arts are modified by a regard for these. And not only is he an artist, but of all beings and things he is the best fitted to be the subject of art. Of all beings, he is originally the most unformed, and the most susceptible of formative influences. And shall man labor for beauty and completeness upon the rigid and insensible marble, and shall he do nothing to realize these in the flexible and living material, which is capable of a beauty so much nobler and higher? Rightly viewed, education is the highest among the fine arts.

Education, conducted on these principles, is, indeed, regarded by some as not practical. But what can be more practical than to make a true man? I distrust that practicalness that would take from the man, to add to his possessions. I believe that this universe is so constructed, that he who seeks legitimately a higher end in any department, will so best secure those that are lower; and facts show that the best practical results to society have originated in the kind of activity of which I have spoken.

Another end of a liberal education is to gain some general acquaintance with the circle of literature and the sciences. There is no department of literature, there is no single science, to which a man may not devote his life without exhausting it; and it is desirable that he should ultimately concentrate his powers on some one department. But before thus selecting one, it is desirable that he should have a general acquaintance with all. This enables him to know his own tendencies; it tends as nothing else can to liberalize his mind, and gives position and standing among literary men. In some things there must be thoroughness and discipline, and an acquaintance with them sufficient for practical purposes. With others, the acquaintance must be what you may call superficial, if you please; but yet it will answer a most valuable purpose. The knowledge of chemistry that can be acquired from the course of lectures given in any of our Colleges, may be, and is superficial, and inadequate to the wants of the practical chemist; but it is sufficient to open to the general student one great department of the works of God, to give him its principles, and enable him to bring them into harmony with the rest. Here is a science at the opposite pole of astronomy, as considering forces that act at imperceptible distances; and yet the wonder and delight with which we trace the definite combinations of atoms, and the laws and forces that govern them, are hardly less than those which we experience when we trace the laws and forces that govern the heavenly bodies. Indeed, it may yet be found that the forces which govern both are the same. While, therefore, the College may not teach chemistry so as to make it the means of fame or gain, it yet does make it an open avenue to these; and especially are its teachings adequate for all the purposes of man as an emotive and contemplative being, striving to bring unity into all his knowledge, and to connect the physical universe with its Creator. So with the mathematics, as an instrument of investigation; so with astronomy, and geology, and the various branches of natural history. A general view of these can be given, which will not only liberalize the mind, and elicit tendencies, but which will bring into activity, and bring out in their full proportions, all the faculties, and thus lay the foundation for the study of any particular profession.

It may be observed further, that while the studies of such a course are always appropriate, there yet seems to be special provision made for them in that formative period between mere boyhood and the time when professional studies and active pursuits may be best entered upon.

But if there is to be a system of liberal education, chiefly for persons in their forming period, I think it will be generally agreed that it should involve some religious instruction and training, and a general supervision of manners and of morals. At no period of life can these be more needed, than during that which generally occupies the college course; and many parents will never consent to send their sons from them at that age, without something of the kind. It is true, the college system implies confidence in the character of the student; and no young man should enter upon it who has not some maturity of character and strength of principle. It is true, also, that the means of supervision in Colleges are not as effective as would be desirable, at times when the general tendency is downward, and when there is artful and determined vice. Still, let a young man meet the same instructors three times a day for recitation, and twice for prayer, and be obliged to give an account of himself if he is unprepared or absent, and let the record of his attendance be reviewed once a week by a college faculty; and if they are discerning and faithful men, they will soon understand the tendencies of every individual, and will be able, by kind suggestion and by discipline, to exert an invaluable influence in arresting evil, and in forming aright the general habits. Any thing that would tend to remove this feature from the system, or to diminish its effect, would be undesirable. More, far more, if possible, ought to be done.

So far, under this head, I should hope for a general agreement. I may not hope it, however, when I say, that the course of study in a liberal education should be, as a whole, a prescribed one.

Without a prescribed course that shall be substantially pursued by all, there can be no pursuit of any study with reference to symmetry of development in the faculties. Let studies be optional, and men will choose that to which they have some natural or accidental bias. He who is fond of mathematics, will take mathematics and pursue them. This I would have him do, ultimately; but if he is to be *liberally* educated, the very thing he needs now, is to have whatever germs of taste and perceptions of beauty there may be in him, stimulated to some such growth as shall be a counterpoise and relief to his mathematical tendencies. So again, is a man imaginative, susceptible, poetical, capable of becoming an orator and a poet? I would have him follow his bent; but while he is the last man that would choose mathematics, and perhaps metaphysics, he is the very one whose happiness and usefulness would be most promoted by a judicious discipline in those studies.

It is said, I know, that if a study be really beneficial, it will stand on its own merits; and so far as it is so, will be pursued. But this proceeds on a supposition not sustained by facts. Do mankind always, do the young especially, make sacrifices, and deny themselves for what they know will be for their good? How is this with the studies of children? How with early rising? How with the taking of a cold bath? How with physical exercise? How with abstinence from narcotics? How is it with uncivilized and heathen nations, in their relations to civilization and Christianity? In these, and similar cases, of which the present seems to be one, the best results can be reached only by subjection to a prescribed course. There is in man a tendency to choose present ease; to defer, and avoid labor and difficulty; and this tendency it should be one object of education to counteract. By adopting a prescribed course, we submit to nothing compulsory or slavish. We simply avail ourselves of the experience and wisdom of those who have gone before us.

Again, the idea to be realized here is a specific one ; nearly as much so, as in professional education. The reading and lines of thought in each profession may branch into infinity, no less than in a liberal education ; but if it would be folly not to prescribe a course in the one, why not in the other, especially as the students are younger and less able to choose for themselves ? But if we abandon this feature, we say that there is no specific idea, and the whole system must lose its unity, and dignity, and power. There will indeed be no *system* of liberal education, and education itself will be displaced from among the fine arts. Its teachers will cease to be professional agents, and will do work to order.

Without a prescribed course, also, there would be no benefit from the collision, the comparison and the general discipline of a college class. In most cases, this is of great value. Meeting with others week after week, and year after year, on the basis of perfect equality, and grappling with the same difficulties, an individual can scarcely fail to gain a knowledge both of his absolute and relative strength. For this end, no better system could be devised. Besides, peculiarities and weak points, especially in the various forms of vanity and self-conceit, are generally modified, or disappear under this discipline.

It may be mentioned, too, that without a prescribed course there would be no community of literary men, standing on common ground, as the graduates of our Colleges now do. The whole of the present order, with all the strong associations connected with it, which work many desirable results, both social and literary, would have to be given up.

But such a system, it is said, must require all to proceed at the same rate, and limit them to the same acquisitions. By no means, unless we suppose the student to be the merest automaton. We would, indeed, require certain things; but would encourage the student to attain as much more as possible. We would not teach him that his object is to "cram" for an examination, and to pass an ordeal as soon as he could reach a given standard. We would rather give some time and scope for growth and breadth in a natural way; for general reading, and the indulgence of individual taste. Our graduates should all be men; but we would cramp nothing, and dwarf nothing, and would have them differ as much in their intellectual, as their physical stature.

But while we would thus have a standard for a liberal education, it should no more be a fixed one, than that for professional education. What would be a liberal education in one age, would not be in another; and no man should wish, however good it might be for the time, to stereotype any such system. Clearly the standard, and the whole system of education, can be true to its end only by being flexible to the advancement and wants of the age.

May I not say, then, that we need institutions that will give a liberal education, including regard to manners and morals, and to religion; that shall be adapted, in restraint and discipline, to the period between the confinement of the school-room and the perfect freedom of manhood; and that shall have a prescribed course, based on the wisdom of the past, and adapted, by good sense, to the wants of the present? Such institutions I suppose our Colleges were intended to be; and institutions that will do substantially this, it seems to me, the community not only need, but will have.

That the Colleges have always realized this idea, need not be asserted. They have, perhaps, been too numerous; they have lacked means; students have been poor, and obliged to teach; there has been a strong tendency to rush into active life, and at the same time a desire to have the name of having completed a liberal course of study. There has, too, been a popular cry against Colleges as too rigid and exclusive; some of them have pursued a mistaken policy, and it has been difficult to keep the standard where it should be.

Nor do I suppose that any of the Colleges either have pursued, or do now pursue, the very best methods of realizing this idea. To do this, the studies selected should be those best adapted at once to immediate and practical utility, and to the discipline of the mind ; they should be arranged in a course, the preceding parts of which should prepare the way for those that follow ; and they should be pursued in such proportions, at such times and in such a manner, as is best suited to those laws of thought on which all philosophical education must be based ; as will best facilitate acquisition, and give knowledge that shall be at once permanent and readily at command.

Into such a course, to refer very briefly to this much agitated question, I have no doubt the ancient classics should enter. By the study of these we gain, indirectly, much knowledge of ancient history and of man ; we become conversant with the finest models ; rendering carefully and elegantly from one language into another we adopt the best method of attaining a copious and exact vocabulary as an instrument not only of communication but of thought ; we gain some insight into the philosophy of language ; and from the intimate connection of the Latin and Greek with the composition and structure of our own language, especially in professional and technical terms, we gain a knowledge of that which could be acquired in no other way.

We admit fully that there are men of great distinction and usefulness who have not studied the classics; but we say there are some things they cannot do as well as they otherwise might, and some which they cannot do at all. Webster, and Everett, and Choate, would doubtless have been distinguished men without classical study ; but they could never have done what they have done. There is an element in their speeches and writings which every scholar sees could not have been there without this, which is felt by the whole public, which gives them now a higher place as English classics, and will give them a firmer hold on posterity. These men have not only studied the classics, but, occupied as they have otherwise been, it is understood that they have lived in communion with them. After a speech by Mr. Choate, strong, indeed, in thought and in logic, but for its beauty and power of language the most extraordinary I ever heard—certainly, I think, no man living could equal it—he said, in conversation, that he found some time every day for the reading of Greek.

With this view of the classics we would retain them; but it would be a great point gained, if, as is now the tendency, the preparation in them could be more thorough.

In minor matters there is a good deal of diversity in the course pursued by the different Colleges, and doubtless room for improvement in them all. If I might venture to state my own impressions, I should say that the physical system has not been sufficiently cared for. In many cases, where health has not actually failed, the vital energies and general tone of the system have been depressed. I should say, too, that habits of observation, or, in other words, the senses, have not been sufficiently cultivated. I would make drawing a part of the course, and, if possible, music, and have an early study of some science requiring observation and description, furnishing series of natural objects for this purpose. Perhaps, too, sufficient attention has not been paid to method in the arrangement and distribution of the studies.

With these remarks on a liberal education, we now pass to a second general proposition, to which, I think, most will assent, which is, that the means of such an education should, as nearly as possible, be made accessible to all.

This is a second great idea which those, who have founded and sustained our Colleges, have endeavored from the first to realize. They have struggled on in the endeavor to attain these two ends, which, with inadequate means, must always conflict. They have wished to furnish every facility, from books, and apparatus, and teachers to give the best possible education, and yet make it so little expensive as to be accessible to all. This is the true idea of a College in this country; and surely nothing can be more in accordance with our common school system, and with the whole spirit of our institutions.

The people ought to have, they must have, accessible to all—I would gladly see them as free as our common schools—institutions furnished with every facility for the very highest education; so good that no man, whatever may be his wealth or station, can send his son elsewhere, except to his own disadvantage. The feeling that this is so, should be a great and pervading element in our social and civil state. For this it is that the State has bestowed its bounty. For this, public spirited and far-seeing individuals in former times and our own, the Harvards, the Williamses, the Browns, the Lawrences, and the Willistons, have labored and made sacrifices. It is not a mere equality of right that will keep society in a state of stable equilibrium; there must also be a strong tendency to equality of condition and of social position. But knowledge and wealth are the two great means by which men gain standing and influence; and where the means of attaining these are guarded from practical monopoly, there the institutions will be essentially equal and free. There you will have all the equality that is compatible with a healthy stimulus and just reward of individual enterprise. In the old world, the spirit of monopoly has generally reigned, both in respect to wealth and knowledge. In some instances they have, indeed, thrown open the road to the highest knowledge more freely even than we have yet done; but this has been so done by the government, that they have held the patronage and direction of talent, and, under the form of popular education, have endeavored to bias, indirectly, the finest minds in favor of monarchical institutions. But in this country, whatever may be said of wealth, there should be no monopoly of knowledge. Its fountains should be practically and equally open to all. This will draw out the latent talent and genius, the intellectual pith and manhood of the whole country, and bring them into free competition. It will bring, side by side, the son of the poor widow and of the millionaire. Side by side it will bring the hard-handed, sun-browned, coarsely clad youth, who, with the exception of some help from home in clothing, expects to work his own way; who furnishes his room with two chairs and a table, and goes to work; who does not so far approximate a carpet on his floor, or a picture on his wall, as even to desire them; and the youth delicately brought up, whose mother comes on with him, and sees to the fitting up of his room, and indulges him in some things which she herself thinks rather extravagant, because other young men have them, and she has always observed that her son studies best when he has things pleasant about him. Now, a young man will present himself elaborately fitted, well informed and gentlemanly in all respects; and now, one who has started up, perhaps, from some nook in the mountains denominated Green, who has acquired, in an incredibly short time, the Latin, and Greek, and mathematics, necessary to enter College, but who knows nothing of literature, or history, or the world. He does not know that such a man as Addison, or Johnson, or Walter Scott, ever lived. Going to the president's study for the first time, he sits with his hat on, evidently as innocent of any conception of manners, as of the tricks that await him from those far inferior to him in true worth and in promise, who may laugh at him now, but who, before three years are past, will be very likely to "laugh on the other side."

   A system like this, really felt by the whole people to belong to them, must be among those things which will make every man proud of his country, and make it dear to him. It must tend powerfully to preserve and foster a genuine spirit of equality and independence. It is capable of abuse; but they must know very little of its real spirit and bearings, who can call it aristocratic. It would be impossible to devise a system more entirely the reverse.

The next proposition I would make, is one to which many would gladly assent, if they do not. It is, that such a system would not require a very large expenditure of money. I say this because there is, in some quarters, a contrary impression; and because, if true, it is important to this enterprise, and to the whole system, that it should be so understood.

In a single, well-devised, thorough, undergraduate course, very large libraries, a great amount of apparatus, and a large body of instructors, can be of no essential service. This follows from the position of the young men when they enter, and from what it is possible they should do in four years. A specific work is to be done; and it is reasonable to suppose that it would be better done by a few, well-qualified, thorough, working men, than by a large number. The excellence of a course will not depend on the amount of science there is in connection with an institution; but on the faithfulness and skill with which the instructors bring their minds into contact with the mind of the pupil, and lead him along those paths of thought and investigation where their own minds have been. It is the characteristic of an instructor, that he causes the mind of the pupil to go where his mind goes. He is not to tell the pupil *about* things, as he might tell about a fine prospect; and attempt to make him see it through his eyes; he must go himself, and stand where the prospect is, must see that the pupil follows him step by step, and cause him to stand where he stands, and to see with his own eyes. But to do this requires time, and acquaintance with individuals,—on some subjects, it requires a great expenditure of thought and emotion; and if the instruction be greatly divided, very little of this will be possible. Responsibility will be divided, and the danger will be, that there will be in the course but little depth and power. A few such men, every institution should be able to command and to retain. It should pay them well. Obtain the right men, and let their hearts be in the work, and the great difficulty is surmounted. But to do this, surely need not require a very great expenditure. Williams College has now stood nearly sixty years. From the question of its removal, and from fire, it has passed through periods of great difficulty. It is not for me to say what it has done; but it has lived, and has educated nearly fifteen hundred men, and is now educating more than two hundred. But it never has had, it has not now, I do not know that it ever will have, charity funds and all, a productive capital of fifty thousand dollars. This ought not so to be. These brethren are quite right in seeking to lay broader foundations for the great West, and I desire to aid them in doing so. For its stability and greatest efficiency, such an institution should have from seventy-five to a hundred thousand dollars. The latter sum would be the limit of my wishes, unless classes are to be divided; and for double that we could educate gratuitously, if not all who would come, yet more than our present number. This shows that if the Western States, or any other States, choose to put their college system on the same footing with their common schools, they can do it.

But the question now arises, whether this system would supply all the educational wants of the country. To this, I have no hesitation in saying, No. The time I think has come, when we need an institution, one or more, of a different order. We need a University. Of this, the nucleus and basis should be professional education, meaning by this not merely that for the three professions technically so called, but education in any branch of literature or science, or art, which would fit an individual for a specific line of life.

Here men from the different Colleges, and others desiring to be fitted for practical life, should meet, and stand chiefly on their own responsibility, and be free to learn, and, as far as practicable, to teach whatever they might choose. Here should be a library of a million or a million and a half of volumes, and cabinets, and collections in the arts, and facilities for prosecuting, to any extent, any branch of knowledge. Here the scientific farmer, the mechanic, the miner, the engineer, the chemist, the artist, the literary man, should find ample means of instruction. As far as possible, they should have access to all that the experience and genius of the world has yet contributed in their several departments.

Of the causes and indications of such a want, I need not now speak. They are to be found in the immense expansion of the industrial and commercial interests in connection with the application of science to the arts; in the quickening and extension of thought and activity in all directions; and in the general advancement of society and demand for a higher culture. For a long time this want has been felt, and has been increasing; and the attempts by some of our Colleges to supply it have been praiseworthy.

How this want may be best met, is a broad question, which we cannot now discuss. Clearly it cannot be done by each separate College; and so far as I can form an opinion, any attempt to blend the two courses into one, will but produce an expensive, complex, incongruous and inadequate system.

The question will then arise, whether such an institution, really distinct, should stand wholly by itself, or be engrafted on some one of our Colleges. If it should be thus engrafted, the object would be, not the benefit of the college course,—for no one supposes that the professional schools connected with some of our Colleges can be of any advantage to that,—but that the University might avail itself of the means already in possession of the College. How far this consideration should weigh at the East, it would be difficult to say; but if a new system were to be formed, it would be my decided impression that it would be better if they were wholly separated. The whole object, and scope, and economy of a collegiate and of a professional course, must be entirely different; and there cannot but be practical evils, where young men, having such different objects, and under such different regulations, are associated.

Nor would the establishment of such a University require too great an expenditure. No buildings would be needed, except for a library and cabinets, and lecture rooms; and from the greater numbers, the lectures would pay for themselves, or at least would require less endowment than if scattered in separate schools. There are men in this country who could found such an institution, and put it well on its way, and have an ample fortune left. This would give us an educational system efficient and complete; there are movements toward it in various quarters, and such an one I trust we may yet have.

I have thus indicated some things which I should regard as essential to a complete educational system. This has been done very briefly and imperfectly; but I hope sufficiently to show, what was said must be shown in order to legitimate this Society most fully—that is, that the Institutions which it would establish at the West, will be an essential link in such an educational system as a great and free people ought to have. Its specific object, indeed, is to provide ministers for the churches; but we contend that the general education which they need is precisely that which is fitted for man as man—that which any judicious parent would wish to give his son, to fit him for usefulness and distinction in the world.

There is here, there can be but one great point of difference, and that is the extent to which religious instruction and influence shall enter into these Seminaries. This is a point on which this Society can have no hesitation and no compromise. Man has a moral and religious nature, by which it was intended his other qualities should be controlled. To this, the intellect and all its acquisitions should be subservient; upon the right direction of this, will depend his individual well-being here and hereafter, and the well-being of society; and it is absurd to think of educating him as a man, and neglect this. No man, especially no Christian man, has a right to send his son to an institution where provision is not made and care taken for this. In this, the period of college life is often a critical one, often a turning point. What a man is when he leaves College, he generally continues to be.

What we need, then, and must have, are institutions on the broad basis of Christianity, with a course of study thoroughly liberal,—institutions of which no one can complain for sectarianism; and yet having connected with them such religious instruction and influence as should satisfy Christian people, as will tend to foster piety, and lead men to God. These are the two great features, and the only ones on which we insist. Retain these fully, and we are willing our institutions should be modified, should be *Westernized*, if you please, to any extent.

That there may be such institutions, is shown by our New England and other Colleges. Who complains of Yale College, or of Princeton, as sectarian? If there can be any ground of complaint, it must be only from the connection with them of Theological Seminaries. Experience shows that Colleges may be so conducted as to be highly favorable to growth in piety, and to revivals of religion. There are no communities where revivals have been more frequent, or more powerful, or more free from questionable elements, or more happy in their results. From the first, the Colleges generally have sympathized fully with the religious community in this; and more especially since the annual observance by the churches of a day of fasting and prayer on their behalf.

Modern times do not furnish, scarcely can ancient times furnish more signal instances of answer to prayer. It has been wonderful to see the great mass of such a community swayed by an invisible influence, as the trees of the wood are swayed,—an influence gradually awing down all opposition, and producing in every mind the solemn conviction that it was from God. It has been sublime to see young men, in the face of such a community, in the perfect stillness of the crowded meeting, rise and in few and simple words state their convictions of sin, their hope in the mercy of God, and their determination to serve him in future. Such scenes we have witnessed the past year, and also the present. They have been witnessed in many other Colleges; and this Society would establish institutions where they may be witnessed without a miracle.

And such institutions are needed not merely for the sake of religion, but of education itself and of the state. God made the intellect and the moral nature to work in harmony, to act and react on each other. He never intended the intellect should reach its perfection, except under the control of the moral faculty; it never will; and to seek to make it, is like seeking to roll up the stone of Sisiphus. It is time this principle was fully recognized, especially in our western States, where it is sad to see such immense educational resources in danger of perversion and loss. Nothing can be more beautiful than the theory of a College as an institution where every facility is provided, and young men have nothing to do but to come in the freshness, and strength, and ingenuousness of their youth, and devote themselves to self-improvement. A more gratifying sight could hardly be presented, than that of two hundred or more young men, devoting themselves faithfully to self-improvement, in the enjoyment of such advantages. But he must know little of human nature, who does not perceive that there must be connected with such institutions tendencies and influences that are strong to evil, and which, unresisted and uncontrolled, would render them a curse rather than a blessing. There is danger that they will become the abodes of indolence and vice, danger of physical, and social, and moral deterioration. If any one supposes that there will be generally, among such a body, faithful devotion to study, and moral purity, without the restraints of religion, and, I may say, the presence of the Spirit of God, he has only to look below the surface to be fully undeceived. No; if there ever was an institution that needed the prayers of God's people and every good and holy influence, that institution is a College. States may endow Colleges as they will; but constituting them so as virtually to exclude these influences, there will be heard a voice, and there ought to be, saying, "Come out of them, my people." And they will come out and endow institutions for themselves, and such institutions will be preferred by the great mass of those who have sons to educate. If political bodies, in those States where there are large educational funds, cannot secure and perpetuate such influences, it would be better that they should let collegiate education alone, except as they might aid permanent boards of trust established for the purpose, and that they should give their strength to the upbuilding of a University on the plan above mentioned.

In the mean time this Society has a work to do. Let it do it well; let it strengthen the bonds of kindness; let it add to the ties of blood the assimilative influence of kindred literary institutions; let it select wisely the points where the fortresses shall be cast up, on what may be the moral battle-field of the world; let it furnish clear light for the guidance of the unequalled strength that is there growing up; let it provide such a ministry for the church as she will need in the day that is coming.

A

DISCOURSE

COMMEMORATIVE OF

AMOS LAWRENCE,

DELIVERED BY REQUEST OF THE STUDENTS,

IN THE

CHAPEL OF WILLIAMS COLLEGE,

FEBRUARY 21, 1853.

BY

MARK HOPKINS, D. D.
PRESIDENT OF THE COLLEGE.

PUBLISHED BY THE STUDENTS.

BOSTON:
PRESS OF T. R. MARVIN.
1853.

Entered, according to Act of Congress, in the year 1853, by

T. R. MARVIN,

In the Clerk's Office of the District Court of the District of Massachusetts

DISCOURSE.

JOB XXIX. 11-13.

WHEN THE EAR HEARD ME, THEN IT BLESSED ME; AND WHEN THE EYE SAW ME, IT GAVE WITNESS TO ME; BECAUSE I DELIVERED THE POOR THAT CRIED, AND THE FATHERLESS, AND HIM THAT HAD NONE TO HELP HIM. THE BLESSING OF HIM THAT WAS READY TO PERISH CAME UPON ME, AND I CAUSED THE WIDOW'S HEART TO SING FOR JOY.

THE patience of Job, in connection with such signal afflictions, has, in some measure, drawn attention from the general excellence of his character. That patience was no isolated virtue, having its root in some special aptitude for it of the constitution; but a manifestation, under varied circumstances, of that rational and central excellence that had shone forth under a different form in prosperity. It was but the circling round to us of the completed orb of his character. Not from his conduct in affliction, but in prosperity, it was, that he was called by God 'a perfect and an upright man.' Scarcely, if at all, has the world shown a finer example of all that goes to make up a complete manhood — of vivid and refined feeling, of elevated and tender sentiment, of enlarged benevolence, of parental faithfulness, of intellectual power in the high form of genius, and of an exalted religious character.

Up to the time mentioned in the history, these excellences had been manifested in connection with high distinction in life, with great wealth, and uninterrupted prosperity. God had, as it is said, 'made an hedge about him, and about his house, and about all that he had on every side.' He had 'blessed the work of his hands,' and 'his substance was increased in the land; — so that this man was the greatest of all the men of the east.'

Thus exalted and prosperous, he was, of course, subject to the usual temptations of pride, and vanity, and voluptuousness, and avarice. But these he resisted. He did not for a moment forget his great moral relations to the Creator and to his fellow-creatures. He abused no power intrusted to him; and in the *acquisition*, the *right estimate*, and the *right use of property*, he set an example for the world.

There is no indication that he was the possessor of hereditary power, or that he had any position or advantage that was not due, under the blessing of God, to his own exertions and force of character. But that his wealth was of his own acquisition is clearly indicated by what is said of God's having blessed the work of his hands, and of his substance as increased in the land; also where he says, "Because mine hand had gotten much," showing that it was his own hand that had gotten it.

And this wealth he acquired honestly. No part of it was gained by any process of which any one could complain. No furrow turned for him could bear witness against him, either that the soil was dishonestly acquired, or that the wages of the laborer were withheld. "If," says he, triumphantly, when the unjust suspicions of his friends wrung from him his vindication,—"if my land cry against me, or that the furrows likewise thereof complain; if I have eaten the fruits thereof without money, or have caused the owners thereof to lose their life; let thistles grow instead of wheat, and cockle instead of barley." Nor did he, as is too often done, either gain or save any thing by any form of hard dealing with his servants or dependants. How noble and solemn is his recognition of their claims to equal justice! "If," says he, "I did despise the cause of my man servant, or of my maid servant, when they contended with me, what then shall I do when God riseth up? and when he visiteth, what shall I answer him? Did not he that made me in the womb make him? and did not one fashion us in the womb?"

Having thus acquired his property rightfully, he saw its true relations to human life, and placed upon it no undue estimate. Between the idolatry of wealth and of the other creatures of God he made no distinction. "If," says he, "I have made gold my hope, or have said to the fine gold, Thou art my confidence; if I rejoiced because my wealth was great, and because mine hand had gotten much; if I beheld the sun when it shined, or the moon walking in brightness; and my heart hath been secretly enticed, or my mouth hath kissed my hand, — this also were an iniquity to be punished by the Judge; for I should have denied the God that is above."

And the property thus acquired, and thus estimated, he knew how to use. He employed it in establishing his children "about him," who seem to have lived in harmony, and to have been to him a source of great comfort. He employed it also in sustaining the bountiful hospitality of the east. "The stranger," says he, "did not lodge in the street, but I opened my doors to the traveller." And especially did he employ his wealth in providing for the wants of the poor. "If," says he, "I have withheld the poor from their desire, or have caused the eyes of the widow to fail; or have eaten my morsel myself alone, and the fatherless hath not eaten thereof; if I have seen any perish for want of clothing, or any poor without covering; if his loins have not blessed me, and if he were not warmed with the fleece of my sheep; if I have lifted up my hand against the fatherless, when I saw my help in the gate, — then let mine arm fall from my shoulder blade, and mine arm be broken from the bone."

Of such a man it might well be expected that he could say, as he says in the text, "When the ear heard me, then it blessed me; and when the eye saw me, it gave witness to me; because I delivered the poor that cried, and the fatherless, and him that had none to help him. The blessing of him that was ready to perish came upon me, and I caused the widow's heart to sing for joy."

These words, thus spoken by Job, could have been applied to themselves by few men who have since lived, more appropriately than by a distinguished Benefactor of this College, who has recently been taken from the earth. It is known to his friends that Mr. LAWRENCE stood in the first rank among men in those qualities, both of the head and of the heart, that adorn humanity, and to some of these I may hereafter refer; but he was known to the public chiefly for his *acquisition*, his *estimate*, and his *use of wealth*. With an integrity as unsullied as that of Job in the acquisition of property, and with a heart as large and a hand as open in its distribution, if we make allowance for the different length of human life, his charities were probably not less extensive.

Among the men of great wealth who have died in this country, he stands, so far as I know, in some respects alone; and rising as he did from moderate circumstances, there cannot but be involved in his course lessons of instruction, great principles demanding not only careful, but special attention in this day of the vast increase, the rapid acquisition, and the selfish and reckless expenditure of wealth. Perhaps one purpose for which he was raised up was to call attention to these lessons and principles. Perhaps the time may be near when higher and more rational views in regard to property and its uses shall prevail; when numbers shall escape from that weary and monotonous round of mammon — the toilsome and careful accumulation, till death, of sums that generally depress the manhood, and often ruin the character, of those for whom they are laid up; when it shall be seen that it is not money, but the 'love of money,' that is the 'root of all evil,' and that property is a great trust. Concerning all this, Mr. Lawrence made no new discovery, but he did what is often quite as important. He saw, as by intuition, great practical principles, and by embodying them in actual life, he gave to some that had fallen much into desuetude the freshness and force of a new discovery. He did in his department and sphere what Howard and Mills did in theirs.

Like most men in this country who have possessed great wealth, Mr. Lawrence was indebted for it to his own exertions. His parents were of the old Puritan stock, and the formative influences of his childhood were those of a religious New England family. His father shared deeply in the spirit and perils of '76. He belonged to a company of 'minute men;' and on the very day of his marriage the alarm was given, his company was called for, and he left his bride, and without returning, gave himself for months to the service of his country. He was a farmer, and a man of standing and influence both in the town and in the church. Above poverty and dependence, he was yet unable to do more for his children than to give them the means of education accessible in their native town, and place them in favorable positions to be the artificers of their own fortune. With the stern manliness that oftenest overlies the deepest and tenderest feelings, he showed them that he was willing to make any sacrifice for their good, and they reciprocated the feeling.

At the usual age, Mr. Lawrence was placed in a store in Groton as a clerk. This clerkship he regarded as the turning point of his life, and was wont to trace back his success to the course he then took. He was placed with a man past middle age, who had been long in business, and was supposed to be wealthy. This man spent the most of his time in the store, but did very little, employing several clerks. It was the usage in those days to 'treat' customers after they had traded, the clerks preparing the various mixtures, and often drinking with them. To this usage Mr. Lawrence conformed for a short time, but soon observed that the owner of the store generally showed before night that he had gone too far, and that the older clerks were fast following in his footsteps. His mind was soon made up. Understanding perfectly the ridicule he should meet with, and which for a time he did meet with in its fullest measure, he yet took at once the ground of *total abstinence*.

Such a stand, taken at such an age, in such circumstances of temptation, before temperance societies had been heard of, or the investigations had been commenced on which they were based, was a striking instance of that practical judgment and decision which characterized him through life. About the same time, he came to a similar decision in regard to tobacco, and never used it in any form. In the wisdom of his course on both these points he was confirmed by all his subsequent observation. The man in whose store he was, died a drunkard; and every one of those clerks, together with other young men in the village similarly situated, had long since found drunkards' graves. In a letter received from him last summer, which accompanied fifty copies of " Stories on Tobacco, by Uncle Toby," after stating that he had never used it, he says, " To this abstinence from its use (and from rum) I owe, under God, my present position in society. Further, I have always given the preference, among such persons as I have employed for more than forty years past, to such as avoided rum and tobacco, — and my experience has been to confirm me that it is true wisdom to have done so. The evil is growing in a fearfully rapid ratio among us, and requires the steady course of respected and honored men to prevent its spread, by influencing the school children of our land against becoming its slaves." Who can tell the bearing upon his business of thus employing men of unclouded intellect, and steady nerves, having the power of self-control? Who can tell how many young men, without knowing the reason, failed to obtain a place which would have been to them a fortune?

At twenty-one, Mr. Lawrence went to Boston, not with the purpose of remaining, but to learn the fashions; and see how business was done there. This was in April, 1807. Instead, however, of returning to Groton, as he had intended, he was induced to remain in Boston as a clerk. Here he so commended himself to his employers, by his energy and business talent, that they very soon offered him a place in the firm. Much to their surprise, and without any definite knowledge of their affairs, he declined the offer. He did not like their manner of doing business. Here, again, the result showed his sagacity. In less than six months they failed, and he was appointed by the creditors to take charge of the sale of the goods. This he did; and in December went into business on his own account.

He was now exposed to the temptations of a city. But he stood firm. His days were spent in business, and his evenings in useful reading. He avoided the *appearance* of evil, treading on no questionable ground; and no stain or suspicion of vice ever rested upon him.

Of his business career I know no particulars. I have never understood that he was, in the ordinary sense of that word, a fortunate man. His wealth came to him by no lucky chances, but by a skill and an energy that commanded uniform and great success. His judgment was shown, not merely in the purchase of goods, and in the lines of business on which he entered, but also, as has been said, in his selection of agents, clerks, and partners; and in deciding whom he might safely trust. He made no bad debts. It is said there has been no man in Boston who took hold of business with the same grasp and energy. Quick in his perceptions, deciding as by intuition, and prompt in action, he is said to have had in those days little patience with the slow, the inefficient, the dainty, or those who felt above their business. So energetic young men, in every department, are apt to feel. They think these things need not be. And perhaps they need not; but in time they become more tolerant of them, finding, as the Saviour said of the poor, that we have them always with us.

The first year his gains were small, but he dealt so promptly and honorably that his customers returned and brought others; and thus the rills began to come in that formed the river. In a few years he placed himself at the head of a house that, for wealth and mercantile honor, was among the very first in Boston, and which continued so till the firm was dissolved by his death.

For twenty-five years he continued in active business. At the end of that time, he was suddenly prostrated by drinking cold water when heated. There seemed to be a paralysis of the stomach, and for many days he was not expected to recover. After that, he was subject to sudden attacks, which deprived him, sometimes for hours, of all consciousness. From that time, he was obliged to be most careful of his diet. His food was of the simplest kind, was eaten by weight, and for twenty years he sat down at no meal with his family. His attacks often came without warning; he expected to die, as he did, in one of them, and hence expressively called himself, in military phrase, 'a minute man.' From this time he gave no attention to the details of business, but remained the senior partner of the firm, giving counsel and general direction, and being consulted and relied on in all questions of difficulty and importance.

In speaking of the acquisition of his property, and as indicating his sagacity and enterprise, it may be mentioned that Mr. Lawrence was among the earliest and most successful of those who engaged in manufactures.

Of his *estimate* of property, and of the modes in which it can be made to contribute to the enjoyment of its possessor, and to human well being, we can judge only from the use that he made of it.

It has been supposed by some that his habit of giving largely commenced with his ill health; but this was by no means the case. It is known that it extended back to the period of his early prosperity, and kept pace with that. He had a sense of religious obligation, and a benevolent heart; and then, with the same sagacity that governed his business transactions, he perceived the tendency there is in accumulation to increase the love of money, and guarded against it. In his busiest days, he had pasted, in large letters, in his pocket book, passages of Scripture inculcating liberality, and the obligation of good stewardship.

But while this was so, we cannot suppose that his views were not modified by the loss of his health. Often struck down in a moment, and awaking to consciousness as from the sleep of death, and then remaining for weeks so feeble that neither he nor his friends expected his recovery, he was led to look fully and calmly at death, and must have gained views of life and its ends which another discipline would not have given him. This was doubtless a part of God's preparation of him for the work he was to do, and he so regarded it. Thenceforth he lived to do good.

When it was that he came to the determination not to increase his property I do not know. Nor do I know the whole amount of his charities. Probably that will never be known. I am, however, safe in saying, that, since 1840, his benefactions have not been less than FIVE HUNDRED THOUSAND DOLLARS.

This he did not dispense at random, nor yet by any rigid and inflexible system that could not be moulded and shaped by the calls and aspects of each new day. He wished to know his duty as a Christian man, and to do it, and to gratify his best affections. He aided family connections near and remote, and old friends and acquaintances. If any of them needed a few hundred dollars to help them over a difficult position, it was sure to come. But his sympathy was not limited at all to kindred or acquaintance, or in any way narrowed by sect or party. He was a true man, in sympathy with suffering humanity, and was always glad — it gave him real pleasure — to find a worthy object of his bounty. He sought out such objects. He learned histories of reverses, and of noble struggles with adversity, that were stranger than fiction. Those thus struggling he placed in positions to help themselves, furnishing them, if necessary, with sums from one hundred to a thousand dollars, or more, as freely as he would have given a cup of cold water. He visited almshouses, and hospitals, and insane asylums, and retreats for the deaf and dumb, and the blind, and became deeply interested in many of their inmates. He was watchful of every thing needed there for comfort or for instruction, and his presence always carried sunshine with it. He distributed useful books. He aided genius, and encouraged promising talent. A true son of New England, he appreciated education, and gave his money and his influence to extend it, and to elevate its standard in every grade of our institutions, from the primary school in Boston to the College. Not only the Academy at Groton but several Colleges, and more particularly this College, were largely aided by him.

Other persons have aided this College generously, and have our thanks and those of the public; but he was its chief benefactor. With one exception,* he is the only person who has ever given the College, at any one time, a larger sum than one thousand dollars, and the only person who has thus given more than that to its unrestricted use.

As your request that I should address you on this occasion had its origin in his benefactions to the College, some account of them will be expected.

In October, 1841, the building known as the East College was burned. Needy as the institution was before, this rendered necessary an application to the legislature for funds, and when this failed, to the public at large. Owing to a panic in the money market, this application was but slightly responded to, except in this town. In Boston the amount raised was less than two thousand dollars, and the largest sum given by any individual was one hundred dollars. This sum was paid by Mr. Lawrence, who was applied to by a friend of the College; and this, it is believed, was the only application ever made to

---

* Woodbridge Little, Esq., who gave $2,500, and bequeathed $3,200, to aid indigent and pious young men.

him on its behalf. This directed his attention to the wants of the College, but nothing more was heard from him till January, 1844. At that time, I was delivering a course of the Lowell Lectures in Boston, when his son, Mr. Amos A. Lawrence, called and informed me that his father had five thousand dollars which he wished to place at the disposal of the College. As I was previously but slightly acquainted with Mr. Lawrence, and had had no conversation with him on the subject, this was to me an entire surprise; and embarrassed as the institution then was by its debt for the new buildings, the relief and encouragement which it brought to my own mind, and to the minds of others, friends of the College, can hardly be expressed. Still, this did not wholly remove the debt. On hearing this casually mentioned, he said, if he had known how we were situated, he thought he should have given us more; and the following July, without another word on the subject, he sent me a check for five thousand dollars. This put the College out of debt, and added two or three thousand dollars to its available funds.

In January, 1846, he wrote, saying he wished to see me; and on meeting him, he said his object was to consult me about the disposition of ten thousand dollars, which he proposed to give the College. He wished to know how I thought it would do the most good. I replied at once, "By being placed at the disposal of the trustees, to be used at their discretion." He said, "Very well;" and that was all that passed on that point. So I thought, and knowing his simplicity of character and singleness of purpose, I felt no embarrassment in making that reply. Here was a beautiful exemplification of the precept of the Apostle, "He that giveth, let him do it with simplicity." Such a man had a right to have for one of his mottoes, "Deeds, not words." This was just what was needed — not all that was needed, but it gave us some breadth and enlargement, and was a beginning in what it had long been felt must sooner or later be undertaken — the securing of an available fund suitable as a basis for such an institution.

His next large gift was the library. This came from his asking me, as I was riding with him the following winter, if we wanted any thing. Nothing occurred to me at the time, and I replied in the negative; but the next day I remembered that the trustees had voted to build a library, provided the treasurer should find it could be done for twenty-five hundred dollars. This I mentioned to him. He inquired what I supposed it would cost. I replied, five thousand dollars. He said at once, "I will give it." With his approbation, the plan of a building was subsequently adopted that would cost seven thousand dollars, and he paid that sum.

A year or two subsequently, he inquired of me the price of tuition here, saying he should like to connect Groton Academy with Williams College; and he paid two thousand dollars to establish four scholarships for any who might come from that institution.

His next gift was the telescope, which cost about fifteen hundred dollars. The history of this would involve some details which I have not now time to give.

In 1851, accompanied by Mrs. Lawrence, he made a visit here. This was the first time either of them had seen the place. In walking over the grounds, he said they had great capabilities, but that we needed more land; and authorized the purchase of an adjacent piece, of four acres. This purchase was made for one thousand dollars; and if the College can have the means of laying it out, and adorning it suitably, it will, besides furnishing scope for exercise, be a fit addition of the charms of culture to great beauty of natural scenery.

In addition to these gifts, he has, at different times, enriched the library with costly books, of the expense of which I know nothing. Almost every thing we have in the form of art was given by him.

In December, 1845, I received a letter from him, dated the 22d, or 'forefathers' day,' which enclosed one hundred dollars, to be used for the aid of needy students, in those emergencies which often arise. This was entirely at his own suggestion, and nothing could have been more timely or appropriate in an institution like this, where so many young men are struggling to make their own way. Since that time, he has furnished me with, at least, one hundred dollars annually for that purpose, and he regarded this expenditure with much interest.

Thus, in different ways, Mr. Lawrence had given to the College between thirty and forty thousand dollars, and he had expressed the purpose, if he should live, of aiding it still further.

Understanding, as he did, the position and wants of this College, he sympathized fully with the trustees in their purpose to raise the sum of fifty thousand dollars, and at the time of his death was exerting a most warm-hearted and powerful influence for its accomplishment. In reference to this great effort, we feel that a strong helper is taken away.

The aid which Mr. Lawrence thus gave to the College was great and indispensable, and probably no memorial of him will be more enduring than what he has done here. By this, being dead, he yet speaks, and will continue to speak in all coming time. From him will flow down enjoyment and instruction to those who shall walk these grounds, and look at the heavens through this telescope, and read the books gathered in this library, and hear instruction from teachers sustained wholly or in part by his bounty. Probably he could not have spent this money more usefully, and there is reason to believe that he could have spent it in no way to bring to himself more enjoyment. The prosperity of the College was a source of great gratification to him, and he said, more than once, that he had been many times repaid for what he had done here. That he should have thus done what he did unsolicited, and that he, and, I may add, his family, should have continued to find in it so much of satisfaction, is most grateful to my own feelings, and must be so to those of every friend of the College. In doing it, he seemed to place himself in the relation, not so much of a patron of the College, as of a sympathizer and helper in a great and good work.

Having thus spoken of the use of his property by Mr. Lawrence, I observe that it was distinguished by *the* three characteristics, which seem to me essential to the most perfect accomplishment of the ends of benevolence; and that in two of these he was preeminent.

The first of these is, that he gave the money in his lifetime. No man, I presume, has lived on this continent, who has approximated him in the amount thus given; and in this course there are principles involved which deserve the careful attention of those who would act conscientiously, and with the highest wisdom. There may, doubtless, be good reasons why property destined for benevolent uses should be retained till death, and he is justly honored who then gives it a wise direction; but giving thus cannot furnish either the same test, or discipline of character, or the same enjoyment; nor can it always accomplish the same ends. By his course, Mr. Lawrence put his money to its true work long before it would have done any thing on the principle of accumulation, and to a work, too, to which it never could have been put in any other way. He made it sure also that that work should be done, and had the pleasure of seeing its results, and of knowing that, through it, he became the object of gratitude and affection. So doing, he showed that he stood completely above that tendency to accumulate which seems to form the chief end of most successful business men, and which, unless strongly counteracted, narrows itself into avarice as old age comes on, almost with the certainty of a natural law. He did stand completely above this. No one could know him without perceiving that in his giving there was no remnant of grudging or of reluctance; that he gave not only freely, but with gladness, as if it were the appropriate action of a vital energy. And in so doing, and in witnessing the results, and in the atmosphere of sympathy and love thus created, there was a test, and a discipline, and an enjoyment, as well as a benefit to others, that could have been reached in no other way.

The second peculiarity in the bounty of Mr. Lawrence, and in which he was preëminent, was the personal attention and sympathy which he bestowed with it. He had in his house a room where he kept stores of useful articles for distribution. *He* made up the bundle, *he* directed the package. No detail was overlooked. He remembered the children, and designated for each the toy, the book, the elegant gift. He thought of every want, and was ingenious and happy in devising appropriate gifts. In this attention to the minutest token of regard, while, at the same time, he could give away thousands like a prince, I have known no one like him. And if the gift was appropriate, the manner of giving was not less so. There was in this the nicest appreciation of the feelings of others, and an intuitive perception of delicacy and propriety. These were the characteristics that gave him a hold upon the hearts of many, and made his death really felt as that of few other men in Boston could have been. In these we find not a little of the utility, and much of the beauty, of charity. Even in his human life, man does not live by bread alone, but by sympathy, and the play of reciprocal affection ; and is often more touched by the kindness than by the relief. Only this sympathy it is that can establish the right relation between the rich and the poor, and the necessity for this can be superseded by no legal provision. This only can neutralize the repellent and aggressive tendencies of individuals and of classes, and make society a brotherhood, where the various inequalities shall work out moral good, and where acts of mutual kindness and helpfulness may pass and repass as upon a golden chain, during a brief pilgrimage and scene of probation. It is a great and a good thing for a rich man to set the stream of charity in motion, to employ an agent, to send a check, to found an asylum, to endow a professorship, to open a fountain that shall flow for ages; but it is as different from sympathy with present suffering, and the relief of immediate want, as the building of a dam to turn a factory by one great sluiceway, is from the irrigation of the fields. Both ought to be done. By Mr. Lawrence both were done.

The third characteristic referred to, of the bounty of Mr. Lawrence, was, that he gave as a Christian man, — from a sense of religious obligation. Not that all his gifts had a religious aspect. He gave gifts of friendship and of affection. There was a large enclosure where the affections walked foremost, and where, though they asked leave of Duty, they yet received no prompting from her. Whether he always drew this line rightly, whether in the measure and direction of his charities he was always right, whether so much of diffusion and individuality was wise, it is not for me to say. Certain it is, that this form of charity holds a place in the church, now, less prominent relatively than it did in the early ages; and it may be that the proportions of Christian character, in portions of the church, need to be remodelled and recast in this respect. These are questions for each individual. It is sufficient to know that Mr. Lawrence looked the great doctrine of stewardship full in the face, and prayed earnestly over it, and responded to it practically as few have done.

This is what is chiefly needed by us all, as intrusted by God with our various gifts and means of influence. This it is that is needed by men of wealth. The feeling of the absolute ownership of property, and of the full right of its disposal within the range of human law, is entirely different from that of stewardship — of a trust held under another, and to be administered with reference to his will. This position is one which the man of wealth is most slow to take. Every natural feeling resists it. But not till this position is taken will the man himself find his true place, or wealth its true uses, or the wealthy themselves the highest and the appropriate blessedness which it can confer.

That Mr. Lawrence took this position, will appear by an extract from one of his letters. "If," he writes, "by the consecration of my earthly possessions to some extent, I can make the Christian character practically more lovely, and illustrate, in my own case, that the highest enjoyments here are promoted by the free use of the good things intrusted to us, what so good use can I make of them? I feel that my stewardship is a very imperfect one, and that my use of these good things might be extended profitably to myself."

Hitherto wealth has been a great corrupter. It has inflamed the passions, and narrowed the heart, and made it sordid. It has been harder for a rich man to enter into the kingdom of heaven than for a camel to go through the eye of a needle. The probation of wealth has been more perilous than that of poverty. But let this broad position of stewardship be taken, and under it let the characteristics before mentioned come in; let the rich man no longer reverse in its spirit the precept to do with his might what his hand findeth to do because there is no work in the grave, and refuse to do any thing *till* he goes there, and *because* he is going there; let him hold always his own heart close to the beating heart of humanity, so that they shall throb with a common pulsation, — and these evils will vanish, and will bear away with them many of the chief evils of society. The man rich in this world will be "rich in good works, ready to distribute, willing to communicate." He will not do a vain work, that shall have no relation to the great plans of God; and "at his end be a fool." He will lift up his eyes upon a world lying in wickedness, and in consequent suffering, and will seek to remove the wickedness, and to relieve the suffering. The accumulated and concentrated water that had before carried desolation in its course, and left its channel dry and dusty, will now show a long track of verdure where it flows; it will find its way to the roots of a thousand flowers, that shall cover the earth with their beauty, and fill the air with their perfume.

In what has now been said, some traits of the character of Mr. Lawrence have been indicated. Something more of him you may wish to know, and it may be proper for me to state; but it must be with a painful sense of its inadequacy. Words and descriptions must fail to convey to others an impression of what he was to his friends. This must always be so where the strength of a character lies so much as did his in the affections. You may give to the perished flower its botanical name and scientific description, but this is not to see it in its living beauty, and to enter the sphere of its fragrance.

Undoubtedly he was a man of great original powers. On this point I have had but one opinion since knowing him. His mind was not speculative, discursive, metaphysical; but in the high moral qualities, in decision and energy, in intuitive perception and sound practical judgment, in the sensibilities and affections, and in the imagination, he was great. Like all remarkable men who are not one-sided, he had large faculties, which found their harmony in their conflict, or rather in their balance. He was quick and tender in his feelings, yet firm; ardent in his affections, yet judicious; large in his gifts, yet discriminating; he was a keen observer, yet kind in his feelings; he had a fertile and shaping imagination — he built air castles, and they vanished, and then he built others; but when he decided to build any thing on the ground, it was well planned and promptly finished.

His tastes were natural and simple, his habits plain, and his feelings always fresh, genuine, and youthful. Not even the smell of the fire of prosperity had passed on him. He shunned notoriety. He had a strong repugnance to all affectation, and pretence, and misplaced finery. A young man with rings on his fingers had small chance of employment or favor from him. He was impatient of talk when action was called for, and of all attempts to substitute talk for action.

His command over the English language, especially in writing, indicated his power. Style is no mechanical product, that can be formed by rules, but is the outgrowth and image of the mind; and his had often great felicity and strength. When he wrote under the impulse of his feelings, he seemed to impregnate the very paper, and make it redolent of them.

He loved nature, and instead of becoming insensible to it as years came on, it seemed rather to open upon him like a new revelation. It was full of life and of teaching, and the charms of natural beauty were heightened by those associations which his quick imagination connected with its objects and scenes. After the death of two of his children, he says, "Dear S——, and R——, speak in words without sound through every breeze, and in every flower, and in the fragrance of every perfume from the fields or the trees." Years ago, after a long confinement, with little hope of recovery, he visited, when first able to get out, the Panorama of Jerusalem, then on exhibition in Boston, and remained there till the scene took full possession of his mind. Shortly after, on a fine day, he rode out to Brookline; and as returning health threw over those hills a mantle of beauty that he had never seen before, they were immediately associated in his mind with the Panorama of Jerusalem, and then with the glories of the Jerusalem above. This association was indissoluble, and he would take his friends out to see his 'Mount Zion.' In 1850, he says, "It really seems to me like the sides of Mount Zion, and that I can cling to them as I view them."

Soon after the death of his youngest son, a storm rent a large bough from one of the oaks that sheltered his grave. The oak bled, and when he saw it, he applied it to himself. The next time he visited Mount Auburn, the gardener had removed all appearance of injury, and covered the wound with what seemed to be bark; and he fancied that the remaining portions of the tree had now a more vigorous growth. This thrilled him — it was a sermon, and his application of it will be seen in the following extract: "And then again the calls, as I visit Mount Auburn, speak to me with an eloquence that no tongue can equal, when I see the old oak holding its head erect, its opposite branches more extended; its leaves have been greener, larger, and more numerous, as its whole nourishment has gone into one side of the tree the past year, and thus have taught me that my precious ones secured, would encourage me to cheer on such as need the shade and encouragement this old oak can supply."

Hear him again, at the close of 1851, associating natural beauty with social blessings. "The closing of the old year," says he, " was like our western horizon after sunset, bright and beautiful; the opening of the new, radiant with life, light, and hope, and crowned with such a costume of love as few old fathers, grandfathers, and uncles can muster."

Thus sensitive to the pulsations and suggestions of nature, it might be expected that he would be still more so within the sphere of the domestic affections. He was; and in these, few men have been as happy. His home was all that a home could be; and then, like Job, he had his children about him, and his children's children. Bereaved of two of his children, he could still say, " And with all these precious ones left, it seems as though I had sources of enjoyment that any man might be justified in craving. If I starve my body, I feed my spirit, and thus receive my full share of the good things of life. My greatest trouble is, not rendering due returns for these." This is a charmed circle with which the stranger may not intermeddle; but perhaps a single extract, showing his feelings on the return of his son from abroad, may be allowed. "The intelligence of son W——'s arrival in New York preceded his arrival in Boston only one hour; and the effect of the intelligence was like the gas which is called laughing gas, only with me it was crying. In truth, it was more than I could stand; and I allowed nature fair play, and cried, and gave utterance to my feelings aloud and alone, as I did not wish my wife to know how it was with me. By the time W—— came, I was self-possessed in a good degree, and for three days I have lived, in the matter of enjoyment, full three months."

With such avenues of enjoyment open, though sometimes pitied as an invalid, he might well be, as he was, a most cheerful and happy man. As intimated in an extract above, his abstemiousness may have made him more keenly alive to the higher sources of enjoyment, and even in sensitive good he did not regard himself as a loser. "If," says he, "your young folks want to know the true meaning of epicureanism, tell them to take some bits of coarse bread, (one ounce and a little more,) soak them in three gills of coarse meal gruel, and make their dinner of them and nothing else, beginning very hungry and leaving off more hungry. The food is delicious, and such as no modern epicureanism can equal."

But man has wants deeper than can be supplied by wealth, or nature, or domestic affections. His great relations are to his God and to eternity. This Mr. Lawrence felt, and he was a deeply religious man. His trust in God, and his hope of salvation through Christ, were the basis of his character. He believed in the providence of God as concerned in all events, and as discriminating and retributive in this world. He felt that he could trust God in his providence where he could not see. "The events of my life," he writes, "have so far been ordered in a way to make me feel that I know nothing at the time except that a Father rules; and his discipline, however severe, is never more so than is required." He believed in the Bible, and saw rightly its relation to all our blessings. "What," he writes again, "should we do if the Bible were not the foundation of our system of self-government? and what will become of us when we wilfully and wickedly cast it behind us?" He read the Bible morning and evening in his family, and prayed with them; and it may aid those who are acquainted with the prayers of Thornton, in forming a conception of his religious character, to know that he used them. Family religion he esteemed as above all price; and when he first learned that a beloved relative had established family worship, he wept for joy. He distributed religious books very extensively, chiefly those of the American Tract Society and of the Sunday School Union. He believed in revivals of religion, and prayed for them. In 1848, he wrote, "This religious awakening among your college students is among the blessings that our Father vouchsafes to his servants who labor faithfully in their work, and I can see his hand as plainly in it as though it was thrust before my face as I write this sentence. Let us, then, bless his holy name, and thank him as disciples and followers of Christ the beloved, and urge upon these young men to come forward as 'doves to their windows.' If my work and my trusteeship have in any manner been instrumental in this good work in your College, it will be matter of grateful thanksgiving while I live." Of the religious movement in Boston, in 1849, he says, "Our dead Unitarianism of ten or fifteen years ago is stirred up, and the deep feelings of sin, and salvation through the Beloved, are awakened where there seemed to be nothing but indifference and coldness, and my hope and belief is, that great good will follow." Still later he says, "And now let us turn to matters of more importance — the awakening of the young men of your College to their highest interest, the salvation of their souls. I have been moved to tears in reading the simple statement of the case, and I pray God to perfect the good work thus begun." Of creeds held in the understanding, but not influencing the life, he thought little; and the tendency of his mind was to practical rather than doctrinal views. He believed in our Lord Jesus Christ as a Saviour, and trusted in him for salvation. He was a man of habitual prayer. The last time I visited him, he said to me that he had been restless during the night, and that the only way in which he could "get quieted was by getting near to God;" and that he went to sleep repeating a prayer. During the same visit, he spoke strongly of his readiness, and even of his desire, to depart. He viewed death with tranquillity, and hope, and preparation, for it was habitual with him.

What need I say more? At midnight the summons came, — and his work was done.

The vacancy caused by such a death is wide, and cannot be filled. It cannot be filled to affection, to friendship, to those who were cheered and strengthened by his sympathy and aid. If it can possibly be filled to this College, it cannot be to some of us. It is not now a branch from the old oak that is rent away; itself is laid low, and those upon whose heads the sun of trouble "beats heavy," can no more find shelter under its broad branches. The vacancy cannot be filled; but his name will stand high among the benefactors of the race, and his example and influence will live through all time.

The sphere of Mr. Lawrence and his line of life were different from those contemplated by the most of us. But success in life, in all departments, depends on the same general qualities; and in these, as I have now spoken of them, he may well be an example to us. Especially would I ask you to go back to that period when he was of the age of many of you, and when, as he uniformly said, the foundation of his prosperity was laid. Of this he had then no distinct foresight; but when the lines of life that seemed almost parallel had diverged widely, he could see it, and could say, as he did, "*The difference between doing exactly right and a little wrong, makes all the difference between success and failure in life.*" Oftener than young men suppose, when they know it not, their destiny is sealed by the processes and decisions of their own minds before they are twenty. How great and precious the results of such a life! How different from those of a different course! How striking that such consequences should depend on what was passing in the mind of a lad in a country store! Who can estimate the capabilities wrapped up in any such lad? Who, especially, can say of any one of you, what may be depending upon the course that he shall take from this time onward? I feel, my friends, that this will take hold, not on time only, but on eternity; and I entreat you to be wise.

Let me add a single word on the position of young men in our Colleges whose facilities of education are thus furnished by a spirit of self-sacrifice, and enlightened patriotism, and Christian benevolence. It cannot be, my friends, that you are under no obligation to regard the spirit in which these are given, and to do your part in securing the results contemplated. Of this young men are too often reckless. They sometimes think that they pay for their education. No one pays for it. If paid for in money, few could afford it; but for the sacrifices that have been made, and are making, in this cause, money cannot pay. There is in them a spirit of love that contemplates high results, intellectual, moral, spiritual; that yearns for these, and can be satisfied with nothing less. Such results must be realized in our institutions, or they are a failure. Who, and what, then, is the young man, indolent, self-indulgent, profane, vicious, who can enter such an enclosure, and exhale an influence of disaster and of moral death? Only in and through you, my friends, with your intelligent and voluntary coöperation, can the results thus sought be secured. Who, then, will not work together with these noble benefactors? Who will not be a co-worker with God?

God's Provisions and Man's Perversions.

A

DISCOURSE,

DELIVERED BEFORE THE

CONGREGATIONAL LIBRARY ASSOCIATION,

IN THE

TREMONT TEMPLE, BOSTON,

MAY 29, 1855.

BY MARK HOPKINS, D. D.
President of Williams College.

BOSTON:
PRESS OF T. R. MARVIN, 42 CONGRESS STREET.
1855.

NOTE.

It has been suggested that the following Discourse might have a controversial aspect. In yielding it for publication, the author would say that he has never been a controversialist, and does not intend to be. He desires to guard himself, and, if possible, others, against the common weakness and wickedness by which Christians are alienated in their feelings as they approximate each other in their views. What they need to contend against is not so much Popery, as that in man from which Popery springs; and if controversy respecting minor points could be conducted in the light of this higher truth, its bitterness would cease. We should not then see Englishmen and Frenchmen uniting for a common object, and Christians contending with each other. It would then be easy for those mutually conceding to each other the essentials of Christianity, to discuss modes and forms in the kindest spirit. God has made great and common provisions, and we simply inquire by what modes, under these, of government and training, the greatest intelligence, efficiency and piety of all the members of a church may be produced. Our view is, that the highest training can be had only through freedom and responsibility; that if men are to be trained for freedom they must have freedom; if for responsibility, that it must be laid upon them; and that with Christian men at least, this may be safely done. They "are called unto liberty." They are best governed by principles, rather than by rules and forms. It is not controversy, but the establishment of this great principle, that we seek.

WILLIAMS COLLEGE, JULY 23, 1855.

Entered according to Act of Congress, in the year 1855, by T. R. MARVIN, in the Clerk's Office of the District Court of the District of Massachusetts.

DISCOURSE.

To secure the well-being of man, is the great practical problem of life; and we are met to-day, Fathers and Brethren, because we believe that the principles which bind us together, are intimately connected with that well-being. For this, in all its forms, physical and mental, individual and social, temporal and eternal, God has provided the materials and the conditions. In doing this, as in creating the earth and the heavens, and in moving the planets in their orbits, he has asked of us neither counsel nor aid. So, in the solitude of his own resistless and unmodified agency, does he often work, but not so does he consummate his purpose of securing human well-being. Having provided the materials and conditions, for their adjustment and application, he waits for the free and intelligent coöperation of man; and without this, the end cannot be reached. It is at this point that man may become an intelligent co-worker with God. This he can do, either as he comprehends, and so adopts, the plans of God; or as he exercises a rational faith, where he cannot comprehend; and the capacity thus to work with God, is his highest distinction, and thus to work is his *only* wisdom.

There can be no well-being except through the materials furnished, and the conditions appointed by God, and when these are adjusted in accordance with the nature of any being, he will enjoy all the good of which he is capable. The ephemeris that is born into the right adjustment of light and warmth, and sports its day, has all the well-being it can have. The measure of its moments and of its capacities is full. Throughout the creation of God, materials and conditions of good are set over against capacities. He creates no want which may not be met, capacity which may not be filled. If there be failure, it is not in his provision, but commences with the agency of the creature in securing the materials provided by him, and in conforming to his conditions.

Like all other well-being, that of man must result from a normal activity. This may be, either of susceptibilities excited by an appropriate stimulus, or of powers acting upon an appropriate object; and when every susceptibility is thus awakened, and every power thus goes forth, each observing its own time and measure, then does man reach all the good of which he is capable. Such essential stimulus and object, as of light to the eye, and God for the soul, must be distinguished from mere instrumentalities and means, which are to be valued only as they place man more readily and fully in the right relation to these; and it is from the failure to make this distinction, that we have latitudinarianism on the one hand, and bigotry on the other. He who is indifferent to essential elements, who believes that we can see by darkness as well as by light, is a latitudinarian; and he who believes that no light is fit to see by that has not been refracted through his prism, is a bigot. Certain conditions must be complied with, or there will be no well-being; but yet the system under which we are, is, in this respect, one of great flexibility and leniency. Perfect health can be insured only by a perfect conformity to organic law; and still there may be devised, under that law, different combinations of food, and systems of regimen, that shall be equally good; while tolerable health is compatible with even a wide range of partial and temporary violation of law. It would be difficult to say, either what a perfect system of tillage is, or what it would produce; and yet a very poor form of it may prevent starvation. In these, and all similar cases, provisions are made and conditions established by God; and the benefits received will be in proportion to our application of the provisions, and compliance with the conditions.

The materials which God has provided for the physical well-being of man, are light, warmth, air, water, and food. Not one of these can be spared, for no one can there be a substitute. It is upon an interaction between these and the vital powers, that physical well-being depends; and the object is, so to adjust them, that this interaction may best take place. But what a field does this open for human industry and skill! What is the larger part of the labor and the movement of life,—its tillage, its building, its dress, its commerce, its travel, but attempts either to procure or to adjust the light and warmth and air and water and food, which God gives? Having health, only the right application of these is needed to preserve it; and when it is impaired, much may be done through these for its restoration. Here there is room for every variety of opinion respecting climate and exposure, ventilation and dietetics; and perhaps it can be said of no one system, that it is absolutely the best. The materials appointed by God we must have; but whether our houses shall be warmed by wood or coal, by furnaces or fire-places; whether we shall have our water from aqueducts, or cisterns, or wells; whether our light shall come through a plain window, or a bow-window, through one that is square, or one that is pointed, matters little. Even light through painted glass may be pleasing to the children, and do very well to see by. Only let the materials provided by God be used, and it is of little moment what contrivances we may adopt in their application.

To secure the intellectual activity of man, and so his well-being intellectually, God has surrounded him by objects of a structure the most beautiful, and varied, and complex, and wonderful; and has placed him in the midst of a succession of orderly, and yet ever-varying changes, that bear upon his well-being, and can scarcely fail to quicken his investigations into causes, and structures, and processes, and results.

And here again the mind is benefited, not directly by means—as schools, and colleges, and teachers; but only as it is brought into direct contact with the materials provided by God, and tries its strength upon the questions involved in the structures and processes of this amazing scene of things.

The neglect and perversion by man, of God's provisions for his physical and mental well-being—his gluttony and drunkenness; his voluntary ignorance and error, need no illustration.

For the social, and civil, and religious well-being of man, besides the teachings of natural religion, God has ordained in his Word three institutions, in signal accordance with our constitution and wants. These are Marriage, Civil Government, and the Church. As God gave them, they are perfectly adapted to man. They are not, indeed, like air and food, the very things by which we live; but they are, in some form, the indispensable channels of those things upon which our spiritual nature does immediately fix and depend. Only in and through them can we have, first, the joys of domestic life, and families trained up for society and for God; secondly, security in the enjoyment of all rights, and the best sphere and training for action; and thirdly, conformity to God, and fitness for heaven. These are the ends; and here, too, to them should all forms be subordinated. The institutions are from God, but all of them may have different forms, which here become, not merely forms, but methods of reaching the ends just mentioned; and it is this question of methods, under the name of forms, that is now deeply agitating the world. Of these, all are not equally adapted to our nature. Those originally instituted by God, are so adapted in the highest and best sense. They furnish the least possible occasion and excitement for evil passions; they open to all the widest sphere of activity and of responsibility; and their whole tendency is, to elevate the individual and the species in the highest degree. But when man lost sympathy with God, and sought to work out, through his institutions, as through his natural gifts, ends different from those proposed by him, it became necessary to change the original forms for those which could be more readily and efficiently wielded by selfishness and passion. Thus have arisen systems, adapted to our nature indeed, and with consummate skill, but only as they have encouraged and given scope to the evil passions of men, and have addressed themselves to their fears and weaknesses; systems which have perpetuated themselves, not by the elevation, but by the degradation of the people. They claim to be either identical, or substantially the same with the original institutions; but they have been so changed, and so adapted to other ends, that it is as if a ploughshare, which is *substantially* the same as a sword, should be gradually beaten into that, and should claim, all through the process, and at the end of it, to be a ploughshare still.

Now in respect to these changes and perversions, we hold that all the provisions made by God, and especially the three great institutions mentioned above, have had an analogous history. Selfishness and passion would naturally work alike through them all. In each, we say, that God has either established or indicated the general form which he prefers; and that it may be shown by an examination of our nature, and of the past—by philosophy and by history—that if the full benefit of the institutions is to be reached, we must adopt, not only them, but the general forms in which they were given; or, which is the same thing, those which are best adapted to the nature of man. These points, particularly the analogy of their history, we now propose to consider.

The object of Marriage, as has been said, is to secure domestic happiness, and the right nurture and training of children for society and for heaven. Doubtless, also, it was intended to be an emblem of the spiritual union between God and his people under the old dispensation, and of Christ and his church under the new. As originally instituted, it consisted in the union of one man with one woman for life, without the power of divorce, except for one cause. In this form, and prompted by affection, it could not well be perverted to the purposes of lust and avarice, but was perfectly adapted to promote the highest and purest earthly happiness. So would the earth be most rapidly replenished; so would instinct and passion be most ennobled by a union with affection; so, having the whole care of both parents, would families be best provided for and trained; so would the example of parents incite children to a similar union, and symbolize one still higher. The institution was from Heaven, its spirit was that of Heaven, it tended to Heaven. After the introduction of sin, it was indeed impossible that all the benefits originally intended to flow from the institution should be enjoyed; but it was still an institution of God, calculated in its form to counteract the spirit of selfishness and unkindness and passion, and to remain the source of the best earthly happiness left us by the fall.

But this institution, in the form which God gave it, man would not retain. How soon he departed from it we do not know; but very early, and in its place, he substituted polygamy, and the power of divorce by the husband almost at will. And so far was the original spirit of the institution lost, even among the Israelites, that its announcement by Christ in its strictness, was received by his disciples with the greatest surprise, and with the strange assertion that it would be better to have nothing to do with marriage, than to be under such restrictions. For ages, God had permitted, as he still permits, his own institution to be thus perverted, because of the hardness of men's hearts. Rather than put an end to human probation, he chose to give a wide range to passion and selfishness, and to suffer them to work out, in some measure, their results. In the mean time God had always had a witness in the higher instincts and better promptings of at least a portion of the race; and through these, and the authority of Christ, the institution has been preserved in the earth.

Respecting the conflict between marriage as God gave it, on the one hand, and polygamy and those forms of licentiousness by which its spirit is repudiated, on the other, we can enter upon no details. We can only observe in general,

1. That the institution, as God gave it, has been rejected by the majority of the race. Learned writers have shown that polygamy was allowed, not only among the Hebrews, but also among all the ancient nations. It is now allowed in all Mohammedan, and in most, if not all heathen countries, to say nothing of a portion of our own; and it is well known that in some countries where marriage is sanctioned by law, faithfulness to its obligations has been the exception, rather than the rule.

2. But we remark secondly, that the tendency to evade the true spirit of God's institution, has been especially strong among the great, the wealthy, and the fashionable. These classes have seemed to claim a particular dispensation to disregard this institution. In general, heathen and Mohammedan kings and rulers, nobles and men of high standing, have had wives limited in number only by their

ability to support them; and in Christian countries, the tendency in this direction, of a court and an aristocracy, of wealth and fashion, is but too well known.

3. Polygamy can plead a high antiquity, and the example of men distinguished for piety. The teachings of our Saviour respecting marriage and divorce, plainly imply the condemnation of polygamy; but so ancient was it then, so had it been practiced by the Jewish Fathers, even by Abraham himself; so had it become incorporated into the habits of thought and action among the Jews, that nothing but divine authority could, in that day, have withstood the force of such examples, and of the argument from the antiquity of the institution.

4. As marriage places a restraint upon the passions and the selfishness of men, its adherents have always been, if not persecuted, yet ridiculed, by those who discard it, as over-strict and puritanical, as behind the age and wanting in large and liberal views. Marriage claims to be a divine institution; a true regard to it involves the recognition of a divine, invisible and holy superintendence, and it is this which has always met with the most decided hostility of a portion of the race.

5. History condemns polygamy. This shows that while there may be a measure of domestic happiness and national prosperity in connection with polygamy, yet that it is incompatible with the full blessings of domestic life for the married pair, with the best nurture and training of children, and with the high and permanent prosperity of a state. It must make the rich voluptuaries, and deprive the poor of their rights; it must sell and degrade woman, and cause alienations of affection, and contentions in families, and the neglect of children. Wherever it has been established, there has been stealthy, if not visible decay; and as the institution of God has been more and more widely departed from, society has tended more and more to dissolution.

With these general considerations, we next proceed to consider Civil Government. This, irrespective of any particular form, springs so directly from the nature of man, and his necessary relations, that it is generally conceded to be from God. Its ends are security, scope, and training—the fullest security of all rights of person and property, the widest scope compatible with this, for all activity, and the training of the powers to submission to law on the one hand, and to self-respect on the other. Of these, security has been chiefly regarded, and has too often been attained by abridging the sphere of individual responsibility and activity; thus cramping energy, and repressing the growth and distorting the natural form of society.

That these ends may be best secured by a republican form of government—by free institutions fairly applying the principles of liberty and equality—need not be proved in this country and at this day. This, therefore, is the form, as we contend, indicated, if not instituted, by God; and while we concede that much of good may be enjoyed under other forms, we yet say that only through this can the three great ends just mentioned be fully attained.

That this is the form indicated by God, is evident, not from speculation merely, but from that form of government which he gave his own people, and from the circumstances attending their change of that form. As instituted by God, the government of the Israelites was a Commonwealth; and from their division into tribes, it bore, in some respects, a resemblance to that of these States. Though Moses was brought up in a court, he made no provision for monarchy, or for any permanent order of nobility. Joshua, after the conquest of Canaan, retired, as did Washington, to private life, with no attempt to secure for himself, or his descendants, hereditary advantages; and the nation, except as they were punished for their idolatry, prospered as a Commonwealth for more than four hundred years.

Some have said that this was a theocracy. But how was it a theocracy, more than any republican government must be? A republican government is not one of force. The moment it becomes so, though the form may remain, the spirit has departed. It implies principle, and a subjection to the rule of conscience and of God. God did, indeed, give the laws of the Jewish state; but the question about the form of a government, does not turn on the origin of the laws, as given directly by God, or indirectly through the people, but on the mode in which they are administered. God did not appear, in person, to administer these laws. He instituted a commonwealth, a republic, in distinction from a monarchy; its laws were formally adopted by the people,* and though requiring for its full success, as republics now do, a recognition of the supremacy of Jehovah, yet it was to be administered by men, precisely as governments are now.

But of this form, the Jews became weary, and asked Samuel to give them a king. They wished to be like the heathen around them. And here again, as in polygamy, God permitted them to try the experiment, because of the hardness of their hearts; but his expressions of displeasure, and his warnings of the consequences, were as full and explicit as we anywhere find against polygamy. It was regarded by God as a rejection of himself, and of the same character as the rebellions in the wilderness. "For they have not," said he to Samuel, "rejected thee, but they have rejected me, that I should not reign over them. According to all the works which they have done since the day that I brought them up out of Egypt, even unto this day, wherewith they have forsaken me, and served other gods, so do they also unto thee. Now therefore," that is, because of the hardness of their hearts, "hearken unto their voice: howbeit, yet protest solemnly unto them, and show them the manner of the king that shall reign over them." Then follows a statement of the results of

---

* Exodus xix. and xxiv.

such a change—of the concentration of power and wealth, of the heavy burdens of taxation, of the change of men and women from independence and freedom, to be the dependents and tools of power, and of the organization of standing armies to perpetuate that power; and they were told, "Ye shall cry out in that day because of your king, which ye shall have chosen you. And the Lord will not hear you in that day."* But though thus fully warned, "the people refused to obey the voice of Samuel, and they said, Nay, but we will have a king over us, that we also may be like all the nations." Could God have indicated more explicitly his view of the tendencies of monarchy, or his preference for free institutions?

But here, too, we observe, 1st, that those who have adhered to the form of Civil Government thus evidently preferred by God, have been in the minority. When the object came to be the selfish acquisition of power, without regard to the rights and best good of the people, it was to be expected that the forms best adapted to give free scope to their activity, in the pursuit of individual welfare, and to react favorably upon their whole spiritual life, as rational and free, would be superseded by those which, while they might confer security from others, should make the ruled the tools and the prey of the rulers. Selfishness operates uniformly, and the constant pressure of a corrupt tendency has been too powerful for the vigilance of principle; and thus the great mass of the race have been monarchists by interest, by principle, by habit, by association, or by necessity. Here, too, the higher instincts of humanity could never be wholly repressed. Always among the nobler races, there have been yearnings for liberty, and those who have been ready to lay down their lives for her sake.

2. Monarchy has been sustained by the wealth, and pomp, and fashion of the world. From its concentration of power, and consequently of wealth, from its control of

---

* 1 Samuel viii.

the labor and property of the masses, it could not fail to surround itself with all that is striking and magnificent in architecture, with all that is costly and splendid in dress and equipage, with all that is beautiful and exquisite in art. It has naturally established artificial points of etiquette, and entrenched itself within ceremonies and forms; it has addressed itself to the imaginations of the people by pomp and shows; it has set up the doctrine of a divine right, and maintained it by "the last argument of kings," thus claiming the sanction of God, and sometimes even divine worship. All this has gathered around it the talent of the country; has been connected, in the minds of the people, with the real blessings they have enjoyed in connection with it; has associated with the court and its usages, refinement, elegance, taste, fashion; and has created a thorough distaste for the natural plainness and simplicity of free institutions, and an aversion to them.

3. Monarchy can claim a high antiquity, and the support of illustrious men. It goes back to the time of Abraham, and aside from the Bible, it might not be possible to show that it was not the primitive form. So soon had the forms of freedom disappeared under the love of power and the general corruption.

4. Free institutions, those preferred by God, have been persecuted. The ends of polygamy do not require that it should persecute marriage, but monarchy forms to itself an interest distinct from that of the people; it becomes a permanent, embodied, self-perpetuating thing, with quick instincts for self-preservation, esteeming no crime so great as interference with itself, and utterly unscrupulous in its use of subtilty or force for the attainment of its ends. With such a separate interest, it naturally becomes a persecuting power. So has it ever been, and, where it can be, so is it now. It has driven freedom into the fastnesses of the mountains, into dens and caves, often leaving upon the earth scarcely a place for the sole of its foot; and

it was only by being removed across the ocean, and into the wilderness, that the germ of a great republic could be nursed into a strength that monarchy could not crush.

5. Free institutions are sustained, and monarchy is condemned, by history.

The Jews were prosperous, at times, under a monarchy; but the form of a government is one of those constant elements involving tendencies that will, sooner or later, become effect, and the general habits of the people, and the alternations inevitable where so much depends upon one man, show the disastrous tendency of the system. Under forms of its own choosing, the same amount of wickedness will work more effectively; and they went on, fluctuating, till they reached a point of corruption which God could not tolerate in his people, and till he gave them up to captivity. So only could he effectually teach them to renounce idolatry and monarchy. And as with polygamy, so has it been with monarchy everywhere. Everywhere under it have the masses been degraded; nowhere have security and an adequate sphere and right training been attained as they should have been. If the civilization has been high, it has been limited and partial. The people have not been educated. Security from outward foes they have had, but not from the exactions and oppressions of tyranny; and by being deprived of all participation in political affairs, they are excluded from a great and indispensable field for both training and action. A republican government is of itself a great school, and involves a training, and opens spheres for honorable ambition, unknown to a monarchy. There is in it a quickening power pervading the whole mass. Hence, imperfectly as the theory of a free government has been understood, the highest achievements in arts and in arms, in poetry and eloquence, the brightest spots in the history of the race, have been where there was the most freedom. And so it is now. Wherever monarchy now is, there is either an ignorance and degradation too deep to appreciate their own wretchedness, or an uneasiness and restlessness, from a deep consciousness of great and radical misadjustments in the arrangements of the social order.

We now come to the Church. Here we find the highest and most central interest of man, and hence that to which all others must ultimately be subservient—about which they must revolve. The object of the church is, to produce likeness to God, as he was manifested in Christ; thus originating and strengthening affinities which will insure peace on earth, and a holy and happy heaven. It is to give, not outward security, but inward peace; to furnish a sphere for spiritual activity, to train men for such activity here, and to fit them to dwell with God.

And here the analogy we would trace requires that we should consider both the old dispensation and the new, because the conflict under the old, chiefly respected the object of worship, and under the new, its forms.

Under the old dispensation, as always, God presented himself as the sole object of worship. But if men would reject the forms proposed by God, much more would they reject God himself; and, accordingly, they almost immediately lapsed into polytheism and idolatry. "When they knew God, they glorified him not as God." "They did not like to retain God in their knowledge." "Professing themselves to be wise, they became fools, and changed the glory of the uncorruptible God, into an image made like to corruptible man, and to birds, and to four-footed beasts and creeping things."

And here again, more emphatically than under the other heads, we observe, first, that the worshipers of the true God were greatly in the minority. With the exception of the children of Israel, the whole world fell away to polytheism and idolatry; and even the Israelites were retained in their allegiance to God, only by his constant and special interpositions. Such was at one time the apostasy of the ten tribes, that the prophet of God said, "I, even I only, am left."

2. Idolatry has been sustained by the wealth, and art, and pomp, and fashion of the world. Among most heathen nations it has been to illustrate and glorify their religion, that wealth has been poured out most freely, and that their highest forms of art, whether in architecture, sculpture, or painting, have been reached. What, but for their mythology, would have been the art of the Greeks?

3. Idolatry can claim a high antiquity and the support of illustrious men. Solomon was an idolater for a time. The heathen sages were idolaters. The Egyptians, the Assyrians, the Persians, the Greeks, the Romans, all the chief nations with their great men, were idolaters. And so great was the antiquity of their idolatry and so was it sustained, as now among the Hindoos, by a fabulous literature, that for thousands of years, it would have been impossible, except by divine revelation, to show that it was not the primitive form of belief and of worship.

4. The worshipers of the true God were persecuted. The various forms of false religion tolerated each other, but they were agreed in despising and persecuting the true worshipers. These were regarded as illiberal, intolerant, over-scrupulous, as behind the age and unfashionable. So was Elijah regarded at the court of Ahab, and they sought his life. These are the very men who "had trial of cruel mockings and scourgings, yea moreover of bonds and imprisonment: they were stoned, they were sawn asunder, were tempted, were slain with the sword." As idolatry always connected itself with the state, it could wield the civil power; and when it chose, want of conformity became rebellion, and prayer to God a capital offence.

5. Idolatry is condemned, and the true religion is sustained, by history. When men changed the object of

worship, they necessarily changed its forms. These were lowered and debased, and made subservient to the selfishness of the priests, and to the fanaticism and sensuality of the worshipers, till the character of the gods, and the forms of religion became the most dreadful source of corruption, and the most formidable obstacle to the progress of truth and of purity. ''The light that was in them became darkness, and how great was that darkness.' Man cannot be stationary. If not elevated, he will be debased. But he can be elevated only by communion with that which is above him; and when the true idea of God is lost, permanent progress is hopeless. The true ends of society never have been, and never can be reached under polytheism and idolatry. However imagination and poetry may gild certain forms of heathen mythology, it has yet been true of those who did not like to retain God in their knowledge, that he has given "them over to a reprobate mind, to do those things which are not convenient; being filled with all unrighteousness, fornication, wickedness, covetousness; full of envy, murder, debate, deceit, malignity; whisperers, backbiters, haters of God, despiteful, proud, boasters, inventors of evil things, disobedient to parents, without understanding, covenant breakers, without natural affection, implacable, unmerciful."

Till the coming of Christ, then, God had given men marriage, and they made it polygamy; he had given republicanism, and they made it monarchy; he had given the worship of the One Only Living and True God, and they had made it polytheism and idolatry. How wonderful his forbearance! How great the mystery that he should suffer his own institutions to be thus overborne and comparatively lost, and idols to be substituted for himself!

But when Christ came, he introduced a new dispensation and a radical change. Forms, as no longer typical, lost their importance. The new wine of his religion he would not put into those old bottles, the new cloth he would not join to the old garment. The middle wall of partition between Jew and Gentile was taken away, and a universal and spiritual religion, applicable to all times, and places, and persons, and sublimely simple in its forms, was introduced. In its spirit, as expressive of the principles of God's moral government, it was identical with the former dispensation; but in its universality, and indifference to forms, it was its opposite. All that was national, technical, local, formal, it rejected; all that was spiritual, holy, universal, it retained; and in this mingled uniformity and contrariety we see strong evidence that both were from God. It had nothing to do with building up hierarchies, or constructing organizations through which ambition and avarice might be gratified. It went to the individual; it knew no man except as a sinner; and, not by sacrifices, or penances, or works, but as a free gift through the one perfect Sacrifice, it offered deliverance from the dominion and the penalty of sin, a moral and vital union with God through Christ, and a consequent place as a child and subject in his one family and in his eternal kingdom. Making the law of God the rule, and Christ the model of life, it required love to him, and love to his followers for his sake; and having thus laid the basis of moral union and progress, it left men to the freeest activity of their own powers, and encouraged the largest individual responsibility as essential to the highest training of those powers. As it knew men before they became Christians only as sinners, so afterwards it knows them only as holding the same relation to God, and as equally bound to use all their faculties for him. All were received on the same conditions, bought with the same price, had been changed into the same likeness, had access to God in the same way, and were preparing for the same heaven. For such, the simplest possible rites were provided, to remind them of the sin from which they had been washed; of the sufferings by which they had been redeemed; and to give visibility to the church; pastors and teachers were given for their instruction and edification; and there was laid down a code of discipline, easy of application and wholly moral in its power. If the offending person would not hear his brother alone, or with one or two others, the church was to be told, and no provision was made for a further appeal. This was all. The ends for which the church was instituted required nothing more, and its unity was to be found, not in any external organization extending over different countries, or even over the same, but in the moral likeness of its members to each other, and in a common relation to Christ.

And must these forms and arrangements, so simple, so beautiful, so worthy of God and accordant with the character of Christ, so well adapted to promote the spirituality of the individual and the efficiency of the church, and through which her great primitive conquests were made—must these too be perverted? Must the last and greatest manifestation of the divine mercy be the occasion of the last and greatest exhibition of human perverseness and malignant ingenuity? So, if the old leaven of wickedness were not destroyed, we might anticipate that it would be; so prophecy foretold that it would be—the man of sin must be revealed; so all Protestants believe that it has been.

In this perversion we suppose the first step to have been a gradual distinction, unknown in the first century, between presbyters and bishops, and the growth, from that, of prelatical Episcopacy. When once there was a bishop, with a diocese, the same principle would require an archbishop; for as the world was then situated politically, who was to limit or define the diocese, or to settle the conflicting claims of bishops? And if pastors require an overseer, why not bishops? Then again the same reason that would require an archbishop, would require a supreme head, and thus the system naturally culminated in patriarchates and in popery. With the exception of these United States, where circumstances have hitherto rendered it impossible, the Episcopal system has everywhere protruded a supreme head. In the Church of England, that head is the reigning sovereign, whoever it may be, without regard to religious character, or the choice of the church—a monstrous anomaly which the Puseyites are right in attacking.

But the assumption by the bishops of the power originally belonging to the congregations, and then gradually of power over other bishops, was not the most important element in the corruption which inaugurated popery. That element lay in the attempt, nearly simultaneous, to clothe Christian teachers with the same prerogatives as the Jewish priesthood—to make them priests and sacrificial mediators. This gave to the churches altars, and to the officiating ministers vestments; it invested them with an awful sanctity, made them the objects of a superstitious veneration, and the sole medium through which grace and salvation could be imparted. This was an entire perversion of the original idea of Christianity; or rather, it was a change in its very substance, and the laying of another foundation. Here we find the true root of the papacy, of the clergy as a distinct order, of transmitted grace, and of an apostolical succession; and wherever this sacrificial element is, in connection with these claims, there is the man of sin, taking his seat in the temple of God. Of these elements, either would be pernicious by itself; but in combination, the priestly power wielding the civil, either directly or indirectly, they are at the basis of a double tyranny, the most awful this world has seen, and only the more awful as assuming to be the religion of the merciful Saviour. Most sad is it that such transcendent wickedness should be connected, and in the minds of many, identified with such a religion; but the best gifts of God can be perverted only by a hardening and searing process, more dreadful than any other. Those who fall from a great height, must sink to a corresponding depth.

And here we remark once more, that those who have adhered to the institutions of God, as he gave them, have been in the minority. We have, first, the Primitive Church for a hundred and fifty years or more; and when the struggle commenced which led to popish usurpations, we have the ancient Cathari, or Puritans, bearing singularly enough the same name that modern intolerance fixed on our Fathers as a reproach. Of these, the history is not known as it should be.* They not only rejected prelacy, but declined the offer of Constantine to be connected with the state. They were a numerous and powerful body, and had descendants and representatives throughout the dark ages, and till the Reformation. We have also the great majority of the Reformed Churches since the time of Luther; but the number of these is small, compared with the Coptic, and Nestorian, and Armenian, and Greek, and Papal, and English Churches.

We observe, secondly, that the prelatical system has been upheld by the wealth and art, and pomp and fashion of the world.

The religion of Christ is not cynical. It does not object to wealth, or to any thing beautiful in art, or elegant in fashion. It simply ignores them as aside from its great end.† Its sphere is far deeper, in that which is spiritual. It is emphatically the gospel to the poor. Its work is by the bed of sickness, and of death, in the hut of poverty, among the jungles of India and the snows of

---

* See an able article by Dr. Forsyth, in the "Literary and Theological Journal" for January, 1855.
† If the end of Christianity could be accomplished, the highest art and elegance would spring from it; but as a means of accomplishing that end it rejects everything not necessible to all. It is the knowledge of *Christ* that makes a man a Christian, and in him "are hid all the treasures of wisdom and knowledge."

Greenland, as well as in the palace. Wherever there is a conscience that is quickened, and the great question is asked, "What shall I do to be saved?" there is its peculiar sphere, and it utters its stern rebuke against any attempt to substitute the emotions awakened by art, for those that spring from an enlightened and quickened conscience. When one of the disciples would have awakened the admiration of the Saviour, for the beauties of architecture, and said to him, "Master, see what manner of stones, and what buildings are here!" the Master did not seize the occasion to discourse upon art, or to found a school of church architecture. He simply replied, "Seest thou these great buildings? there shall not be left one stone upon another that shall not be thrown down." It was upon a temple spiritual and imperishable that his eye was fixed, and the utterance of his religion everywhere is, "The things that are seen, are temporal; but the things that are not seen, are eternal."

But from its concentration of wealth and power, there is an inherent tendency in prelacy, precisely as in monarchy, to associate with itself wealth and art, and pomp and fashion. There is a tendency, illustrated by its whole history, to appeal to the sensuous, rather than to the spiritual part of our nature. It has deified art. It has thought architecture, and sculpture, and painting, requisites to the highest form of the worship of the One Only Living and True God. It has built vast cathedrals, meaningless and useless except as they sustain those two ideas subversive of all Christianity, sacrificial mediation, and auricular confession. It has prescribed ceremonies and vestments and processions, and made of these vital points. It has had its ritualism for the rich and refined, making it easy for them to stand equally well in the church and in the fashionable world; and in all countries except this, social discriminations have been made against those who would not conform; they have been put under the ban of fashion; and to those who would rise in family and fortune, other than religious reasons have been offered for worshiping with the establishment. The slightest knowledge of English literature and society shows us with what distaste and aversion Dissenters, and especially the Puritans, have been and still are regarded by a large set of sentimentalists in the English Church, and what an air of relative gentility they conceive that to be, in which they exist. Whether anything of all this has crossed the Atlantic, it is not for me to say.

But we observe, thirdly, that the prelatical system can claim a high antiquity and the support of illustrious men. Of the great and good men who have lived and labored under this system, particularly in the English Church, I yield to no one in my admiration. I honor them, and shall always be ready to express my indebtedness to them. On this point I am ready to concede all that can be asked; but even if they were as wise as Solomon, they might, like him, be led astray; and then there have always been those opposed to them quite as great and quite as good.

The main point here is antiquity, for we claim to be the true ancients. Recent research has thrown new light on the history of England, particularly of Cromwell and the Puritans; it has greatly changed ancient Roman history; and it has cast a broad light, which cannot now be obscured, upon the free and simple forms and spiritual worship of the primitive church. Here prelacy has made high claims, availing itself much of what are now clearly shown to be forgeries. In the language of Bunsen, "Between us and those fathers, empty phantoms have sprung up, darkening that primitive age."* But those phantoms have been laid; for he says again, "As regards those churches which insist upon hierarchical tradition, both as to dogma and authority, they acknowledge, and cannot help acknowledging, the paramount authority of

---

* Hippolytus, vol. iii. p. 8.

the first links in the chain of that historical development which they call tradition. The undeniable facts of that age accordingly witness against them, as much as they do in favor of a free Christianity."*

Again he says, "The hierarchical party, towards the end of the second century, used the captivating idea of the 'Catholic Church,' as a basis for the doctrine of spiritual absolutism, and foisted the doctrine into all the documents, fathering their unholy tenets upon the ancient bishops, with the same zeal and impudence as, in later times, the papists did in their decretals."†

For the original identity of bishops with presbyters or pastors; for their oversight of but a single church; for the equality of pastors, and of churches; and for their free and spiritual forms of worship, there is a mass of evidence, from the state of things then existing, from Scripture, from the Fathers, and from the researches of modern historians, such that, in its selection, one does not know where to begin or where to end.

To one acquainted with the materials of which Christian churches were composed, and their position in the first century, the supposition of anything like papal, or even episcopal forms of government, and especially of worship, seems preposterous. They had, and could have had no church-structures, no altars, no vestments, no rituals.

The original equality of bishops and presbyters is very evident, and is admitted by many Episcopalians. This is clear from the Scriptures. When Paul enumerated the gifts of the Saviour to the church, he mentioned apostles, prophets, evangelists, pastors and teachers, but not bishops. Indeed, it would appear from the address of Paul to the *elders* of the church at Ephesus, not only that elders and bishops are the same, but that so far from having the oversight of more churches than one, there were some-

---

* Hippolytus, vol. i. p. 307. † Ibid. vol. i. p. 101.

times more bishops than one over a single church,—for he says, "Take heed therefore unto yourselves, and to all the flock over whom the Holy Ghost hath made you Ἐπισκοπους bishops." The word had then acquired no specific meaning, and the same man might be a presbyter or elder, shepherd or pastor, and an overseer or bishop, as he was viewed in different relations. Clement, the most ancient of the apostolical fathers, uses the terms interchangeably. He "was not," says Riddle, an Episcopal church historian, "even aware of the distinction between bishops and presbyters—terms which, in fact, he uses as synonymous." Polycarp, in his epistle, speaks of presbyters, but does not even mention bishops. Irenæus speaks of the succession of the presbyters, and Jerome says they were originally the very same. "Our intention," says he, "is to show that among the ancients, presbyters and bishops were the very same. But that, by little and little, that the plants of dissension might be plucked up, the whole concern was devolved upon an individual."* At the Reformation, all the Reformed churches came on to the same ground, and renounced the principle of any divine right of Episcopal ordination. "The Smalcaldic Articles, in 1533, which strenuously assert the identity of bishops and presbyters, and their equality by divine right in the power of ordination, were signed by nearly eight thousand ministers, among whom were Luther, Melancthon, Bucer," &c.† About the same time, a declaration was made in England, that "in the New Testament, there is no mention of any degree and distinction of orders, but only of deacons or ministers, and of priests or bishops," and this was signed by thirty-seven distinguished civilians and divines, and by thirteen bishops, among whom were Archbishop Cranmer, and the

---

* See Coleman's "Primitive Church," p. 214, where the original is given, and much more to the same effect.

† Christian Spectator for 1830.

leaders of the Reformation. Cranmer says, expressly, "The bishops and priests were at one time, and were no two things, but both one office in the beginning of Christ's religion." In the English edition of Burnet, there are documents, *omitted in the American edition*, showing that this question was carefully considered in those times, and decided by a large majority with us. In these, the answers of individuals to this question is given, and Dr. Redman comes fully on to our ground, and says, that "the authority of preaching and ministering the sacraments is given immediately to the church, and the church may appoint ministers as is thought convenient."* It is historically certain that high-church principles can be traced back in the Church of England only to the last part of the reign of Elizabeth, when they began to be needed against the Puritans. Whitgift himself only wished they might be true, and even long after that, Stillingfleet says, "It is acknowledged by the stoutest champions of Episcopacy, before these late unhappy divisions, that ordination performed by presbyters, in case of necessity, is valid; which I have already shown doth evidently prove that Episcopal government is not founded on any unalterable divine right." Of Archbishop Leighton, Burnet says, "He did not think orders given without bishops were null and void," but "he thought every church might make such forms of ordination as they pleased."† That this general view was originally held by the English Church, both Hallam and Macaulay agree. Nor had the first Scottish bishops Episcopal ordination. "Bishop Andrews," says Burnet, "moved the ordaining them." "But that was overruled by King James, who thought it went too far towards the unchurching of all those who had no bishops among them." ‡

No less evident is it that a bishop had originally the

---

* Christian Spectator for 1830. † Burnet's Own Times, p. 140.
‡ Burnet's Own Times, p. 139.

oversight of but a single parish. Says Clarkson, an Episcopalian, " A bishop, in the best ages of Christianity, was no other than the pastor of a single church. A pastor of a single church is now as truly a bishop." Says Bunsen, " Every town, however small, was a bishopric."* But on this I cannot dwell. I will only add, as applicable to the present times on another account, one of the canons of the Ante-Nicene Church. " A bishop ought not to leave his own parish, and go to another, although the multitude should force him, unless some rational cause compelleth him.—But this he shall not try by himself, but after the judgment of many bishops, and after pressing supplications."†

On these and all the other points on which we are at issue with prelacy, we have with us the learning and thorough research of Germany. Neander, the first church historian of modern times, is with us. So is the Chevalier Bunsen, combining German learning with English good sense, in his great work " Hyppolitus," in which he edits a newly discovered work by Bishop Hyppolitus, and thoroughly discusses the whole subject. Nor is Bunsen merely a historian and a scholar. He is a profound thinker, a diplomatist, and man of the world. With us, too, are Moshiem, and Planck, and Böhmer; nor may I omit to mention the thorough and unanswerable works of our countrymen, Dr. Edward Beecher and Dr. Lyman Coleman, which ought to be in the library of every pastor.

We observe, fourthly, that those who have adhered to Christian institutions as God gave them, have been persecuted.

The primitive church was persecuted by both Jews and Gentiles till prelacy arose, and that has always been, where it could be, a persecuting power. It is so naturally, for the same reason that monarchy is. It forms to itself a paramount interest distinct from that of the church,

---

* Hyppolitus, vol. ii. p. 123.   † Ibid. vol. ii. p. 80.

sometimes so losing sight of the laity, that the clergy alone have been called the church. It is easy to see that precisely the same love of power, and distinction, and wealth, that would change a republic into a monarchy, would destroy the equality of the pastors, and the independence of churches; would change the character of original officers, as bishops, and create new ones unknown to the Scriptures, making its bishops as little like primitive bishops, as the patriarch of Constantinople is like the patriarch Abraham; and that all politicians, favoring monarchy, would also favor such a change. This would bring the institutions of the church and of the state into harmony, and enable the rulers, in both, to aid each other in attaining their personal ends; and when this is done, the results are to be looked for in the Inquisition, and St. Bartholomew's day. Then the two classes of powers can be fully exercised, which it has been seriously maintained were conferred upon Peter by the two commands—"Feed my sheep," and "Arise, Peter, slay and eat." It is really wonderful how few spots there have been on the earth where a free Christianity could be without some form of disability, without molestation and without fear. Nowhere has this been, where prelacy has been predominant, not even in England. Only by being driven across the ocean, and into the wilderness, could a free church, like a free State, have permission and scope to grow strong; and even here we are unchurched, and turned over to "uncovenanted mercies," and the determination to subvert our religious liberties is boldly avowed. Wherever, too, we would plant free churches in countries nominally Christian, we find the true idea of religious liberty, now the great want of the world, utterly unknown; and the most formidable obstacle in our way is persecution by prelacy, in some form, to the extent of its power.

We observe, fifthly, that a free Christianity is sustained, and prelacy is condemned by history.

This opens a wide field, but we have only to glance at the whole field of prelacy, at the Coptic, the Nestorian, the Armenian, the Greek, the Papal and the English Churches, to be satisfied on this point. With the exception of England, and of the Low Church there, the priesthood have every where become ambitious and corrupt, and the people ignorant, superstitious and degraded. It is sickening to read the accounts of the clergy in ancient times, after prelacy had come in, and when, from the wealth and power and distinction connected with it, every body was desirous of entering what then began to be called the priesthood. Says Gregory Nazianzen, in the fourth century, " I am worn out—with contending against the envy of the holy bishops; disturbing the public peace by their contentions, and subordinating the Christian faith to their own private interests." " If I must write the whole truth, I am determined to absent myself from all assemblies of the bishops; for I have never seen a happy result of any councils, nor any that did not occasion an increase of evils, rather than a reformation of them, by reason of these pertinacious contentions, and this vehement thirst for power, such as no words can express."* Still later, Jerome says, " The bishops, by their pride and their base deeds, are a reproach to their name, and whenever they perceive one to have gained an influence by rightly handling the word of God, they seek, by detraction, to oppose him."† When Leighton entered the Episcopal Church, after finding out the men with whom he had become associated, he said, " that how fully soever he was satisfied in his own mind as to Episcopacy, yet it seemed that God was against them, and that they were not like to be the men that should build up his church, so that struggling about it seemed to him like a fighting

---

* Coleman's " Primitive Church," p. 280.   † Ibid. p. 302.

against God. He who had the greatest hand in it, proceeded with so much dissimulation, and the rest of the order were so mean and so selfish."* And so under this false system, it has very generally been, down to the card-playing, wine-drinking, fox-hunting incumbents and recumbents of the English Establishment. There is no sadder chapter in the history of our race, than this fearful perversion of Christianity, and the wide-spread moral and spiritual paralysis consequent upon it. England excepted, there is not a church that has been under prelacy, that is not in need of Christian missions, and to which we are not sending them.

And how has it been with the English Church? Of all the Protestant churches, she is the only one that has retained prelacy; for though the Lutherans have bishops, as the Methodists have, yet they are not prelatical, not a separate order, not by divine right, or apostolical succession. Nor were they originally so in England. There was at first a strong sympathy with other Protestant churches, and foreign churches were recognized as in the fullest sense churches of Christ. "Foreign divines," among them John Knox, " were invited by Cranmer from abroad to aid in the Reformation, and were instantly employed in clerical duties, without one hint of re-ordination;" and it was enacted by Parliament, "that the ordination of foreign churches should be held valid, and that those who had no other orders should be of like capacity with others, to enjoy any place of ministry in England."†
But by that *facilis ascensus*, which has always shown itself in connection with prelacy, high-church principles came in, and what has been the result? According to Hallam, the clergy studiously inculcated, in the reign of Charles I, "that resistance to the commands of rulers was, in every conceivable instance, a heinous sin."‡ In the

---

* Burnet's Own Times, p. 141. † Christian Spectator for 1830.
‡ Const. Hist. vol. i. p. 264.

language of Macaulay, the church became "the servile handmaid of monarchy, the steady enemy of public liberty. The divine right of kings, and the duty of passively obeying all their commands, were her favorite tenets. She held them firmly through times of oppression, persecution and licentiousness, while law was trampled down; while judgment was perverted; while the people were eaten as though they were bread."* She persecuted to imprisonment, exile and death, the Puritans and the Covenanters; she arraigned Baxter, and imprisoned Bunyan; she opposed the Christian Sabbath, which England now owes to the Puritans; she opposed the spiritual reformation, made necessary by her own supineness, under Wesley and Whitefield. Endowed as she has been, she has done next to nothing for the education and elevation of the masses; and while she had originally all England, and while there has been so much to make Dissent discreditable and uncomfortable, yet more than half of the people of England have left her, and are Dissenters to-day. And while many have gone off by Dissent, by the natural tendency of high-churchism, many have recently gone back to Rome, and more ought to go. Making, then, every allowance for the great good contained in the Church of England, and done by her, may we not say that prelacy, even there, is a failure?

But of the Church of England, and of the Episcopal Church in this country, it is difficult to speak without putting ourselves in a false position, because they really contain two denominations, differing more from each other than we do from one of them. With the Church of England, as it was at first, and for many years, when the Lord bishop of Derby could say in a public discourse, " The Gallican, Belgic, Helvetian and German churches reject not us, nor we them, although we differ in rites and discipline;" when he could say further, " For my part,

---

* Miscellanies, vol. i. p. 293.

I freely profess that were my lot cast among any of the Reformed churches beyond the seas, I would presently join in their communion, and not at all scruple to conform myself to their received customs"*—what probably no bishop, even in this country, would now dare to say—with such a church, recognizing other churches, and laboring with them, we would not contend. With such men as Newton, and Scott, and Simeon, and Wilberforce; as Bedell and Milnor, and some of honored name now living among us; with our low-church brethren generally, if they could but stay where they are, we would not contend. They are our personal friends. We honor and love them, and all the more because they seem to be falling into that honored minority in which we have always been. But against the spirit of high-churchism, in whatever form, involving as it does the essence of superstition, bigotry and oppression, we feel bound to contend. Social experiments require centuries, and we cannot afford, the world cannot afford, to try this over again. Our souls have still in remembrance "the wormwood and the gall." Still, the world is what it always has been. No man who has watched the progress of high-churchism in this country need ask how it arose at first.† With the exception, perhaps, of Mormonism, the progress of nothing has been more striking; and such is its adaptation at once to indolence and ambition, to formalism and fanaticism, that we are to be surprised at nothing, and that only the grace of God can save us.

Turn we then to our own simple, scriptural institu-

---

* Hopkins on the Ten Commandments, Ser. 2.

† "It is well known," says Dr. Coleman, "that the introduction of Episcopacy into this country gave rise to a long and bitter controversy. The objection from within the Episcopal churches, as well as from without, was, that its form of government was anti-republican, and opposed to the spirit of our free institutions. The House of Burgesses, in Virginia, composed chiefly of Episcopalians, declared their abhorrence of bishops, unless at the distance of three thousand miles, and denounced 'the plan of introducing them, in the most unexceptionable form, on this side of the Atlantic, as a pernicious project.' Such was Episcopacy after the Revolution, and high churchism did not exist."—*Primitive Church*, p. 261.

tions, adapted in the best sense to the nature of man. And in doing this we recur to the principles stated at the opening of this discussion, and placing ourselves above all forms, and looking only at ends, we recognize Christ as all and in all; and wherever he is found, through whatever forms, there we give our hands and our hearts. We recognize the adaptive and plastic power of the Christian, as of the natural life, and its capability of showing itself with equal beauty under forms that are different. We say that in the application of general principles here, precisely as in regard to health and intellectual well-being, there may be modifications that shall be equally good. Exclude the sacrificial and hierarchical elements, let there be equality of rank among the clergy, let the substantial power and the responsibility rest with the congregations, as with those who are all called to be kings and priests unto God, and we are content. Then, in all things indifferent, as architecture, liturgies, responses, robes, we concede the largest liberty. Those whom our Saviour sent forth to preach were not, indeed, permitted to have two coats, and we do not see that it follows that preachers now should be required to have two robes, or that a Christian teacher should change his garments during service, because the Jewish priest, who slew animals, changed his; but if any prefer this, we only say, " Let all things be done to edification." We admit, too, the paramount importance of a right spirit in the administration of any forms; and that they must be adapted to the capacities and moral state of the people. Still, the form will react upon the spirit, the method will modify the results. As man now is, his character will be formed more by his temptations than his duties, and that must be the best system which will present the fewest temptations to those who have the control, and the most responsibilities to those who have not. If then there are forms, which God has indicated and recognized, it may be expected that the church, as a whole, will be benefited in proportion as she shall conform herself to them, and that only through them her highest efficiency will be reached. That there are such forms, we believe; and what they are, ought to be investigated in the freeest and broadest spirit, without personality, or sectarianism, and in every light of Scripture, of analogy, of history, and of philosophy. Such investigation we invite. Omitting, then, the scriptural argument, not drawing sharp lines, not claiming perfection for our own system, cordially receiving brethren of other names who are really one with us in spirit, with whom we have labored, and love to labor, and mean to labor,—we say that Congregationalism is analogous to the freedom of the winds and the waves, and to all free institutions. We say that she is the mother and model of those institutions; for as Bunsen says, " These Christians belonged to no state, but their father-land in heaven was to them a reality; and the love of the brethren in truth, and not in words, made the Christian congregation the foreshadowing of a Christian commonwealth, and a model for all ages to come."

Her history, to say nothing of primitive times, shows a general intelligence, a love of liberty and of the Bible, a readiness to make sacrifices for education and for missions, a purity and fidelity of the clergy, and an efficiency and unsectarianism of the laity, that have never been surpassed. *She has labored for Christianity, and not for herself*, and far, far be the day when she shall lose her unsectarian spirit. With her originated common schools; with her, foreign missions in England, for the Baptists are Congregationalists; with her, both foreign and domestic missions in this country.

If we apply the test of philosophy, we shall find that she adopts, more fully than any others, *that great principle of individual responsibility, and so of intelligent liberty, on which the hope of the world now rests.*

She bases the security of all upon the culture of all. Thus we rest on a great principle, and this is our strength. Slowly, but surely, it will upheave the nations. We shall find that she is adapted to man, as man, precisely as is republicanism, whether he may live at the North or at the South, at the East or at the *West*. If people are too ignorant to understand their relations, or to assume responsibility; if they are too worldly, or too fashionable, to care for the church; if they wish for an order of men to take care of their religion, and of the interests of Christ in the world, while they are willing to pay for it; then, and then only is Congregationalism not adapted to them. We shall find, and that I did hope to show, that the wit of man cannot devise a system that shall contain fewer elements that would foster *ambition*, or *sectarianism*, or *formalism*, or *superstition*. *It does present the fewest temptations to the clergy, and lays the most responsibility on the laity.*

And finally, we find in Congregationalism the best, if not the only ground of that unity, of which the Bible speaks, and for which the heart yearns—" That they all may be one." Other churches, with centralized forms of government, tend to break into sects; they must have different centres, and jurisdictions, and names; and there can be no unity except, as in the papal church, under one head. But Congregational churches pass over all state limits as water, and would be as little divided by them; and if they could cover the earth, recognizing each other as brethren, Christ as their common head, and heaven as their common home, there would be a unity, perfect and sublime, as of the ocean. Then, when the waters were at rest, would the whole earth reflect the image of Heaven, and when they should be heaved and tossed by holy emotion, 'the sea would roar and the fullness thereof, the world and they that dwell therein.—The floods would clap their hands.'

THE PROMISE TO ABRAHAM.

A

MISSIONARY SERMON.

BY

MARK HOPKINS, D. D.
President of Williams College.

BOSTON:
PRESS OF T. R. MARVIN & SON, 42 CONGRESS STREET.
1858.

NOTE.—The substance of the following Discourse was delivered at Bangor, Maine, in August last, at the ordination of the Rev. E. P. ROBERTS, as a Missionary to Micronesia. It has since been repeated here, and elsewhere—recently at the Missionary Convention held at Pittsfield—and is now published at the request of the MILLS THEOLOGICAL SOCIETY, with the hope that it may strengthen the faith of the friends of missions.

WILLIAMS COLLEGE, JAN. 1, 1858.

SERMON.

ROMANS iv. 13.

FOR THE PROMISE, THAT HE SHOULD BE THE HEIR OF THE WORLD, WAS NOT TO ABRAHAM, OR TO HIS SEED, THROUGH THE LAW, BUT THROUGH THE RIGHTEOUSNESS OF FAITH.

In the passage now read from the word of God, we have, First, the fact that it entered into the original conception of the religion of the Bible, that it should be universal. The promise to Abraham was, that he should be "the heir of the *world*."

We have, Secondly, the grand characteristic, from the first, of the religion of the Bible, and that by which it is fitted to become universal. Abraham was to be the heir of the world *through the righteousness of faith*.

We have, Thirdly, the ground on which the people of God have expected, and do expect, that this religion will become universal. The *promise* was to Abraham.

And we have, Fourthly, as implied in the last, the principle of action which must sustain those who labor to make this religion universal—*faith* in the promise. These points we now propose to consider.

We say then, First, that it entered into the original conception of the religion of the Bible, that it should become universal.

As it is the object of Christianity, and especially of the missionary work, to establish a universal religion, it becomes us to inquire into the origin and history of this idea.

Ideas giving impulse and direction to human thought and effort, may either originate with God, or with man. The idea of the law of gravitation did not originate with Newton. It had been operative in the works of God thousands of years before he was born, and was as really expressed in the movements of those works, as a thought is expressed in a sentence. It lay behind those movements, as the thought behind a sentence; was presupposed by them, was their upholding and informing principle. And so we say that the idea of a universal religion originated with God, was communicated by him to man, and is, to Him, like the law of the planetary motions, one of those great ideas, in accordance with which, and for the realization of which He works. True, this idea may spring at once from a correct conception of the attributes and claims of the true God, and so, when once made known, commends itself to our reason; still, as man was situated, we say it could have come only from God.

It was more than four hundred years after the flood, when the promise referred to in the text, that all the families of the earth should be blessed in him, was made to Abraham. The race had been dispersed over the earth, had been divided into different tribes, with different languages, and idolatry in various forms had become nearly or quite universal. With idolatry is naturally connected the idea of local divinities, and the impression, still prevalent among the heathen, that each religion is good, and the best for its own locality. The earth had not been explored. Nothing was known of its form, or of its extent; nothing of the capabilities of the race for extension, or for various forms of culture and organization. The tendency then was, not to centralization any where, but to wider dispersions, the reach of which no man could foresee, and which might be so wide as to sunder permanently, as they did for ages, the relations of different parts of the race. There was no writing then, no printing, no system of roads or of intercommunication. The race was not only idolatrous, but nomadic and predatory. It was a great thing for Abraham to go out from his kindred and his father's house, to a land which he knew not of; and nothing but the special protection of God could have prevented him from being plundered and slain. War, indeed, not for the purpose of union, but of plunder and subjection, seems to have been then, as it was subsequently, the great business and ground of distinction among men.

Under such circumstances, the suggestion that a universal religion either was then, or ever could become possible, would seem entirely aside from the laws of human thought. It was no light thing thus to claim to know the future for all time; and to recognize the highest and only true bond of unity for the race; and to conceive that that unity might be realized, and to utter this with the simplicity and majesty and unfaltering certainty which we find only in the Scriptures.

And then, if the suggestion were made, it would seem still farther aside from the laws of human motive and effort, that any man should deny himself, and labor for such an end. Aside from the religion of the Bible, such a person as a Christian Missionary could not be conceived of. No motive, merely human, could call men off from their apathy, their toil, their sensuality, their ambition, and lead them to such labors as would be requisite to establish a religion that could become universal. No, my friends, it was not for man, thus situated, to originate an idea so far-reaching and comprehensive, so exciting and elevating, so alien from all that was, and so consonant with all that ought to be, as that of one, true, exclusive, universal religion. It was not for any one individual, especially one who had none of the ordinary grounds of distinction, who built no city, founded no state, conquered no country, wrote no book, who was a wanderer dwelling in tents, to conceive of himself as holding such a relation to all nations, that they should be blessed in him; and the fact that this was foretold of such an individual nearly four thousand years ago, and that it has come to pass to such an extent, is conclusive proof that the Bible is from God, and that the promise will be completely fulfilled.

But strong as this proof is, it becomes more so when we look at the history of this idea. It had no gradual growth, was from no tendency of society, or progress of the mind; but appeared in its completeness, like an apparition from heaven. Like such an apparition, it appeared for a moment, and then departed.

And not only did it thus appear and depart, but it appeared in combination with an idea that seemed its opposite, and departed leaving that idea wholly dominant. The chief marvel connected with this promise is, not its universality simply, but its combination of universality with exclusiveness. The covenant was with Abraham, and its immediate effect was, not to unite him with others, but to separate him from them, even from his kindred and his father's house. This separation continued while he lived, during the lives of the patriarchs, and became still more exclusive under the Mosaic dispensation, one great object of which was to separate the Jews from other nations. Here was a seeming inconsistency, which could have proceeded only on the deepest knowledge of what the completed circle of God's providence would be. It was like Columbus seeking the Indies by sailing in an opposite direction. It was like the change of the egg into a grub, when the promise had been that it should be a butterfly. There was doubtless provision for a three-fold development, as there is in insect life for a three-fold organization; but this was utterly beyond the reach of human ken, and could as little have been foretold by man without experience, as the changes in the insect.

And indeed, when we look at these three-fold organizations of insect life, each preceding one, so slowly and strangely preparatory, so identical, and yet so diverse; when we see it, now creeping upon the earth, now enclosed in its web, and now floating in freedom and beauty in the upper air; and then look at the Patriarchal dispensation passing into the Mosaic; at the Mosaic enclosing itself within its web of rites and ceremonies; and then, at the expansion and glory and universality of the Christian dispensation, it is difficult not to feel that the one is related to the other, though it be but as the slightest sketch of a great master to his masterpiece. May not this be? Is it too much to believe that He who forms in the dew-drop the image of the sun, who has established corresponding ratios of distance between the leaves of the plant and the orbits of the planets, should thus show, as in a glass, through the structure and changes of that which is lowest and most transient in his works, something of the march and glory of that which is highest and most permanent?

But however this may be, the promise was made, not only with no apparent provision for its fulfillment, but in connection with an arrangement by which, in all human probability, it must have been counter-worked.

Originating thus high up upon the hoary peaks of time, and in combination with an element apparently its opposite, this idea, this element of universality, just showed itself, and then, like water that finds a subterranean channel, it disappeared. From that time till the coming of Christ, there was nothing in the history of the world to indicate that such an element existed. There was nothing to show any tendency towards universality. Every thing indicated the reverse. Compared with the nations around them, the people of God were generally a small people, and their system of polity was neither attractive nor aggressive. In the course of events, there was no breath, no token, no movement, to indicate any such principle; and yet we find it bursting up in prophecy, along the track of time, like fountains in the desert, and so as to show a divine and irrepressible force.

And the striking point here, one affording conclusive proof of the truth of the Bible, is that the utterances and overflowings of prophecy became more distinct and full, as the prospect of their fulfillment, on the grounds of experience and probability, became more and more dark. It was when the idolatries of the heathen had become multiplied and confirmed, when the glory of Israel had declined, and the nation was ready to go into captivity, or had already gone, that we find the utterances of her poets and prophets most fully inspired with this idea. With great variety of expression, and with unmistakable clearness, they foretell a time when wars shall cease, and the peaceable kingdom of Immanuel shall be every where established. "Nation," say they, "shall not lift up sword against nation." "The idols He shall utterly abolish." "The mountain of the Lord's house shall be established in the top of the mountains, and all nations shall flow unto it." "The kingdom, and dominion, and the greatness of the kingdom under the whole heaven, shall be given to the people of the saints of the Most High." "The earth shall be filled with the knowledge of the glory of the Lord, as the waters cover the sea." "From the rising of the sun, even unto the going down of the same, my name shall be great among the Gentiles; and in *every place* incense shall be offered unto my name and a pure offering."

The next point to be noticed in the history of this idea, is the place it occupies in the Christian dispensation. And here the marvel is not less, and wholly unaccountable except on the supposition that Christ was what he claimed to be. Like that of the being of a God, this is one of those ideas which the Saviour did not so much formally announce, as take for granted. He assumed it as entering into his religion, as a matter of course, and in this there was unspeakable grandeur. He said, "I am the light of the *world*." "The field is the world." He commanded his disciples to "go into all the world, and preach the gospel to every creature."

Here we find this idea appearing at the opening of the new dispensation, as it had before at that of the old; but whereas it was then a prophecy, it was now a *purpose*. The transition from a mere thought, a conception, an imagination, to a purpose, is a great one; and, in comparing the old dispensation with the new, it is here that we find one of the great points both of identity and of transition. The underlying conception in the old dispensation was an ultimate universality. That was really its glory, and it was only by the adoption of that as an object and a purpose, that the religion of Christ could become the fulfillment, the antitype, the expansion, the transfiguration of the old dispensation. Accordingly we behold Christ—doubtless the one solitary person of the race who had ever cherished, or even formed such a purpose—taking the ancient promise, eliminating its really great element and placing that in front, and then saying to the world, "I am not come to destroy the law and the prophets, but to fulfill." So doing, he became the central point towards which all in the past that belonged to the old covenant converged, and from which all in the great future must radiate and expand. As he alone gave to the law its spiritual interpretation, so did he alone give to the promise its true expansion. If, then, Christ was not from God, how unaccountable in him the idea even of a universal religion! How much more so that he should quietly, and as it were unconsciously, assume it as a part of his system! How much more still, that in him, in him alone, it should become a purpose! And most of all, that he should announce that this purpose would be accomplished by his own crucifixion! "And I, if I be lifted up, will draw all men unto me."

In the history of this idea, but one step remains. Receiving it from Christ now in the form of a purpose, the disciples, immediately after his resurrection, commenced their labors for its realization. Then was seen the true spirit of Christian missionaries; a spirit of self-denial and faith, which, if it could return into the church, would soon cause the gospel to be preached in every nation under heaven. Then every church was of course a missionary society, and every church member held himself ready to serve the church, and the great Head of the church, wherever he might be called.

But those days passed away. The spirit of worldliness and of self-aggrandizement stole in. The man of sin began to assert his supremacy, and the night of the dark ages set in. The Reformation was a great work; but, as its name imports, it was a work within the church, and it was not till recent times that she began again to feel the inspiration of this great purpose. But now the apathy of ages is broken. The church begins to remember that she is the heir of the *world*; the voice of the ancient promise rises and swells upon her ear; it seems like a new revelation, and she feels that it is time to arise and take possession of the promised inheritance. It is almost within our own day, that "the angel having the everlasting gospel to preach to every nation, and kindred, and tongue, and people," has renewed his flight; and we trust that flight shall not cease till there shall be heard in heaven those great voices saying, "The kingdoms of this world are become the kingdoms of our Lord and of his Christ, and he shall reign forever and ever."

Such is a slight sketch of the origin and progress of that great idea which was involved in the promise made to Abraham.

Let us now consider, Secondly, as indicated in the text, that grand characteristic of the religion of the Bible by which it is fitted to become universal. Abraham was to be the heir of the world *through the righteousness of faith.*

And here it is certainly remarkable, that in that transaction with the father of the faithful, in which the old dispensation commenced, there should be found, in such close connection with that idea of universality which was to be the consummation of the religion, the peculiarity by which that religion should be distinguished from all others, and should be fitted to become universal. The promise to Abraham was, that he should be the heir of the world, and it was *the very believing of this that was counted to him for righteousness.* So says the Apostle. " Abraham believed God, and it was counted to him for righteousness." In believing this, he believed in a Saviour to come, and so he became the heir of the world, "not through the law, but through the righteousness of faith."

The term "righteousness," is here used by the Apostle to signify a mode of justification. Ordinarily, " the righteousness of God " would indicate a personal quality in him ; but as used in this Epistle, it indicates the method which he has adopted of constituting and declaring his people righteous; that is, the justification which is of God. Thus in the third chapter, 21st and 22d verses, "But now, the righteousness of God without the law is manifested, being witnessed by the law and the prophets ; even the righteousness of God which is by faith of Jesus Christ unto all and upon all that believe." Certainly, God has no personal righteousness "without the law," or, " which is by faith of Jesus Christ."

Here then we have, brought face to face in the text, the only two modes of justification before God, that are possible ; and we are told that the religion for man—for the race—is not to be through the law, or any of its works, but through the righteousness of faith ; that is, that it is to be a justification wholly free and gratuitous. " It is of faith, that it might be by grace." This it is that makes the gospel to be what it is—the evangel, the good tidings, a proclamation of mercy and of free salvation. This is the central evangelical element. It presupposes the claims of Law, else there could be no salvation. It presupposes the Atonement, "that God might be just, while he justifies the ungodly;" but the salvation itself is wholly free. There is no condition even, but that of acceptance. Repentance and faith are sometimes said to be conditions; but in this it is forgotten that holiness itself is essentially the salvation, and that repentance and faith are but the forms in which holiness must necessarily begin. They are the acceptance.

That this characteristic of justification by faith, that is, of a free salvation, fits the religion to become universal, is plain, because it recognizes man simply as a sinner. It knows nothing of him in any other relation; nothing of age, or sex, or rank, or wealth, or knowledge, or country, or color, or race. There is here, "neither Greek nor Jew, circumcision nor uncircumcision, barbarian, Scythian, bond nor free, but Christ is all, and in all." "In Jesus Christ, neither circumcision availeth any thing, nor uncircumcision, but *faith* that worketh by love." Wherever, therefore, there is a human being who knows that he is a sinner, and desires to be delivered from the power and curse of sin, there this doctrine will be welcome. O, how welcome! It is no system of metaphysics, or of dogmas; it is a proclamation; it is good tidings; it is rest to the weary, peace to the tempest-tossed; it is forgiveness and free salvation.

Here the gospel is broadly distinguished from all mere systems of development, and training, and culture, which require time and a system of appliances. And this distinction is so vital that it was signalized by our Saviour in the salvation of the thief on the cross. Both the thieves reviled him, but one of them had but to turn upon him the eye of faith and say, "Lord, remember me when thou comest into thy kingdom," and instantly the reply was, "To-day thou shalt be with me in paradise." All his relations and prospects were changed in a moment. Hence the gospel may be carried at once to the ignorant, the degraded, the abandoned. Clothed with supernatural power, there is no depth of degradation or extremity of suffering which it cannot reach. To the hut of poverty, it bears a wealth which the world cannot give; to the dungeon of the captive, the liberty wherewith Christ makes men free; and, though rejected till then, yet, in the hour of sickness and death, it can gild the pallid countenance with the light of hope, and the radiance of a celestial joy.

But not merely because it regards man solely as a sinner, and makes salvation a gift, does this principle of justification by faith adapt Christianity to become universal. It thus adapts it because it is as simple as one of the great laws of nature, and is yet as complex in its relations, and as pervading in its results, as are those laws. How simple it is! Only to believe! And yet it will adjust rightly all the relations of man to God, to himself, and to society.

Without faith in God, man is alienated from him, and can neither love nor obey him. With it, the filial relation is restored. This involves a recognition of the paramount claims of God; it involves ultimate heirship, and all essential good.

Without this faith, man rests upon his native goodness and on his works, and thus is fostered *pride*, that primal sin of the spirit, not only in its relations to God, but to itself. But this doctrine strikes at the root of all pride. It leaves man, in respect to salvation, no ground of his own, not the least self-righteousness, and this brings him to the foot of the cross. It is when he feels his own utter destitution, and only then, that he will come and ask at the hand of mercy, free and sovereign, what he needs. This is submission; and when the pride that struggled against this departs, then comes in *peace*, and a cheerful obedience, born of gratitude and love.

But in thus adjusting the relations of man to God and to himself, those of society will be adjusted also. A true religion must include a perfect morality. Self-adjustment implies it. But justification by faith has a special relation to those pervading and unutterable evils in society, which spring from superstition and formalism. These it would sweep utterly away. They always imply works as opposed to faith, and not works from faith. They imply something outward, done on the supposition that it will avail to some extent as the ground of salvation. Of these, especially of the spirit of formalism, how full is the whole world! How full especially of superstition, are the papal and heathen worlds! How appalling the power which these give to man over the conscience of his fellow ; and through this, how mighty the support they have lent to systems of civil oppression ! They have sat as an incubus upon the nations. They have converted the very church and temple of God into a den of thieves and the stronghold of tyranny. But when this has been done, the simple sling and stone by which these giants have been slain, is the doctrine of justification by faith. It was the proclamation of this by Luther, that caused the knees of the papacy to smite together ; and now, there is no doctrine so hated by Rome, and by all who tend thitherward. This is the doctrine that Rome really combats at every point, that heathenism and tyranny every where combat, because this alone brings all men into immediate relation to Christ as the sole Head of the Church, and so, dispenses with all those forms and intermediate agencies through which they have been degraded and oppressed. Before this, would vanish at once the confessional, and indulgences, and penances, and pilgrimages, and masses, and prayers for the dead, and prayers to saints, and mawkish mixtures of modern sentimentalism and mediæval superstitions ;—all the modifications of superstition, in short, whether in the heathen, or the nominally Christian world ; and in place of these there would come the simple worship of God in spirit and in truth, and "the unity of the spirit in the bond of peace."

This, then, is the doctrine for man as a sinner. It is for all, and to be received by all in precisely the same way. It is for the king, for without it he must become poorer and more powerless than the lowest of his subjects who receive it ; it is for the scholar and the philosopher, for without it they have no light that will not go out in the darkness of the tomb ; and this too is the doctrine for the poor benighted heathen, for he too is a man and a sinner.

But while we say that there is thus an adaptation and a tendency in the religion of the Bible to become universal, we yet say that this has not been, and is not now, the ground on which the people of God expect that it will become so. That ground, as is stated in our Third proposition, which we now proceed to consider, is the promise of God. "The *promise* was to Abraham."

In reasoning from adaptations and tendencies, we must regard, not those only, but also obstacles and opposing influences. There is in the seed a tendency to grow, but this may be so checked and thwarted by an adverse soil and climate, that no one would predict of the plant, that it would ever reach its full size, or, perhaps, even maintain a feeble and sickly life. So with the religion of the Bible. Till the time of Christ, neither its adaptation nor tendency to become universal could have been perceived ; and since then, such have been its reverses and perversions, for long periods, that no human sagacity could have predicted its ultimate triumph. Missionary zeal has not been stimulated by a philosophical perception of adaptations and tendencies. There never has been a time when, on grounds of mere reason, and without reference to supernatural agency, it would have been rational to predict even the continuance of a pure Christianity. It would not be rational to predict it now. We hear much, indeed, at present, of civilization and commerce; of science and the arts; of ocean steamers and ocean telegraphs; and it is thought, by some, that these herald and will secure the progress of Christianity. These we would not undervalue. They are the indirect product of Christianity, but there is in them literally nothing to move it forward. They may be as the wheels upon which it shall move, but even then it will be only as the "spirit of the living creature is in the wheels." Let the vitalizing force of Christianity be withdrawn from society, and the car of civilization will be unfastened from its engine, and will come to a stop. But Christianity itself has moved on by a divine energy; it has advanced against all calculations of probabilities, and only by conflict. Its life has been through death. That life has been in God, and from God. It must be so still, and He only can assure us of its continuance, or predict its range.

The future can be known by us only in two ways—either from the experience of the past, or from the promise or prediction of one who has it under his control. These grounds are quite distinct, and may seem, and be, opposed to each other. The prediction of a final conflagration and general judgment, is in opposition to all experience. In such cases, there is a conflict between the evidence for the permanence of the present system and the truth of the promise. This has sometimes been called a conflict between reason and faith, but is really only a question for reason, of evidence and of fact; and it is not difficult to show, on grounds of reason, that confidence in the word of a moral being who can control the future, must be a firmer basis of belief than any experience of the past can be. Only admit that there is a God, and that this universe is controlled for moral ends, as it must be if he be God, and it will be seen at once, from the very nature of the element of experience, that it must be as nothing when opposed to the word of God, and that there can, therefore, be no conflict between faith and reason, respecting any of the great facts of the future, revealed in the Bible. What is it for a particular order in a material system to come to an end? Another, and a better order may succeed it; but if the truth of God fail, that is a subversion of all foundations, and an end of all order, physical and moral. Hence the promise of God is rationally the firmest ground on which confidence can rest; and it is precisely and only on this that we do rest in our belief that this world shall be given to Christ. *We believe the promise; and belief in a promise, from confidence in the promiser, is faith.*

This brings us to consider, finally, the principle of action which must sustain those, and especially missionaries, who labor to make this religion universal—Faith in the promise.

The labors and trials of the missionary are peculiar. This is not, as is often supposed, because he must leave friends and country, and break up cherished associations, and go and dwell among a strange, a heathen, and a degraded people. Others do this, and in great numbers, from the love of gain. His great trial is, when he has reached a heathen shore, in giving himself there, during the best years of his life, with no hope of any thing but a bare support, in singleness of heart, with earnestness, with diligence, with watchfulness and prayer, in the midst of apathy, ignorance, low vice, suspicion and opposition, to the work of enlightening and saving a people whom he knows only as the children of a common Father, and as those for whom Christ died. To do this, is not of nature unrenewed. It requires the support, not merely of a high aim, but of a divine principle; and such is faith.

Here faith is regarded not merely as a ground of belief, nor yet in its relations to a mode of justification by God, but as a principle of action. Being not simply belief, but confidence, and belief only from confidence, it takes hold of the emotive nature, and so may become a principle of action. Being confidence in *God*, it may become the strongest, the deepest, the most pervading, as well as the most rational principle by which we can be moved. This is needed, not by missionaries only. It has been, and is, distinctively, *the* religious principle—the source of strength and endurance to the whole church. This, as was just said, is a divine principle. It is apart from all others; it may be opposed to them. It does not judge by sense, or by past experience. Let its warrant be clear, and it knows nothing of difficulties or impossibilities. It says, "With God all things are possible." If called upon to step out of the ship into the water, it will step out. It believes in a God who is mightier than nature; and hence its range of expectation is not limited by nature, and it can believe in future events, and labor for future consummations, of which nature and experience can furnish no ground of expectation. Hence, too, to those who judge from nature and experience only, its projects must seem madness, its hope delusive, and its labors inexplicable. By those of them who condescend to notice it at all, it is looked upon with a pity, sometimes wondering, but oftener derisive. This antagonism has always existed, and always will. But faith holds on its way, and the mockers die, and the great plans of God, of which they never had even a glimpse, move on. This is no untried principle. At the opening of the old dispensation, in connection with the very promise referred to in the text, God purposely laid upon it a stress and a pressure that tested its power. "By faith, Abraham, when he was called to go out into a place which he should afterwards receive for an inheritance, obeyed, and he went out, not knowing whither he went." "By faith, when he was tried, he offered up Isaac, and he that had received the promises offered up his only begotten son, of whom it was said, that in Isaac shall thy seed be called." "He staggered not at the promise of God through unbelief, but was strong in faith, giving glory to God." "By faith," also, "Moses," the head of the Jewish dispensation, "esteemed the reproaches of Christ greater riches than the treasures of Egypt, and endured as seeing Him who is invisible." "By faith, the Israelites passed through the Red Sea;" by faith the ancient worthies performed their wonders. Nor has this principle lost its power under the new dispensation. It supported the Apostles as it did Abraham. It sustained the martyrs. It carried Luther to the Diet of Worms. It led our Pilgrim Fathers across the ocean; and when modern missionaries have gone out, like Abraham, into some place which the church should afterwards receive for an inheritance, not knowing whither they went, they have gone by faith. And so they go now, thus honoring the Lord Jesus, and giving the best possible testimony to the value of that salvation which he came to bring. No, this principle has not lost its power; it never can lose it while God lives, and man is his child.

Having thus considered the points proposed, I ask you to notice their remarkable combination in the text. We have here, not only the promise of a universal religion, so wonderful; and its freeness by which it is fitted to become universal, not less wonderful; and the promise as the sole basis of our expectation, putting this religion wholly aside from nature and above it; but in our labors to make this religion universal, we have the impulse and strength of that very confidence by which the promise was originally accepted, and by which we ourselves accepted of a free salvation.

From this subject I observe, first, that the object of the missionary is the noblest that can call forth the energies of man. Some labor solely for pay. These are hirelings. Some, again, labor from the inspiration of the idea they would realize. It is in them as a fire in their bones, and if it be a moral one, they are moulded into its image. Such are artists, patriots, philanthropists, heroes; and of the kind of inspiration that is in all these, there can be no more perfect example than the true missionary. His object is wider in its range, and more beneficial in its results, than any other. Men labor for civil liberty and human rights, but a thorough religious revolution and renovation would involve such individual, as well as social and civil changes, as would secure all the rights and the highest well-being of man. Let there but be the spiritual regeneration of all into the image of one who represents a perfect manhood; let there be the mutual attractions which must flow from such a similarity; let there be the subjection of all to the same moral laws, and the union of all in love to the same common Saviour, and the best purposes of all revolutions would be reached. Society would be moulded into the image of heaven.

We see, in the second place, that the missionary work is not chimerical, and the certainty of the ultimate triumph of the religion of the Bible.

This idea of a universal religion, as we have seen, originated with God; its realization was foretold by his prophets in the darkest hours; it was adopted by the Saviour; was made by him a purpose and a command; and we have reason to believe, from the movements of Providence, and from the fact that the religious nature is central in man, that this is the central idea in the administration of the world. Nothing short of this has ever been proposed by the church of Christ; and now, when she is awake to it as but once before, how grandly does the voice of the old promise, that has bided its time for four thousand years, mingle itself with the expectations and hopes of an awakening race, with the portents of change, and with those movements of Providence which have been of late, and are now as the sound of a going in the tops of the mulberry trees.

Only when the time is ripe, do great events spring from little causes. It is but fifty-one years ago, that a few young men knelt in prayer for the heathen, beside a haystack. As their prayers ceased, the sun, which had been hidden by a passing storm, shone forth, and the bow of promise spanned the eastern sky. It was the token of God upon the cloud. From that day to this, his smile has rested on the cause. It is less than fifty years since the American Board, of which that meeting was the germ, was formed, and now it may be said of its missionary stations, as has been said of the military posts of Great Britain, that the sun never sets upon them. As he rises in the farthest East, he beholds them, first, in China, then in India, then in Persia, then in the Turkish empire, then in Western Africa, then among the Indians on this continent, then in the Sandwich Islands, and then in Micronesia; thus belting the globe. Not by the drum-beat, calling to arms, are his morning beams welcomed at all these stations; but by the voice of prayer, and the proclamation of "peace on earth, good-will to men." Every where those walls of exclusion which, fifty years ago, rose to the very heavens, are prostrate. Every where there is a feeling of unrest, and of indefinite yearning, and the moral and social elements of a world wait the plastic hand of a pure Christianity. The period of those dispersions by which relations were sundered, is now past. The divergency was not, as it seemed, in straight lines, but upon a globe, and in a circle which now tends to its completion. The tendency to unity through science, the arts, and commerce, as well as through missionary labors, is not less remarkable than the original tendency to dispersion. The nations are fast nearing a point of intercommunication and reciprocal influence, where that which is effete must be swept away, and that which is artificial must be destroyed; and the feebler moral forces must give way before those which have an undying life from nature and from God. Towards this point there has been a tendency from the beginning. The movement has indeed been slow, and not such as man would have expected; but it has been analogous to the great movements of God in his providence and in his works. So, if we may credit the geologists, has this earth reached its present state. So have moved on the great empires. So retribution follows crime. So rise the tides. So grows the tree, with long intervals of repose and of apparent death. So comes on the spring, with battling elements and frequent reverses, with snow-banks and violets, and, if we had no experience, we might be doubtful what the end would be. But we know that back of all this, beyond these fluctuations, away in the serene heavens, the sun is moving steadily on; that these very agitations of the elements and seeming reverses, are not only the sign, but the *result* of his approach, and that the full warmth and radiance of the summer noontide are sure to come. So, O Divine Redeemer, Sun of Righteousness, come thou! So will He come. It may be through clouds and darkness and tempest; but the heaven where He is, is serene; He is "travelling in the greatness of his strength;" and as surely as the throne of God abides, we know He shall yet reach the height and splendor of the highest noon, and that the light of millennial glory shall flood the earth.

Who then is in sympathy with Christ? What are we willing to do to help forward this great cause?

RELIGIOUS TEACHING AND WORSHIP.

A

SERMON,

PREACHED AT THE

DEDICATION OF THE NEW CHAPEL,

CONNECTED WITH

WILLIAMS COLLEGE.

SEPT, 22, 1859.

BY MARK HOPKINS, D. D.
President of the College.

BOSTON:
PRESS OF T. R. MARVIN & SON, 42 CONGRESS STREET.
1859.

NOTE.

The views presented in this Discourse are in accordance with the views of the Trustees of the College, upon the importance of discussing the truths of revelation, as well as the principles of science.

The President was requested to preach the Dedication Sermon himself, and to make the religious teaching in the College the principal topic.

EMERSON DAVIS,
Chairman of Committee.

At a meeting of Graduates of the College, held in Alumni Hall immediately after the Dedication of the new Chapel, it was unanimously voted to request a copy of the Discourse, delivered on that occasion, for publication.

Entered according to Act of Congress, in the year 1859,
BY T. R. MARVIN,
In the Clerk's Office of the District Court of the District of Massachusetts.

SERMON.

MATTHEW vii. 25.

AND IT FELL NOT; FOR IT WAS FOUNDED UPON A ROCK.

A ROCK is the emblem of stability. The winds sweep over it; the waters glide past it; the sands shift around it; the tree by it grows and decays; the boy looks upon it, and passes into life, and fights its battles, and returns with white locks and a feeble step, and there it remains unchanged. Relatively to all things around it, it seems to be, and it is, stable. And yet, emblem though it be of stability, it is not itself really stable. It is not so in fact, or as related to forces that may act upon it. In common with the earth, of which it is a part, it has a motion far more rapid than a cannon ball, and there are known forces that can heave, and rend, and fuse every rock on the surface of the globe, or within its depths.

What, then, is that which is really stable, and of which a rock is the emblem? It is God, and his purposes. "He is the Rock," He only. With Him there is "no variableness, neither shadow of turning." He is "the same yesterday, to-day, and forever." All matter is fluent. So far as we know, or have reason to ieve, there is not a particle of it in the universe that is not in motion ; and aside from God, and independent of Him, it has no permanent existence. He created and upholds it, and it is entirely flexible and plastic in his hands ; while He abides forevermore. As saith the Scripture, "Of old hast thou laid the foundation of the earth; and the heavens are the work of thine hands. They shall perish, but thou shalt endure : yea, all of them shall wax old like a garment; as a vesture shalt thou change them, and they shall be changed : but thou art the same, and thy years shall have no end." "He is the Rock." He "only hath immortality," that is, hath within himself, and in virtue of his own original mode of being, a permanent, undecaying, and unchanging existence.

But the purposes of God are as unchangeable as his being. "He is in one mind, and who can turn him? and what his soul desireth, even that he doeth." "For I," says he, "am the Lord ; I change not." "His way is perfect," and therefore unchangeable ; but this is the result of his purposes. The reasons on which these are based, can never be seen in a new light, and so they cannot change. As the purposes of God grow out of his perfections, while those perfections abide, his purposes must abide also.

In these purposes of God, so far as we can ascertain them, we find a test of wisdom in all arrangements of men in their individual concerns, and in all founding and ordering of public institutions.

Whatever there is in the purposes and work of any of God's creatures, that coincides with his purposes and work, will be wrought into that structure which God is rearing, and will stand ; and whatever does not coincide with those purposes will not stand. It will be counterworked, will end in disaster, and be buried in oblivion. The works of man, originated in his own wisdom, and conducted for his own ends, may seem to prosper for a time. They may go up, as did the tower of Babel, but they shall not inherit the ages ; God will send confusion upon them, and they shall cease, and perish forever. He therefore, and he only, is wise, who intends to work, and does work, both in accordance with those purposes, and in furtherance of them.

It is true, indeed, that there is a sense in which all things are included in the divine purposes ; and to reconcile this with the free-agency and responsibility of man, has been the labor of many. This we shall not attempt here. For all practical purposes, the view of God and his government given in the parable of the tares, is the true one. The husbandman sowed wheat. It was his purpose to raise wheat. An enemy sowed tares. Here was something not at all so in accordance with his purpose as was the sowing of the wheat—something to be in some way counteracted. For a wise reason, he suffered the tares to grow with the wheat till the harvest. Then they were gathered together into bundles to be burned. So it is now. There is wheat, and there are tares ; they grow together. The purpose of God is the growth and harvesting of the wheat. In these he permits us to aid, and in this, and this only, is there wisdom. The wheat shall be gathered into the garner and be preserved; the tares shall be burned.

The purposes of God are indicated in the structure of his works; in his providence; and in his word; and these conspire in showing that man was made for religion. Aside from the word of God; aside from history, which is, or ought to be, but a record of his providence, and the philosophy of which will always show a religious purpose, there can be no fair analysis of man that will not give the religious powers as deeper and more radical than any others. It is not, therefore, more obvious that the eyes were made for seeing, or the feet for walking, than that God intended that the relation of man to himself, should be his great and central and all-harmonizing relation; and that man should know, and love, and worship, and obey Him. For these man has capacities, these are the highest uses to which those capacities can be put, and the highest use to which a capacity can be put, is always that for which God intended it. But to know, and love, and worship, and obey God, is to be religious. These are the whole of religion. We may, indeed, say that the whole of religion is to know and love God; but from these, worship and obedience emanate as light from the sun, and are so inseparable from them, that they may well be mentioned as its constituent parts.

We cannot then be mistaken in supposing that we are working in accordance with the purposes of

God, and with Him, in doing what we may to lead men to know, and love, and worship, and obey him. It is the business of education in its broadest sense, excluding all that is professional, and regarding man solely as man—that is, of a liberal, in distinction from a professional education—to form man to be all that God intended he should be; or, at least, to go as far towards this as is possible. If this work is beyond the reach of education alone, and the aids of his own Spirit and grace are needed for its accomplishment, then must we recognize the necessity of such aids, we must seek them, and work in harmony with them.

That this is the true view of education, seems self-evident when it is stated. It simply implies that God intended that man should be all he ought to be. It is only thus that man can work in harmony with God. Expressed in a different form, by those who do not care to recognize God, this is really at the basis of all those great changes and simplifications which have been made in the theory of government, in political economy, in the treatment of disease, and in vital and social problems generally, by the system of what is called "letting alone," or "trusting to nature;" implying that there are ends proposed in nature, and that towards those ends there are tendencies and movements which it is the great business of practical wisdom to recognize and aid. To deny that God has a purpose and agency in this matter, would be atheism. But if He has, and we cannot know what that purpose is, there can never be a perfect system of education. The formative agencies would be discrepant, and the result disastrous. But if we can know that it is the purpose of God to bring men, with faculties enlarged and trained, through the knowledge of himself, through love and worship and obedience, into conformity with himself, and so into right relations with all their fellow creatures, then we may be sure that any institution which shall really accomplish this, or aid in it, will be founded upon a rock, and will stand.

This general purpose we wish it to be the object of this College to promote. This is the grand, comprehensive, ultimate object at which we would aim. Nor, in our view of it, would this restrict at all the course of liberal study, but would rather enlarge it. We believe that all scientific knowledge, and all knowledge that ought to enter into a course of liberal study, has a tendency to lead men to God. Let the eye be but purged, and it will do this; and then, the relations of men to God being rightly adjusted, we believe that those of men to each other will fall into harmony of their own accord.

Of the four constituents of religion mentioned above, knowledge is a necessary condition, but may exist by itself without religion; while the other three are essential elements. Of these, love and obedience are wholly individual and personal. Being inward and spiritual, they must come from the affections and will of each individual by an act in which no one else can have any share, or, the conditions being given, can render any aid. In these indispensable, greatest, and most central elements of religion, each individual must be wholly by himself before God. But in gaining a knowledge of God and of religion, we may be aided by others; and worship may be social, and we may be aided in that. In short, in gaining knowledge, and in worship, we may make use of means, while love and obedience are simple acts that do not, strictly speaking, admit of means. Accordingly, provision can be made in our public institutions not strictly for religion in its essence, but only for teaching, and for worship; and the simple question is, what this provision shall be. And first, of teaching.

So far as teaching is concerned, this question has chief relation to revealed theology. In many, perhaps the most, of our higher institutions, some treatise on Natural Theology is studied. Often there is a lesson in the Greek Testament Monday morning, or in Biblical Geography. Perhaps the Evidences of Christianity are studied; but when the question is, whether the inquiry shall be raised in the class-room what Christianity is, and whether, in their connections with that, the highest and deepest questions which connect themselves with human life and God's government shall be there discussed, there is a difference of opinion.

Practically, there has been a great change on this point. Originally, education was almost wholly under the auspices of religion, and its institutions were founded chiefly for the purpose of raising up a learned as well as a godly ministry. Very different from the present, both in direct teaching, and in their modes of interpenetration, must have been the general relation of education and religion when such laws as the following, once those of Harvard College, could have been adopted.

"Every one shall consider the main end of his life and studies, to know God and Jesus Christ, which is eternal life."

"Seeing the Lord giveth wisdom, every one shall seriously, by prayer in secret, seek wisdom of Him."

"Every one shall so exercise himself in reading the Scriptures twice a day, that they be ready to give an account of their proficiency therein, both in theoretical observations of language, in logic, and in practical and spiritual truths, as their Tutor shall require, according to their several abilities respectively, seeing the entrance of the word giveth light," and when the only literary condition of receiving the first degree was that the scholar "is found able to read the original of the Old and New Testament into the Latin tongue, and to resolve them logically."*

Since that time the tendency has been to separate the teachings and discussions of the class-room from religion. This has arisen partly from the larger number of those having in view other callings than the ministry who have sought a liberal education, and from the feeling that young men generally could not be interested in the discussion of the higher questions of theology; partly from the great number of new and exciting subjects requiring to

---

* Quincy's History of Harvard College, pp. 515 and 517.

be taught; and partly from multiplied differences of religious opinion in the community, inducing a fear of the imputation of sectarianism. And this has gone on, till now, in the course of study published by some of our higher institutions, not a vestige of instruction distinctively religious is left.

In the latter part of the last century, the Westminster Catechism was studied in Yale College, and was transferred from there here; for eight out of thirteen of the first Trustees of this College were graduates of Yale. At what time it was discontinued there I do not know, but here it has remained, and has always furnished, and does now, the regular exercise for the Senior Class every Saturday forenoon. So far as I know, we are alone in retaining this, or any thing analogous, in the course of college instruction; and most persons are surprised when it is stated that it is so retained.

Are we then wrong? If not, by what principle are we to be guided?

It is now conceded, that a college course should have chief relation to man as man, and so is to be the common basis and preparation for all the professions. Theology may not, therefore, be studied in College professionally, but only as a part of a liberal education. May it be thus studied? We think it not only may, but ought to be. A liberal education, it will be remembered, is the training of man to be what God intended he should be. Unless this deep and serious view is retained, the business of education will degenerate into a mere trade. Men will cease to work with God and for Him, and will work for money. But aside from this view, in saying what we do, we do not place Theology on ground different from that of the other professions, or of the studies generally. No man has a culture truly liberal, who is not acquainted with the general principles, and great outlines, of all the departments of knowledge. Between these, and the knowledge needed by the professional man, the line is sufficiently distinct, and these it is the business of the college course to give. Thus we do not teach a man to be a physician, but we do teach Anatomy and Physiology—and these lie at the basis of medical practice—so far as to give a general knowledge of the human frame, of its place in the scale of God's works, and of the mode of preserving health. We do not teach men to be lawyers, but we do teach them the Constitution of the United States, giving them a knowledge of the institutions under which they live, and involving the general principles of law; and gladly would we have, as the Institution had in its early history, a course of Lectures on those principles, or have studied, as there formerly was, a book (Vattell) on the Law of Nations. We do not teach men to be engineers, but we teach them the Mathematics by which they may become so. We do not make men specialists, of any kind; but we teach the outlines, and general principles, which give comprehension and guidance in all specialties, and we see no good reason why religion should be an exception.

But while we see no good reason why religion

should be an exception, we see strong ones why it should not. Among these are the relation of religious truths to other truths; and to the human mind.

These, that is, religious truths, are the high table lands. Here arise the great rivers of thought and of influence. Here are the mysteries, and though we may not find the head of the Nile, yet hither must our explorations tend, and in this direction must our approximations be found. To deep thinkers, all other speculations, severed from those that are religious, must seem fragmentary and inadequate.

But it is chiefly from their relation to the human mind, as stimulating and formative, that religious truths are demanded as a part of a liberal education. If education is to be superficial, to consist of accomplishments, and information, and of what can be given by others, then these truths may be dispensed with. But if the human soul has capacities to be reverently approached and drawn out, and the best education is in that; if reflection is to be induced; if the problems of human destiny are to be wrestled with; if its latent powers and highest affinities are to be aroused; if the great deep of an immortal nature is to be stirred and heaved from centre to circumference, so that the deep that is in man shall call back to the infinite depths there are in the universe and in God; then we must have the power, quickening and formative, of religious truth. It is only heavenly bodies that these deep tidal waves obey. Men may refine, and file, and polish as they will; they may cry out Enthusiasm! Fanaticism! Nineteenth Century! to their heart's content; but if they construct a system of education that shall ignore the highest powers and the deepest wants of man, they may set themselves apart in their own niches, quiet it may be, and the forces and movements of society will rise and roar around them, and sweep by them, but with their origin or direction they will have little to do. What we wish is a system of education that shall first be true to our nature, and then in full and living sympathy with the times.

But can there be such teaching without fostering a spirit of sectarianism and of bigotry? If not, it ought not to be. Here, however, it must be observed, that sectarianism has more than one basis; and that the chief one is not doctrines, but rites, and forms, and modes of organization and government; and attention to these would not be required by the objects of a college course. It is in these latter that we find the whole difference and ground of separation between Congregationalists, Presbyterians, Episcopalians and Baptists. I say, the whole difference, because there is no doctrine, properly such, held by either as a test, which would exclude a man from any of the others. So far, then, there would be no objection.

But even if there be a difference in doctrine, it would be sad if a teacher may not so understand his position as to deal fairly with the human mind—if he may not introduce young men to subjects pertaining to God and immortality, and infinity, without being a partisan. Let perfect freedom of questioning and discussion be, as it always has been here, by me at least, not only conceded, but encouraged, and there will be little danger that young men, most of them past their majority, with good native powers and trained minds, will be unduly biased.

The truth is, that through revealed religion we best approach the deepest and most vital problems of life—those which belong to all ages and to men every where, whether Christian or heathen, and in the presence of which every thoughtful man must at some time stand. These problems revelation solves in its own way, and there is no higher task for reason than to find its own limits in connection with these problems, and to reconcile the solutions of revelation with its own independent laws and processes. In this, some diversity of views must be expected; but why should not the teacher and the pupil view Niagara together, and calculate its height, and the mass of its waters, though they may differ as to their source, or the origin of the precipice over which they fall? The interest and power of education must depend on the interest and power of the subjects with which it deals, and no man can feel greatly indebted to his education, or his teacher, who has not found some great want of his nature met, and received aid at the points of severest struggle. And is a liberal education to be deprived of its grandest inspiration, is its whole field to be swept of its mysteries and its sublimities, and left to utilities, so called, and to prettinesses, because of our distrust of each other, and especially because of the objections of those whose distrust of individual men is generally in proportion to their profession of belief in the goodness of the race? We trust not.

As has been said, this instruction was continued here in the form in which it was commenced. When it became my duty to enter upon it, it was with no little misgiving; but I now wish to add the testimony of experience to the views already expressed, and to say, that no study under my charge, and with one or two exceptions I have generally heard all those of the Senior year, has been attended to with an interest either as deep or as general as this. In proof of what is thus said, it may not be amiss for me to confirm the statement recently made, though by no agency of mine, in the public prints, that the classes have, not once, or twice, or thrice, but frequently, requested that they might have an hour and a half instead of an hour for this recitation. This, with any power of teaching I may possess, I will venture to say never could have occurred in any other study.

Thus encouraged, we hope that what has been, will continue to be. And we hope this the more, because, by the munificence and wise foresight of Mr. Jackson, a Professorship of Christian Theology has been recently established in this College. It was indeed the view of Mr. Jackson, that those who should desire to study Theology professionally, without going through the course prescribed by the Seminaries, should have the opportunity of doing so here. This opportunity will be given, as we may be able; but it was also with his full consent and concurrence, that the President was appointed on his foundation, and that its avails should go, in part, to sustain and extend the religious instruction already given in the College.

Thus, while we would welcome every new science, we would not discard the old; we would not, under the guise of progress and enlargement, bring in restriction and diminution; while we rejoice in the progress of physical investigation, while we are doing what we can, and mean to do much to enlarge our means of instruction in this direction, we would yet preserve the balance; we would not mar the circle; we do not believe that the votaries of physical science 'are the only people, and that wisdom would die with them;' and however high they may pile the mountains of their own department, we would say to them, and cause it to be felt, that "there be higher than they."

Having thus spoken of religious knowledge, which is the first great object to which this house is to be set apart, and which it represents, we now turn to the second, which is worship. This is higher than knowledge, because knowledge is for worship. Worship is no unmeaning form repeated by habit, and capable of coalescing with wickedness, or of being commuted for it; it is no blind or mystic impression of awe, engendered by superstition and heightened by craft; it is no mixture of religious emotions with those of art; but has its basis in a rational apprehension of the attributes of a personal, invisible, and holy God. It can be truly performed only by one who is in the image of God, both in nature and in character, and implies the highest possible recognition of his perfections and complacency in them. It is, therefore, the highest act of the creature; and the question is, What aid can be rendered in this act?

And here I observe, that the highest worship may exist with no external aid. The centre and essence of all worship implies a recognition of the personality and holiness of God; and in the discussion of this subject we are never to forget that without this there can be no worship. A pantheist cannot worship; and the moment there is a tendency towards pantheism, worship is enervated, and mysticism and sentimentalism set in. But this recognition of the personality and moral attributes of God must take place in the depths of the soul, and can have no relation to place, or to any qualities or combinations of matter. These, if attractive, as in the fine arts, may be unfavorable, and accordingly we find that private devotion, where every thing of this kind is excluded, is especially mentioned by Christ as acceptable to God. There is no higher worship than that which may be rendered by him who enters into his closet, and shuts the door.

But this, it will be said, is private worship, and we are speaking of that which is social and public. We say, then, that there may be the highest and best social and public worship—if there be but adequate means of expression—

without any thing addressed to the eye, or the taste, to produce an impression. If not, how ought we to pity the Christians of the first two centuries, who had no paintings, or sculpture, or architecture, or artistic music, to aid them in their worship? How should we pity the poor in their log cabins, refined and devoted though they may be, in their family devotions? How those whom, in all ages, persecution has driven into mountains and caves, whence their prayers and their songs have gone up? Is it not enough that man should reject and persecute them, but will God too avert, or half avert, his face, because they are poor and persecuted for his Name's sake? Nay, verily. If there is worship any where that is acceptable, if there is prayer any where that enters into the ears of the Lord of Sabaoth, it is from these. Strange indeed would it be, if He who waters the whole earth from the heavens, making no special conduit that he gives in charge to any, who causes the springs to burst forth from every hill-side, who hears the young ravens when they cry, who, though he dwells in the high and holy place, dwells also with him that is of a contrite and humble spirit, strange if He should find it necessary to wait for his childen to paint pictures, and carve statuary, and frame musical instruments, and build cathedrals, before he could dwell with them, or they could love and adore Him with the fullest acceptance.

But are there no aids to worship? Yes, precisely as there are to music, or rather to musical feeling; and they are social in the same way. For every thing emotional there are negative conditions that are not directly aids, yet indispensable. There must be nothing to distract the attention; and the mind must be in a right tone. These being given, emotion expressed by an individual will communicate itself to others; and the expression of it by a multitude will react upon the individual. In these two statements we have the whole philosophy of this subject. The influence is vital, and not mechanical. Life is from life; and all life is originally from the Living One. As fire kindles fire, as the musical power in another that is superior to ours quickens our power, as the volume of sound from many voices reacts upon us solely because there is in it music expressed, so do the superior devotion of another and the united devotions of many, and they only, quicken our devotion. It is worship expressed that aids worship, and nothing else.

On this whole subject of worship, as connected with the fine arts, entire coincidence of opinion and feeling are not to be expected. The slowness of man to apprehend God as a spirit; his aversion to his character as holy; the tendency to substitute æsthetical emotions for true worship; the disturbing, and often capricious influence of association and habit; and the complexity of those emotions which may be associated, perhaps blended, with a true worship, are such, that men will often mistake their own position and feelings, and misjudge those of others. Still, if a man say that he can worship God better by means of architecture, that is, of matter in the form of a building, he might well be asked how he would answer the man who should say that he could worship God better by means of matter in the form of an idol. Certain it is, if God is to be worshiped, that it must be in the apprehension of his own attributes; certain it is, that as our conceptions of Him as a person become more distinct; as the glories of his holiness and mercy are more revealed; as ideas distinctively Christian, such as repentance, faith, obedience and love, become more immanent and controlling, every thing pertaining to art must either wholly disappear, or dwindle more and more, till we reach that direct and pure worship of heaven in which it is more than intimated that no aid of this kind can come in. "And I saw," says John, "no temple therein; for the Lord God Almighty, and the Lamb, are the temple of it."

It is with views like these that we desire and propose, on this occasion, in the name of the Trustees and Faculty of the College, of the Alumni and Donors who have contributed to its erection, to dedicate this house to the service of Almighty God, to be used for religious teaching, with the fullest proclamation and encouragement of the right of private judgment; and for the worship of God in spirit and in truth.

The building to be thus set apart will be the third Chapel used by the College. The first was in the south end of the second and third stories of the West College. That was used till September 2d, 1828. At that time, the Chapel in the building opposite was dedicated. That building was erected through the extraordinary zeal and labors of Dr. Griffin. Besides the Chapel proper, it contained a room for a Library, for a Cabinet, for the Philosophical Apparatus, and for Lectures. Also the Conference Room, the Senior Recitation Room, a room for the Libraries of the Societies, and a Chemical Laboratory and Lecture Room ; and was supposed to contain provision for all the wants of the College in these departments for many years, if not for all time. But soon the Society Libraries outgrew their quarters ; then the Chemical department spread out into a wing ; then the place for the books of the College Library became too strait, and they migrated to Lawrence Hall; and under the command of Dr. Emmons, the older records of the creation wheeled into their places. Then the Seniors were obliged to swarm into the Conference Room, and the classes, at prayers, to scatter themselves, which was never anticipated, about the gallery of the Chapel, and finally, while other reasons conspired, it was seen that the increasing demands of Physical Science required that the whole of that building, the Conference Room excepted, should be given up for its illustration and cultivation. In thus deciding we have not felt that it would be turned aside from the general purpose for which it was erected, and we would now use the language of Dr. Griffin, respecting it, and say, "Let it be devoted to science as subservient to the Redeemer's kingdom."

This having been decided, through the zeal and

generosity, and, in many cases, I may say, the self-denial of the Alumni and other Friends of the College, this building arose. We are thankful for it, and for all there is in connection with it of architecture and of beauty. It was intended to have in it, and we think we have, as much of these as our means would allow. Would there were more. Because nature has done much for us, we would not do the less. We would rather seek to make what we do, respond to what she has done. We value architecture in connection with education. We would invoke the spirit of beauty in its every form. We think of that spirit as worthy of heaven; we believe she descended thence; but we remember that she has also been thrust down and debased even to hell. We simply wish to give everything its place. We do not think of architecture as a means, or direct aid of worship; nor of the spirit of beauty as the Spirit of God.

From the form of this building its parts have a relation that may be said to symbolize, not inaptly, the proper relation of ideas and ends in a College. In front, prominent and beautiful, is the Chapel, which represents the great ideas of religious instruction and worship. Separate from this, yet connected by the tower and spire, heaven-ward pointing for both, are the rooms for the instruction of the two upper classes; and over these, united with each and all, is the Alumni Hall. So, through worship and instruction, religious and secular, but both pointing to heaven, would we raise our Alumni to their own place, and send them thence into the world.

Of this whole building it may be said literally, that it is founded upon a Rock; for there was not a stone in its foundation, that did not reach the rock. In this respect, we trust and believe, that it is a symbol of the Institution itself. So the providence of God would seem to indicate, for the rains have descended, and the winds have blown, and beat upon it, but it still stands firmer than ever. And if those who shall control it shall but order it in accordance with the purposes of God, if they shall respect the great laws and wants of mind, as modified by the changes of society, we know that it shall be founded upon a rock, and shall not fall. So may it be. To this beautiful valley may young men, ingenuous and aspiring, continue to come. Here may there be known those joys of a student's life that leave no sting, and no stain. Here may health mantle the cheek; here strength and beauty blend in the character. Here, O here, may the Spirit of God descend, and the Saviour be found, and the love of self be overmastered, and Christians learn to "stand up for Jesus," and to stand by each other. Hence may all go forth well equipped for service in life; and especially, as heretofore, may *they* go, whose "feet shall be beautiful upon the mountains" of heathendom, who shall "publish salvation."

A

DISCOURSE,

COMMEMORATIVE OF

NATHAN JACKSON,

DELIVERED BY REQUEST OF THE STUDENTS,

IN THE

CHAPEL OF WILLIAMS COLLEGE,

MAY 17, 1863.

BY

MARK HOPKINS, D. D.
President of the College.

BOSTON:
PRESS OF T. R. MARVIN & SON, 42 CONGRESS STREET.
1863.

DISCOURSE.

PSALM xcii. 14.

THEY SHALL STILL BRING FORTH FRUIT IN OLD AGE.

In the passage now read, man is compared to a fruit-bearing tree; and what it is for him to bear fruit will be seen from the analogy here implied. A tree has two products — the leaves and the fruit; but these are of a different order, and stand in relations entirely different. The leaves are for the sake of the tree. They are its lungs. They absorb nutriment from the air; they draw up and elaborate its juices, and prepare the materials for its growth. But the fruit is not for the sake of the tree. It is wholly a gift of the organization to a system of things out of itself, beyond itself, and having no relation to its individual well-being. The object and end of the leaves is the well-being of the tree; the end of the tree itself, individually, and of the whole species as fruit-bearing, is the *fruit*, as a gift for the use of systems beyond itself.

In the same way, there are two forms and products of human action. There are those which have sole relation to self, as self, and not as a part of the general system; and there are those which have relation to a system entirely out of and beyond self. To his own well-being every man must have some regard, were it only that he may do good to others; but this regard and its results are not so much fruit-bearing, as a preparation for that; and if, as is often the case, the regards of a man do not extend beyond himself, he does not bear fruit at all. He is, according to the Scriptures, "an empty vine; he bringeth forth fruit unto himself."

That a man should bear fruit implies, then, that he should do something freely, intentionally, wholly, for the good, the enlightenment, the elevation of others. He who does this, bears fruit in the sense of the Scriptures; he who does not do this, does not bear fruit.

This distinction between the fruit and the leaves as of a different order, and so between the different kinds of action they represent, was expressly recognized and signalized by our Saviour in that act of his, so striking and significant, of cursing the barren fig-tree. That bore leaves only. That it bore leaves, was no objection to it. It was made for that. But it bore leaves *only*. It lived to itself, and so was cursed and withered away. In this act of our Saviour towards a thing unconscious and irresponsible, there was nothing splenetic or capricious; but he taught the universal and solemn lesson, that that thing or being in God's universe that does not bear fruit, that is, does not answer the end for which it was made, is accursed, and fit only to be destroyed.

Having thus seen what it is for a man to bear fruit, we next inquire who they are that do this. These, we are told in the context, are the righteous. The object of this Psalm is to contrast the righteous and the wicked, and the dealings of God with them, that his character as a righteous Moral Governor may be vindicated. The wicked, we are told, do not recognize God as he is manifested in his works, and do not study or regard his thoughts and purposes. "O Lord," says the Psalmist, "how great are thy works! and thy thoughts are very deep." But he adds, "A brutish man knoweth not, neither doth a fool understand this." "A brutish man" and "a fool"! What terms could better designate one so absorbed in his own selfish ends as to have no apprehension of this glorious universe in the midst of which he is placed, or of those great ends and purposes which God proposes? Instead of apprehending the works and the thoughts of God, and thus becoming a part of his holy and imperishable kingdom, the wicked live like the brutes, and like the brutes they die. "When the wicked spring as the grass, and when all the workers of iniquity do flourish, it is that they shall be destroyed forever." "But the righteous shall flourish like the palm-tree; he shall grow like the cedar of Lebanon. Those that be planted in the house of the Lord, shall flourish in the courts of our God; they shall still bring forth fruit in old age; they shall be fat and flourishing; to show that the Lord is upright: he is my rock, and there is no unrighteousness in him."

Not only, then, do the righteous bring forth fruit, they also, and which is the specific point here noticed, bring forth fruit in old age. In this they are contrasted, not only with the wicked, who do not bring forth fruit at all, but even with the tree; for while the tree bears fruit when we call it old, yet in what is really the old age of the tree, its powers become enfeebled, and it is not equal to the effort of fruit-bearing. Then, with vessels rigid, and trunk decaying, and branches withered and dry, and leaves sparse, it simply struggles for a weary time to sustain its own life. So is it with every thing that runs the circuit of what is called nature, and has not beneath it the undecaying strength of God, and in it the power of an eternal life. Having beneath them this strength, and in them this power, the righteous are an exception to all other beings and things on the earth. They are the one great exception. " Even the youths shall faint and be weary, and the young men shall utterly fall, but they that wait upon the Lord shall renew their strength; they shall mount up with wings as eagles; they shall run, and not be weary; and they shall walk, and not faint."

Regarded solely as a product of nature, man, like other beings, has his periods of development and of decay. Of these, each has its own characteristics, and they have been carefully noticed by dramatists and essay writers. For the purpose of poetical description, rather than from any accurate line of division, Shakespeare divided the life of man into seven stages or acts. The more common and accurate division is into childhood, youth, manhood, and old age. When man is left to himself, the ruling passion commonly assigned to him in youth is that of pleasure; in manhood, of ambition; and in old age, of avarice. This will do for a classification, but the exceptions are numerous. Still, each has his cycle, till we come to him who is really linked by faith to an eternal world, and so comes under " the powers of the world to come." He is in a measure taken out from the influence of these natural cycles, and will move on not only in the formation of character, but in its mode of expression, in one line. Hence, having begun to bear fruit, he will continue to bear it. He will bear it in old age. So long as his faculties remain, they will work under this law. Instead of moving according to any routine, and completing a circuit, and being subject to the law of habit, the faculties will work according to a free principle that shall be always ready to adapt itself to new circumstances, to avail itself of new possible combinations, to appreciate, to enter into the possession of, and to enjoy all new discoveries in science, or inventions in art, or opportunities of usefulness, or vistas newly opening in the developments of divine Providence. For a man thus to keep himself free from incrustations, and from the contractedness so often caused by routine, and by the numberless pettinesses of human life, and, though the outward man may perish, to have the inward man renewed in its original freshness and capacity for action, day by day, is a great thing. Only thus can man assert his prerogative as having in him something higher than nature. Within her domain, whatever draughts a man may take, he shall thirst again; but he who drinks of the water that Christ gives, shall never thirst, but the water that he giveth shall be in him a well of water springing up unto everlasting life.

Of this fruit-bearing in old age we have an eminent example in a prominent benefactor of this College, recently departed. It was not till Mr. JACKSON had reached the bound allotted by the Psalmist to human life, of threescore years and ten, and had passed five years beyond, that he made his first donation to this College; and so far as I know, the first that required public notice, or that would, if known, have been likely to cause special remark. This donation consisted of three thousand five hundred dollars,* and was given, not directly to the College, but to a Society always fostered by it, as furnishing facilities and a discipline in the study of Natural History that could be gained in no other way. When young men have their own organization, write their own papers, carry on their own discussions, describe their own specimens, and originate their own expeditions, their knowledge becomes incorporated into them, it becomes practical; and by doing what

---

* The whole amount given for Jackson Hall was between four and five thousand dollars.

he did, Mr. Jackson gave an impulse to this system that will be felt while the Institution shall stand. This donation was made from no besetment, or pressure of solicitation, but from simply reading a circular prepared by his grand-nephew, Mr. Orton.

If this donation had stood alone, it would not have been so remarkable. It might have been imputed to a momentary impulse, or caprice, or to vanity; but, taken in connection with what followed, it is clear that it sprang from a principle vital in him, and that his main motive was that assigned by him in his communication to the Trustees. "I esteem it," says he, "a privilege, as well as a duty, to devote a portion of the means wherewith a beneficent Providence has helped me, to the encouragement and promotion of science in connection with an Institution under sound moral and religious influence, as I believe Williams College to be, under the profound conviction that knowledge obtained and accompanied by such influence, is to be the future safe-guard of our free institutions." This was his great motive. The particular direction of his bounty was determined by his family connection with the Founder of the College, and by his birth and early associations in this County.

In accordance with the principle thus acting,

and the motive thus stated, three years afterwards Mr. Jackson gave the College twenty thousand dollars more. Of this, six thousand dollars were given for the purchase of a house and grounds for the President, which he thought would be more suitable than those then occupied, and on condition that the rest of the purchase money should be made up. The remaining fourteen thousand dollars were for the support of a Professorship of Christian Theology, and also to pay the bills of the sons of missionaries. This last provision was most appropriate. It was fitting that here, where the first foreign missions from this continent originated, there should be provision,—would it were ampler,—for the sons of those who devote themselves to this grand and self-sacrificing work, and that thus the cause itself might receive strength whenever in the current and phases of its circling influences it should touch the spot of its origin.

The idea of purchasing the house and grounds was original with Mr. Jackson, and in view of the future of the College, showed his sagacity. So too the idea of devoting money to instruction in Christian Theology was wholly his own, and he adhered to it in opposition to the wishes of some of the friends of the College. His impression was, that a modified course of instruction in Theology might be given here with advantage. He thought that a course wholly in the Seminary made men too professional and technical, with less sympathy for the people and their ways, and less power over them, than those who were trained as formerly, by studying with pastors. Whether he was right in this, and if so what would be the appropriate remedy, this is not the time or the place to discuss. The final arrangement was, that till further provision should be made, the President, who, it was his wish should act as the Professor, should give to those who might wish it, such instruction as he could in compatibility with his other duties.

Besides this, Mr. Jackson gave the College two thousand dollars to provide for an annual celebration of the birth-day of Colonel Williams. This was not merely because Colonel Williams was the Founder of the Institution, but because he gave his life for his country in that great struggle which determined the fate of Protestantism and of freedom on this Continent. For a time, and on certain conditions, a portion of the income of this money was to be given to the Natural History Society.

This, besides some minor gifts showing a watchful eye and continual interest in the College, is what he did. He purposed to do more. He had, at his own expense, procured the plan of a Gymnasium, of which he had offered to bear one-fourth of the expense; and he had stated publicly his intention of leaving something for the enlargement of Jackson Hall.

Nor did Mr. Jackson confine his benefactions to this College. He aided liberally in the establishment of a Library in Stockbridge, and was proposing, at the time he was taken sick, to give largely for the endowment of the Academy there.

Now, that a man whose opportunities for education were but limited, the earlier part of whose life was a struggle with difficulties, who had several children to provide for, and whose property was never large — that is, large for a city — that such a man should thus apprehend justly the wants of the country and of the race, and should thus devise liberal things, would be extraordinary at any period of his life. But I lay my finger on the fact that all this was the fruit of his old age. This seems to me the extraordinary thing about it. It was done by a man past seventy-five years of age, who had not previously given at all on such a scale. Of such giving at such a period, cheerful, considerate, judicious, the fruits of which were seen and rejoiced in, so as to shed a sunshine over life, I know of no example. I have never heard or read of one. True, it might be supposed that as man should approach the end of life, he would cling less closely both to life itself, and to its possessions. But experience does not teach thus. On the contrary, and as might, indeed, be anticipated from the law of habit, the grasp of the miser upon his wealth grows but the tighter as age increases, and every habit tends to confirm itself. Naturally, the aged man not only does not go beyond his accustomed circuits, and find enlargement, but those circuits grow narrower; he has less and less interest in the external and the distant; he does what he has been accustomed to do, only with less force, till death comes. Not so with Mr. Jackson. That law of habit, seeming hitherto as inevitable as death, by which the old man not accustomed to give largely, becomes, if not avaricious, yet timid and cautious, and clings to his money, failed to bind him. Instead of being narrowed and chilled, his sympathies were widened by age. Never did he manifest a deeper, or more intelligent, or more gratified interest in all that was passing here, than at the last Commencement; and of his party, who went from here on a pleasure excursion to Lake George, and some of whom were his grandchildren, not one was more prompt, or energetic, or looked forward to its enjoyment with a keener zest. With the exception of some defect of hearing, the responses in him to impressions from the outward world were quick and accurate, and his strength was firm. This must have been from a physical organization originally happy, and from a temperate life. His affections also, as I should judge, were uncommonly kindly and social, and put him in ready sympathy with the young. But more than all this is needed to account for the enlargement and liberality of which I have spoken.

Hence I observe again, that Mr. Jackson brought forth fruit in old age as a Christian man, recognizing his relations to God and to those great spiritual interests which are eternal.

On this point I am not so well prepared to speak as some others, but can truly say that the more I knew of him, and not on this point only, the more my respect and regard for him increased. I knew he had long been a professor of religion in the Dutch Church, but it was not till I heard him read the Scriptures in his own family in the most reverent manner, and pray with a solemnity and fervor which showed that God and eternity were to him great realities, and heard him say with a child-like humility that God had greatly blessed him, both in temporal and in spiritual things, that I understood how deep the springs were from which his bounty was an out-flow. The sympathies of God never decay, and whoever keeps himself in sympathy with him will be in sympathy with all the good, the enlightenment, the blessing that God would accomplish in this world, and must seek to aid in it. This, Mr. Jackson did. In the use of his property he adopted the principle of stewardship, which applies to age and to youth alike, and from a regard to which, as I doubt not, sprung his chief motive in doing what he did.

But a disposition to give, and even a principle of giving, avails nothing without the means; and I observe again, that Mr. Jackson brought forth fruit in old age by adhering, after he had attained property, to that simple and unostentatious life to which he had been accustomed. In every thing that pertained to the necessaries and comforts of life, he was free — entirely removed from any thing like parsimony; but he adhered from principle to the simplicity of his original habits and tastes, and spent comparatively little upon himself. This, and not alone his acquisition of property, was the turning-point in respect to his ability to give.

At this point there is a marked dividing line between men who gain property. Many who gain it, and do not go on in a mere process of accumulating, enter, if not from their own tastes, from those of their families, upon a course of expense required by the demands of fashionable life. Their lives are governed, or come to be, by a reference to the opinion of fashionable circles, and their standing with them. This draws them as into a maelstrom; it opens a gulf that is bottomless. Thenceforward giving will be but the crumbs that fall from their table — it will be slight and incidental. The man says he cannot give, and, if he is to run the race of pleasurable and fashionable life, he cannot. The cry of the horse-leech that is fastened on him saying, Give, give, will drown all other cries. At this point every man must judge for himself. Something is due to position and a regard for appearances, but the great weakness of the times is a readiness to yield personal independence, and principle, and the power of beneficence, to a love of show; to the heartless, and, if your money fail, the contemptuous and derisive goddess of fashion; to the opinion of classes and sets whose standards are merely conventional, and false, and who would be scarcely missed in the great movements of benevolence and of progress, if the whole of them were to be swept away, like a swarm of insects, in a moment. The great want of the times is men, independent men in sympathy with God, and acting from principle as his stewards. Hitherto, plain living and high acting, certainly action of the highest order, have gone together. No doubt they always will. How easy would it have been for Mr. Jackson to spend upon horses and carriages, upon a house and furniture, the money he gave here. But he chose rather to give impulse to thought and right training, to lay the foundation of an influence that shall be perpetual, to act from conscience and the affections rather than from vanity, or for any selfish gratification. In all this, Mr. Jackson was a true man, simple, natural, showing strong sense, and bringing forth fruit.

Once more, Mr. Jackson brought forth fruit in old age in his patriotism. He belonged to a race of men now fast passing away, who were born during the war of the Revolution, whose blood was stirred by the personal narratives of those who took part in that conflict, and all whose associations and hopes clustered around the flag of their country. For that flag his attachment was something like a passion. Early on coming here, and before there was the thought of war, he procured a large and expensive flag for the College, that it might be displayed on the Fourth of July and at patriotic celebrations; and, in accordance with his desire, it has always decorated the room at the celebration of Williams's birth-day. Early in the war, when a Massachusetts regiment marched through New York, he marched with them to the Astor House, and carried the flag. It is among the more touching incidents of the war, that an old man like him, of more than fourscore years, should claim to come in among the soldiers of his native State, and carry the dear old flag through the streets of that city. He provided for the soldiers, at one time, I think, giving a breakfast to a whole regiment. He made speeches to them. He had numerous relatives in the army, for several of whom he provided outfits, and his expenditure in connection with voluntary offerings of this kind, was several thousand dollars. With him all this was as natural as his breathing, for patriotism was a part of his being. With the rebellion he had no patience; he had no tolerance for it; and never had a thought of any thing but that it was to be crushed, and that the old flag was to wave again over the whole country. With a spirit like his pervading the North, such a result would be speedily realized.

Thus did Mr. Jackson, during the period of his relation to us, and in his old age, bring forth fruit; and it was fruit that will remain.

Of the early, and maturer life of Mr. Jackson, I have said nothing, because he was not known by me till after his first donation here, and because I know nothing that has not been already stated in the College Quarterly. As linking him with us, it is important only to state here, that he was born in this County, in what was then the town of Tyringham, now Monterey; that the mother of Ephraim Williams was a Jackson, and his great aunt; and that Ephraim Williams received his education in the family of his grandfather Jackson.

The final sickness of Mr. Jackson was brief. He became ill on Friday, and died the following Tuesday. He was conscious till the last, and died peacefully, trusting in God.

Thus has God given, and taken away, the second great benefactor of this Institution. We are grateful to the immediate giver. His name will always be held in honor here. But we would recognize God in all. We would remember that it is from him that every good and perfect gift cometh down, and would thank him for the increased means of usefulness possessed by the College through these gifts.

Like Mr. Lawrence, Mr. Jackson gave in his life-time. He had the strength to part with money in large sums; and how extraordinary I regard this at his age, and in his circumstances, I have already stated. He opened the spring and cut the channels, in which the waters of his beneficence were to flow, with his own hand, and had the satisfaction of seeing those waters enter upon their glad and lengthening way. That this is often, perhaps generally, the best mode of giving, there can be no doubt. There is need of men who can give thus. They are indispensable to our Colleges, or to the most of them, and will be for some time yet. With us, other branches besides Natural History, as Physical Education, and Modern Languages, need to be fostered and endowed. Men who give thus, work in accordance with a great analogy set before them by God. In gathering and distributing water to meet the wants of the earth and of man, God has two methods. In his widest method, he draws up the water, little by little, from a broad surface, that he may give it again in dew and in showers. He takes it, indeed, chiefly from the ocean, where it is not needed; but he takes its fair proportion, also, from every lake, and pool, and moist spot. Every part of the earth is made to contribute to the rain and the dew. And so God needs men who will contribute freely to sustain the current charities of the day — those which are gathered and dispensed like the clouds. These are a system by themselves, and are best sustained by the whole people. We all need them for our own moral growth—to keep us in vital connection with something higher than those sordid pursuits to which men gravitate; and the wider and more even the surface from which these charities come, the more healthful they are, and the more likely to be efficient. No one of these could be sustained by a few; and if it could, it would be to the general loss. But water is also gathered in fountains, and wells, and reservoirs, for supplying the more immediate wants of man; and he who digs a well, as Jacob did, where the people may come a thousand years afterwards, like the woman of Samaria, and draw, and remember that it was their father Jacob who gave them the well, does a very different and more permanent, and in many respects a nobler work, than he who simply contributes to the rain and the dew—to the passing wants of society. Now, Mr. Jackson dug a well—one like those in the East, to which men gather from far, that they may drink. This is a great work; it is not every man who can do it; and we need men who can and will dig wells where they are needed. This they may provide for, and leave to others to do, but they lose the satisfaction of seeing and enjoying their own work; they lose the benefit of it in their own moral improvement, and in the sympathy and kindness and honor that are drawn out from others.

We now turn from what has been done by Mr. Jackson, to ourselves and its relation to us as connected with this College. What he did had respect to the future. There is no good man who does not hope the time is coming when the world will be better than it is now, and who does not wish to do something to make it so. His life would be an impertinence, and an insufferable weariness, if he could suppose he was only turning a tread-mill. But in this, his hope rests, not on those whose characters are formed, and who are passing off the stage, but on the young; and the problem is to know what can be done for them. We are willing to give money and labor, but the question is how these can be so applied as to secure the result. In answer to this we have the different theories of education. Among these, however, two things are in common. One is, that the means of the best intellectual culture are to be furnished as widely as possible; and the other, that we must have the co-operation of the young.

This is the theory of our Colleges. Of these, the last—the co-operation of the young—is the most important. We may, we do, need at some points more and better means; but that is not the greatest difficulty. Why, my Friends, all these buildings are for you. This apparatus, and these libraries are for you; these instructors are here for you. The munificence of individuals and of the State is for you. For you the Trustees consult and provide, and their desire is that every thing here may be so for your use and at your disposal as to make you the best generation of students and of men that has yet lived. Why should you not be? Why should you not, in accordance with the whole theory of our government, so put yourselves into intelligent and voluntary co-operation with what others are doing and praying for, as to give you the greatest wisdom for self-direction, and the greatest power of self-control? This is what is most needed. It is an independent, manly, faithful use by yourselves, of the means provided. The turning point here is with you. When the questions come, as practically they do come every day,—What indulgence will you forego? What evil habit will you abandon? What unworthy custom that has been handed down will you suffer to sink into oblivion? What higher ideal of manhood will you form and seek to approximate?—the decision must rest with you, and on this, every thing will turn. Without a high and true manhood in you, there must be failure. No implements or skill can form a pillar of society out of a poor stick. But whatever you may choose to do, it is obvious that the more ample the means are that are provided, and the greater the generosity and the self-sacrifice in providing them, the greater must be the shame, the guilt, the deserved scorn and condemnation, if they are not improved. For every sacrifice that has been made for us here, and for every means and privilege offered, we shall be held responsible; and I put it to you as from the faithful and self-denying men who have labored for this College and given to it; I put it to you as from God himself, who giveth to all, and watcheth over all, and requireth all, whether you will not seek, with a spirit of hearty co-operation, to do your part in this great work.

What I have now said chiefly respects our relations here, and as scholars, but the text brings to our thoughts a wider relation—it is that of fruit-bearing wherever, or whatever we may be, in this universe of God. Not every man is required to bear fruit by bestowing large sums of money. There are few who can, and the value of this, in the sight of God, depends on the disposition from which it flows. Let those who can, do this; but the fruits which we may bear, if we put ourselves in right relations to God and our fellow creatures, are very various, and very precious. They are all those clusters, appropriate to every period of life, that are called in Scripture "the fruits of righteousness." That he might bear these, man was made, as was the fruit-bearing tree for its fruit. Without this the life of man is in vain, and towards this every movement and process ought to tend. If we take the fig-tree, selected by our Saviour as a type of its class, of what use is it if it does not bear fruit? It is not fit for timber, or ornament, or shade. It cumbers the ground, and the voice of common sense approves and echoes the sentence—cut it down. So a man that does not bear fruit cumbers the earth. Fruit, fruit is what is needed. " By their fruits ye shall know them." " Every tree that bringeth not forth good fruit, is hewn down and cast into the fire." You, my Friends, are planted as in the garden of God. What fruit will you bring forth? Will you stand barren and wait for the axe? or will you bring forth fruits meet for Him by whom such a garden is dressed? You are young. Many years may be before you; I know not. But bring forth fruits of righteousness now, and you shall continue to bear them. As the years pass they shall be more golden in hue, and richer in flavor, and if God spares you, you too " shall still bring forth fruit in old age," you shall bring it forth forever.

www.ingramcontent.com/pod-product-compliance
Lightning Source LLC
Chambersburg PA
CBHW022109300426
44117CB00007B/647